C2 000000909092 56

CW00435327

NatWest Small Business Bookshelf

This series has been written by a team of authors who all have many years experience and are still actively involved in the day-to-day problems of the small business.

If you are running a small business or are thinking of setting up your own business, you have no time for the general, theoretical and often inessential detail of many business and management books. You need practical, readily accessible, easy-to-follow advice which relates to your own working environment and the problems you encounter. The books on the NatWest Small Business Bookshelf fulfil these needs.

- They concentrate on specific areas which are particularly problematic to the small business.

- They adopt a step-by-step approach to the implementation of sound business skills.

- They offer practical advice on how to tackle problems.

The author

Gary Jones is a coordinator of small business courses at Blackpool and the Fylde College, and has also originated and developed PEI business enterprise courses for young people. He has considerable commercial experience in retail management, has run his own small business, and is the author of *Starting Up*.

Other titles in this series

A Business Plan
Book-keeping and Accounting
Exporting
Franchising
Hiring and Firing
Managing Growth
Selling
Small Business Survival
Starting Up

NatWest Small Business Bookshelf

Retailing

Gary Jones BA(Hons), Cert Ed(Dist)

Pitman

Pitman Publishing
128 Long Acre, London WC2E 9AN
A Division of Longman Group UK Limited

First published in Great Britain in association with the National Westminster Bank,
1989

© Longman Group UK Ltd 1989

British Library Cataloguing in Publication Data

Jones, Gary
    Retailing.
    1. Great Britain. Retailing. Management
    I. Title   II. Series
    658.8'7'00941

ISBN 0 273 03101 5

Typeset, printed and bound in Great Britain

Contents

Preface

Thinking about opening a shop?
Already running or managing a shop but want to do better?
Buying another shop or expanding an existing one?

In this book every major aspect of retailing, from choosing a location to electronic tills, is discussed in detail. You will find many useful techniques that can be applied to your business to improve profitability and sales, with clear language and numerous examples to help your understanding.

The book consists of three main sections.

Part one: *Making a Start*, helps you consider in detail the various retailing alternatives. In the first chapter you will find a wealth of information and discussion on: newsagents, convenience stores, off-licences, specialist food shops, clothes and fashion stores, and a summary of the choices available in other areas of retailing. Help is given to enable you to select the type of shop that is right for you. This section will also introduce you to some of the realities of running a shop – a chance to learn from other people's mistakes and start to plan for a successful start up.

Part two: *Opening*, provides the means to establish whether your shop will stand a good chance of success. You will be asking and answering the following:

- Who are my customers and what motivates them to buy?
- How can I plan my business to serve my customers most profitably?
- Which will be the best location for my shop?
- Will my shop make sufficient profit?
- How much money will I need – can I afford it?
- What kind of finance will I need – how will I go about raising it?
- What store image, display and layout of merchandise will appeal to customers and maximize sales and profit?
- What should I check for when buying an existing shop?
- How will I deal with the Inland Revenue and VAT?
- How will I trade – as sole trader, partnership or limited company?
- How can I protect my shop's name from being used by others?

Part three, *Open for Business*, considers what has to be done to successfully manage your business – to keep things running smoothly and take action to expand sales. Amongst other things you will learn how to:

- Do your accounts
- Make your business grow through adopting simple but proven marketing techniques
- Collect and make sense of sales information
- Select suitable suppliers
- Monitor and improve profitability
- Devise and use stock ordering systems
- Select and effectively use electronic tills
- Monitor stock losses and improve security
- Stay on the right side of the vast legislation affecting retailers.

At the end of the book you find:

- Computer spreadsheets for use by small retailers
- Further sources of information, help and advice
- Additional accounting information, including a series of tables to help you make pricing decisions.
- A helpful glossary of terms and jargon used in retailing and in business in general.

You can simply read this book from cover to cover to give you a general understanding of what is involved, or work slowly through each chapter and section building up your business plan as you proceed. You can, however, refer to each chapter in the order that suits you best. Further, each chapter ends with a concise summary and most have detailed checklists to help you monitor your progress and as far as possible make sure you don't leave out a vital element in your preparations.

This book is based in part on my own experience of managing a number of retail businesses both large and small and starting my own small business. I hope I have given you a practical, usable book that will become a friend in the hard, interesting and, finally, personally and financially rewarding task in front of you.

Gary Jones
February 1989

Dedication

To Ann, who I will always love, whose smile kept me going, and to Andrea for all those helpful interruptions. Love to you both.

1 What kind of shop?

What's on offer □ Popular retail trades: newsagent, convenience stores, off-licences □ Specialist food retailing □ Clothes, fashion and shoe shops □ Other non-food trades □ What kind of shop is right for me? □ Should I buy an existing business? □ Franchises and voluntary groups □ Summary □ Checklist

It is likely that you have already decided to some extent what type of shop you would like to run. However, you may be at the stage where you have decided to go into retailing but are not sure what type of shop is best suited to your requirements. This chapter will help you consider the various options open to you and then consider them in relation to your motivation, interest, needs, skills and resources.

What's on offer

There is a multitude of shop types to choose from, ranging from the popular retail trades such as CTNs (confectioner, tobacconist, newsagent), off-licences and general convenience stores, through the more specialist food trades such as greengrocery and butchery, to the retailing of furniture, clothing and other household goods or the retailing of services such as TV hire and repair. Maybe you are considering something more 'original' and 'specialised', presenting a much more difficult challenge, such as starting a new type of shop from scratch, hoping to match the success of the high street innovations of 'Sock Shop', 'The Body Shop' and 'Tie Rack'.

Although it is true that some sectors of retailing are faring better than others it is impossible to say that one type of shop is better than another. National trends do not take into account local conditions and individual entrepreneurial flair. What kind of shop is 'right for you' is very much dependent on your skills, interests, personal commitments, financial resources and local market conditions. First let's look at some broad areas of retailing in some detail before getting down to the business of selecting one that is 'right for you'.

What follows is a fairly detailed but far from exhaustive look at a variety of shop types. In each section you will find information relating to sales, gross profits and stock holdings. The information given should be useful to you when assessing prospective businesses and comparing one shop with another. However, this information is not a substitute for your own detailed market research. Sources of the information given are principally the *Retail Business Monitor, Family Expenditure Survey, Monthly Digest of Statistics* and *Annual Abstract of Statistics* (all HMSO publications) which you should investigate further. More information is given on the use of such information in Chapters 3 and 4. A glossary of terms is provided at the rear of the book for those who are not familiar with the terms and definitions used.

Popular retail trades

Collectively CTNs (confectioners, tobacconists and newsagents), off-licences and small convenience stores are the most popular retail trades with the newcomer to retailing. Because of their largely enduring nature they are sometimes referred to as 'bread and butter' shops. Providing one is selected with care and properly run then the risk of failure is relatively low. However, if you are looking to get rich quick this is not the area for you.

Newsagents

The number of newsagents operating within the UK has seen a slight decline other the last few years but still remains perhaps the most 'protected' small retailer. This is largely because most wholesalers will only supply to established newsagents, unless of course there is no or relatively little provision in an area. If this type of shop appeals you will undoubtedly have to buy an existing business. However, you must take care to establish that the current wholesaler will continue to supply you after the business changes hands (this is not automatically guaranteed!).

Generally speaking you can expect pay more for a newsagents than off-licences or convenience stores. This is due in part to their continuing popularity with newcomers to business, but more to the fact that it is often viable and profitable to expand a newsagents by selling general groceries and obtaining a licence to sell wines and spirits.

In this type of business perhaps the greatest investment you will make is time. You can expect to be open from 6.00 am onwards (sometimes until 10.00 pm if you expect to operate an off-licence in tandem with the main business), 360 days a year. For most newsagents this can add up to a working week in excess of ninety hours. If you are not a 'morning person' don't go into this type of business!

A good deal of care should be taken when employing and instructing your newspaper boys and girls. Importantly, you should not employ any child under the age of 13 and you must comply with any byelaws relating to the employment of children (consult with your local authority). As with all employees you should conform to health & safety regulations and with children you should take even greater care. For instance, instruction should be given on road safety, perhaps even insisting that a cycling proficiency certificate is obtained and reflector strips attached to newspaper bags in the winter months. Remember an action in negligence brought against you in respect of an injury to one of your newspaper delivery staff could be ruinous.

Newspapers carry a healthy profit margin of 27 per cent (see the summary at the end of this section). You therefore want to be looking for a newsagent with a large turnover in newspapers comparative to other sections of the business. This will ensure a steady trade, the potential to produce a good overall gross profit and a 'solid' basis on which to diversify/expand the business into other product areas if so wished.

It should be noted that the sale of tobacco products by newsagents (currently representing between 25 and 40 per cent of total money sales) is a rapidly contracting market. After discounting the effect of inflation tobacco sales are falling at an approximate rate of between two and three per cent per annum.

Convenience stores

Since the 1950s because of the change in life style, the advent of the modern supermarket, the more recent growth of the out of town hyper-market and the 'large mixed retail business', the number of local or so called 'corner shops' has reduced dramatically and the ones that are left have changed. The trend now is towards the American style of 'convenience store', typified by:

- Colourful, bright, well designed shops along the lines of their larger competitors the supermarkets.
- A broad range of merchandise, including: grocery, video hire, beers, wines and spirits, household items, confectionery, household medicines, and even newspapers.
- Early to late opening hours (e.g. 8.00 am until 10.00 pm) and six to seven day trading.

The success of such business is based on the benefits to the customer of place and time rather than the individual benefits of the products it sells. The bread, milk, headache pills and toilet rolls you buy from your local convenience store at 9.30 pm on Wednesday night might be exactly the same products you can buy at a lower price from the supermarket the next morning, but the total package of benefits to the customer such as accessibility and opening times, show that the convenience store has survived not by competing directly with the supermarket, but by offering a different service. However, you should be aware that the current trend with supermarkets, hypermarkets and superstores is to open longer (often until 8.00 pm) and where local bye laws allow to trade on a Sunday (see Chapter 15). Obviously this presents a new threat to the local shop by reducing the effect of its long opening hours. Consequently the main determinants of success are location (see Chapter 4) and extent of product range. The convenience store should incorporate at least two retail trades to stand a reasonable chance of success, for instance general grocery and off-licence or general grocery and newsagency. In each case the additional trade hopefully ensures regular custom.

You can expect to pay considerably more for a convenience store if it includes an off-licence or newsagency. As noted before you will find it difficult if not impossible to find a wholesaler to supply you with newspapers if there is already an established newsagent in the area. It can be equally difficult to obtain an off-licence (see 'Off-licences').

You should note that if you do not possess an off-licence the Shops Act 1950 and/or local byelaws may require you to close by 8.00 pm. The regulations in 1988 regarding Sunday trading are given in the final chapter 'Keeping on the Right Side of Law'.

Off-Licences

The licence

A common misconception with newcomers to this trade is that when you buy the business the licence is automatically transferred to the new owner. This is not the case; the licence is held by the individual and not the business. The licence is granted by the local Licensing Justices, to which the prospective new owner must make an application. To cover the possible eventuality that the licence may not be granted to you it is imperative that an escape clause is inserted into the contract of sale to cover this possibility. Once the licence is obtained it must be renewed annually. If you do not conform to the rules and regulations appertaining to the operation of the licence or there are valid objections from the police or local residents there is every chance that the licence may not be renewed.

Applying for a licence

An alternative to buying an existing off-licence is to buy an empty shop or compatible retail trade and apply for a licence. There is of course no guarantee that one will be obtained but they are easier to obtain than most people think. Generally, the success of your application will depend on how well you can demonstrate the following.

1. First and foremost you will have to demonstrate conclusively that there is a need for an additional off-licence in the area. The best way of demonstrating this is to get local residents and other potential customers to sign a petition stating that they would use/approve of the off-licence if granted. Another, if applicable, is to point out the considerable distance local residents have to travel to existing off-licences or that elderly local custom has to cross busy roads to visit the nearest existing off-licence and so on. Generally speaking you may well have trouble obtaining a licence if there is an existing off-licence within quarter of a mile of your shop (particularly if it is on the same side of the street).
2. You will have to show that you are a 'fit and proper' person to hold a licence. The production of character references from 'credible people' in the community might help your case. You will also have to show that you will be in a position to control/manage the sale of the alcohol.

In applying for a licence, or in attempting to identify suitable premises for a new off-licence, you are advised to consult a solicitor. He or she will be able to give you some indication (based on their local knowledge and experience) whether the application will stand any chance of success. When selecting a solicitor make sure that you choose one who deals in this kind of legal work frequently.

In making the application, in brief, this is what will have to be done:

1. A detailed proposal will have to be compiled, inclusive of:
   - Full details about your shop, inclusive of who owns it and the product ranges you plan to and/or are selling
   - Layout of the shop, in particular where exactly the alcohol sales and storage areas will be – detailing how they will be secured and controlled.
   - Map showing the location of the shop and giving details of the area, inclusive of all off-licences within quarter of a mile of the shop, housing, parking facilities, transport, etc.
   - Evidence showing that there is a need for an off-licence at the proposed site.

- Details about yourself showing that you are a 'fit and proper' person to hold a licence.
All these details must be made available to the Clerk of the Justices a minimum of 21 days (4 to 6 weeks is preferable) before the application is heard.
2. A minimum of three weeks before the hearing you must inform the local authority, the police and the fire service of your application. Each may then make a visit to your premises without prior warning.
3. You must notify the general public of your application by:
   - Placing the notices of formal application in your shop (where they can be seen) for at least seven days during the 28 days prior to the hearing.
   - Placing an advertisement in a relevant local newspaper.

Opening times and legal restrictions

- The permitted times for the sale of alcohol are:
  Monday to Saturday: 8.00 am to 11.00 pm
  Sundays: 12 noon to 3.00 pm and 7.00 pm to 10.30 pm.
- No sale of alchohol may be made to anyone under the age of 18, or to any person who appears drunk or who is acting in an unruly manner.
- It is worth noting that the sale of goods (including alcohol) is at the discretion of the retailer.
- You must not allow any person to consume alcohol on the premises.
- You cannot employ anybody under the age of 18 to sell alcohol.

All of these rules must be strictly adhered to. Any breach many well lead to criminal prosecution, loss of licence and, of course, have ruinous consequences for the business.

Useful facts and figures for newsagents, convenience stores and off-licences

Gross profit

Depending on the type and extent of your stock range you can expect a gross profit profit margin of between fifteen to twenty two per cent. The average profit margins and mark ups for broad groupings of products are given in Fig. 1.1 as a guide.

Product group	Average margin %	Average mark up %
Grocery	20	25
Confectionery	25	33
Soft drinks & ices	30	43
Alcohol	15	18
Tobacco	8	9
News and periodicals	27	37

(*Source:* Author's own research)

Fig. 1.1 Approximate percentage profit margins and mark ups

Stock holding

Depending on the type and extent of your stock range you can expect to have to hold the following stock levels to maintain sales:

- Grocery – four weeks stock (a rate of stock turn of 12 per annum).
- Confectionery, tobacco and newsagents – five weeks' stocks (a rate of stock turn of 10 per annum).
- Off-licences – 7 weeks stocks (a rate of stock turn of 7.5 per annum).

This is perhaps as you would expect, a high rate of stock turnover in low value items (grocery) and a low rate of stock turnover in high value items (wines, spirits and beers). The amount of money you will have to invest in stock is of significance to any business. Take for example a grocery shop and off-licence with identical sales of £100,000 per year. The off-licence with a relatively low rate of stock turn can expect to have £13,333 (at retail prices) invested in stock whereas the grocery business with a high rate of stock turn can expect to have a lower figure, £10,000 (at retail prices) invested in stock. Obviously, the higher the rate of stock turn the lower the stock holding required and therefore the less money you will have tied up in stocks.

The market

It is a well known fact that many small retailers have lost a lot of their trade to the large stores, supermarkets, hypermarkets and large multiples retailing through small outlets. However, in some product markets the small retailer has retained a reasonable proportion of the overall sales.

Figure 1.2 gives some indication as to respective product market shares of small retailers operating in this area.

Product groupings	Small Retailer %	Supermarket %
News and periodicals	61	less than 1
Confectionery	48	20
Tobacco	43	21
Grocery & soft drinks	20	72
Alcohol	18	39

(*Source:* Based on Tables 7 and 10, *Retail Business Monitor*, SDO 25, HMSO)

Fig. 1.2   Percentage of overall sales captured by the small single outlet retailer

As you can easily see from Fig. 1.2 the small shop fares best in the sale of newspapers and confectionery where there is effectively little or no price competition with the large retailers. The price of newspapers and periodicals is set by wholesalers and confectionery is largely bought on 'impulse' when purchasing other goods. As you might expect, the small retailer does less well where price is an important factor, as is the case with grocery.

The small off-licence's share of alcohol sales is much more difficult to predict. Government statistics indicate that small retailers (collectively) capture some 18 per cent of the market with 39 per cent being taken by large grocery retailers such as supermarkets. However, off-licences in general, inclusive of the multiples such as Cellar Five Ltd, Thresher and Co. Ltd, Victoria Wine Co. Ltd, etc. take some 44 per cent of the total sales. Therefore, as an off-licence your share of total consumer expenditure off-sales of liquor is likely to fall somewhere between 18 per cent and 44 per cent, depending on how well you compete with the multiples such as Victoria Wine, Thresher and Cellar Five.

It will be useful for you to note the general sales trends in *real terms* (i.e., after discounting the effect of inflation) of the principle merchandise groupings. Figure 1.3 gives a brief summary of overall changes between 1980 and 1986.

You will note that the sales in food show a slight increase, with a fairly static picture for the consumption of alcoholic drink, and, not surprisingly given the increasing concern about health risks, an overall decrease in tobacco consumption of 23 per cent over the space of six years. The overall fall in the sale of newspapers and books is substantiated by readership figures for newspapers and magazines given by *National Readership*

Merchandise group	Percentage increase/decrease in real terms 1980 to 1986
Consumer consumption of all goods and services:	up by 17%
Food:	up by 6%
Alcoholic drink:	up by 3%
Newspapers & books:	*down by* 5%
Tobacco:	*down by* 23%

(*Source:* Based on Table 6.11, *Social Trends*, 18, 1988)

Fig. 1.3   Sales trends in real terms 1980 to 1986

Surveys. With a few exceptions there has been an overall decline in the readership of all major newspapers and magazines since 1971, and the trend is likely to continue. All this does not paint a rosy picture for the retailer operating in these markets facing competition from larger organizations. Overall the principal product markets in which you will compete can be collectively summed up, at best as slightly increasing, at worst as stagnant or on the decline. This does not necessarily mean that you will do badly in this type of business but it does signify that for you to increase your overall sales in real terms year by year, you will actively have to seek a larger share of the existing market. Finally, you should note that these trends are for the UK as a whole and ignore the possibility that the locality you are considering may be far from typical!

Further information may be sought by contacting relevant trade associations and reading trade papers.

Associations
National Federation of Retail Newsagents, 2 Bridewell Place, London.
Tel: 01-353-6816
Retail Confectioners & Tobacconists Association Ltd, Ashley House, 53 Christchurch Ave., London. Tel: 01-445-6344

Trade papers
The Grocer
Retail Newsagent Confectioner and Tobacconist
Self-Service and Supermarket
Supermarketing

Convenience Stores, CTNs and Off-Licences – the main points

1. Profit margins between 15 and 22 per cent of takings.
2. The hours are unsocial and often in excess of ninety hours.
3. The best profit margin is to be found on newspapers and periodicals.
4. Wholesalers will not supply newspapers to a new outlet where there is an existing newsagent in the vicinity – this protects your sales but makes it difficult to start from scratch.
5. The sale of papers and/or liquor helps ensure regular repeat sales – if you are planning a convenience store you will be well advised to include one of these in your operation.
6. There is continuing long term decline in the sale of newspapers and periodicals.
7. The sales of confectionery and food remain buoyant but without any significant increase over the past years.
8. Off-licences are not automatically transferred to the new owner on the sale of the business.
9. It is not impossible to apply for a new off-sales licence to enhance the sales of a convenience store.
10. As with all retail businesses great care must be taken when choosing a location.

Specialist food retailing

To run a butchers, greengrocers, fishmongers or bakery shop requires quite extensive trade skills and knowledge. Unless you possess these or are highly motivated to attend courses and/or gain the relevant experience before going into business I strongly advise you to avoid this type of shop.

One of the main problems with this type of business is associated with the highly perishable nature of the stock and the sometimes unpredictable 'whims' of the market in terms of supply, customer demand and prices. All these factors combined, without very careful management, can create a high degree of stock wastage sufficient to turn a good week's trading into a sizable loss. However, the potential profit margins (if wastage is controlled) compared to other types of business are comparatively high:

Butchers	24
Fishmongers	26
Greengrocers	25
Bread and flour confectioners	44

In another way the perishable nature of the stock works to the advantage of these types of business by keeping stock holdings low. On average the typical stock levels you will have to carry are as follows:

Butchers	1 week's stock
Fishmongers	2/3 days' stock
Greengrocers	1 week's stock
Bread and flour confectioners	1.5 weeks' stock

Such low stock holdings substantially reduce the amount of money you have to have invested in the business. For instance compare two businesses, a general grocery shop with a rate of stock turn of 12 per annum (4 weeks' stock holding) with a greengrocers with a rate of stock turn 52 (1 week's stock holding), both with sales of £100,000 per annum. The general grocer would have to have £8,333 invested in stocks whereas the greengrocer would only have to have £1,923 invested, a 'saving' of some £6,000!

It should be obvious that a great deal of attention must be payed to hygiene when storing and handling fresh foods. In fact there are detailed Food Hygiene Regulations that you must conform to in selling any food (see Chapter 15). The regulations are available from any HMSO bookshop. You should study these with care and make sure your business conforms. If you breach any of these regulations you may be prosecuted by your Local Authority Health Department, who will periodically send an inspector to check your premises. The consequences of failure to comply with these regulations are dire. The Local Authority has the power to close your business (in extreme cases) and if you are prosecuted the story does not end with a fine as it is most likely that the local press will pick up the story and ruin your trade, perhaps to the point of bankruptcy. My local butcher was doing good trade until he was reported in the local paper (with great relish!) for breaches in food hygiene regulations. He struggled on for six weeks as trade all but disappeared and then closed down. For further details on Food Hygiene Regulations see Chapter 15.

The specialist food retailer like other small retail outlets is under continued threat from the large retailer. Figure 1.4 gives you some indication as to the respective market shares of specialist food retailers against their principal competitors.

Generally speaking small retailers of this type have managed to hold on to a large share of their respective markets. The general rule of thumb is the more specialised the market and the greater the skill involved in processing and selling the merchandise, the less interested the larger retailers are in competing. Well over 50 per cent of the fresh fish market is captured by the small fishmonger because of the relatively high level of skill involved and the highly perishable nature of the stock. In this case this has deterred the larger retailers who have preferred to concentrate on frozen fish sales. Small butchers have fared less well with the advent of centralized processing and packaging of meat and poultry enabling the large stores to enter this market in volume. However, out of all the specialized food trades the greengrocer is most open to competition from the supermarket and other food retailers because of the relatively lower level of knowledge and skill required to set up and operate compared to butchering for instance.

SPECIALIST RETAILERS

	Small Outlets	Multiples	'Supermarkets'	Total Sales
	%	%	%	%
Fresh fish:	60 – 70	25	5 – 15	100
Fresh meat and poultry:	40 – 50	26	34 – 44	100
Fresh fruit and veg.:	40	23	39	100
Bakery products:	20 – 35	30	35 – 45	100

(*Source:* Based on Tables 8 and 10, *Business Monitor, Retail*, SDO 25, HMSO)

Fig. 1.4 Market shares and principal competitors in specialist food retailing

In the specialized food trades the small retailer does not necessarily face competition on the basis of price but rather on the basis of quality and convenience. The 'average' customer is more likely to be tempted to buy say their meat and poultry with their main grocery shopping rather than make a separate visit to their local butcher. Therefore, although your prices must be competitive, the quality and range of your merchandise, the location of your shop and the level of personal service will be the main determinants of success or failure.

Fresh food in general is a fairly static market. However, it could be said that in some ways it has done well not to suffer severe contraction when one considers the preference of large retailers (for economic reasons) for food of the processed, pre-packed and frozen nature.

Figure 1.5 shows some quite dramatic changes in the consumption of meat and poultry. The changes have been mostly as a result of the various healthier eating campaigns significantly reducing the household consumption of high fat content meats such as lamb. 'White' and 'leaner' cuts of meat have suffered least with poultry consumption actually showing a slight increase over 1980 levels.

Surprisingly the consumption of fresh vegetables and fruit has not

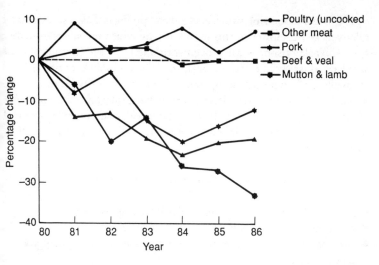

Fig. 1.5 Absolute percentage changes in meat and poultry consumption
1980 to 1986

increased since 1980 (see Fig. 1.6). It appears that the drive towards
healthier eating has led more to an increase in the consumption of 'fruit
products' such as fruit juice (up by some 20 per cent since 1980) rather
than fresh fruit.

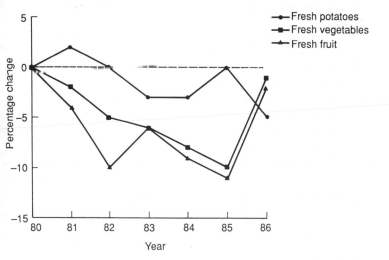

Fig. 1.6 Absolute percentage changes in fresh vegetable and fruit
consumption 1980 to 1986

The consumption of bread and bakery products has also remained relatively static. However, this masks a trend which favours the smaller specialist bakery shop – the movement away from the consumption of standard white sliced loaves to 'healthier' wholemeal bakery products.

Finally and importantly, opening shops of this type presents the possibility for innovation and variety – the chance to project an image that appeals to the consumer and/or offering a service that cannot be obtained from your competitors. The possibilities are endless – here a just a few ideas:

- Plan the cooked meats section of your butchers as a delicatessen or convenience foods counter.
- Feature organically grown vegetables in your greengrocers.
- Offer recipe ideas, cooking instructions and hints.
- Become known as a fresh food shop rather than just a greengrocers, butchers or bakery.

Further information may be sought by contacting relevant trade associations and reading trade papers.

Associations
National Federation of Fishmongers Ltd, Queensway House, Redhill, Surrey. Tel: 0737-68611
Institute of Meat, Boundary House, 91/93 Charterhouse Street, London. Tel: 01-253-2971.
Delicatessen and Fine Food Association, 3 Fairfield, Staines. Tel: 0784-61339.
Retail Fruit Trade Federation, 108/110 Market Towers, Nine Elms Lane, London. Tel: 01-720-9168.
National Association of Health Stores, Byron House, 1 College St, Nottingham. Tel: 0602-474165.

Trade papers
Meat Trader
Fish Trader
Retail Fruit Trade Review

Specialist food retailing – the main points

1. Specialist trade knowledge and skill is required.
2. A high rate of stock turnover makes for a relatively low level of investment in stock.
3. Very careful buying/ordering and management of stock is required to avoid ruinous wastage.

4. The large retailers do not appear to compete with the small retailer on the basis of price.
5. Consistent high quality and personal service are the keynotes of success.
6. A wide range of stock is required to give customers the choice which they are increasingly coming to expect.
7. As with all retail trades careful consideration must be given to location (see Chapter 4).
8. These types of shop may be started from scratch.
9. If started from scratch there may be a large investment required for equipment.
10. They are usually less expensive to buy than say a newsagents or convenience store.
11. In some localities many specialist food retailers, in particular fishmongers, are fast disappearing. The ones that remain have survived either because of excellent reputation based on quality or service or because they have changed their image and approach to meet changing tastes and styles of living – offering benefits to their customers that their larger competitors cannot provide.

Clothes, fashion and shoe shops

The retailing of clothes and footwear is a trade which is increasingly being taken over and monopolized by the large retail units and multiples making it a difficult area for the small retailer to gain a foothold and expand into. In 1984 the largest ten retail companies accounted for 43 per cent of the sales of men's and boys' wear, 46 per cent of women's, girls', children's and infants' wear, 43 per cent of travel goods (handbags, etc.) and over 53 per cent of footwear sales (*Source*: Table 15, *Retail Business Monitor* SDO 25). Collectively small single outlet retailers capture less than 25 per cent of the total consumer expenditure on clothes and footwear (see Fig. 1.7).

	%
Footwear:	18
Travel goods & bags:	24
Men's and boys' wear:	23
Women's, girls' and children's wear:	28

(*Source:* Tables 7 and 10, *Retail Business Monitor*, SDO 25, HMSO)

Fig. 1.7 Small single outlet retailer's share of total consumer expenditure on clothes and footwear

That is the bleak side and there are three good reasons why this should not necessarily stop you going into a business of this type.

1. Set against the relatively poor market shares held by small retailers is the encouraging fact that real consumer expenditure on clothes and footwear increased by 34 per cent from 1980 to 1986. When you consider that total consumer expenditure increased by 17 per cent for the same period, the rate of increase in this area is substantial to say the least.

2. The high profit margins when compared to other retail trades are certainly attractive (see Fig. 1.8). In practice this means you may be able to exist on a lower sales level than another type of shop that has a lower profit margin. For instance a ladies fashion store with takings of £1,000 per week would earn £330 gross profit whereas a newsagent with an expected profit margin of 22 per cent would have to take half as much again, £1,500, to earn the same gross profit.

	Profit margin %	Profit mark up %
Footwear retailers:	42	72
Men's and boys' wear retailers:	37	58
Leather and travel goods retailers:	35	54
Female and infants' wear retailers:	33	49
General clothing businesses:	32	47

(*Source:* Based on Tables 3 and 4, *Retail Business Monitor*, SDO 25, HMSO)

Fig. 1.8 Approximate profit margins and mark ups: clothing and footwear (small retailers)

3. Observers of the high street and the fashion industry will certainly agree that one thing that characterizes this market best is the speed at which it changes. On the plus side the small retailer, knowledgeable and observant of changes in fashion and with access to a range of good suppliers, can be better placed to react to changes – more quickly than the high street giants. The dramatic growth of 'Sock Shop' which had relatively small beginnings is testament to this, showing that there is always room on the 'high street' for new ideas and innovation. On the minus side, it is easy to be caught wrong footed and end up with a lot of high value 'out of fashion' stock – no doubt there have been many would-be entrepreneurs who tried to emulate the success of Next, Tie

Rack and Sock Shop, got it wrong and ended up bankrupt. Also it is worth noting that to some extent the large retailers themselves set fashion trends in terms of the stock they choose to promote and sell.

To stand a reasonable chance of success in a business of this type you will probably have to be located in a shopping centre where there is significant passing trade. This in turn pushes up the cost of the operation in terms of the initial start up money required for the premises and the high rates a high street location will attract. Also, because of the high value of the stock and the breadth and depth of merchandise you will have to carry to satisfy customers, you will have to have quite a large amount of money invested in stock. Figure 1.9 gives you some indication of the number of weeks' stock you will have to carry.

	*RST	Number of weeks stock held
Footwear retailers:	3.6	14 weeks
Men's and boys' wear retailers:	4.0	13 weeks
Leather and travel goods retailers:	4.0	13 weeks
Female and infants' wear retailers:	3.2	16 weeks
General clothing businesses:	3.2	16 weeks

* RST: Annual rate of stock turn

(*Source:* based on Tables 2 and 3, *Retail Business Monitor*, SDO 25, HMSO)

Fig. 1.9 Approximate stock holdings: clothing and footwear (small retailers)

Further information may be sought by contacting relevant trade associations and reading trade papers.

Associations
Independent Footwear Retailers Association, 3 Masons Ave., Wealdstone, Harrow. Tel: 01-427-1545.
Menswear Association of Britain Ltd, Palladium House, 1–4 Argyll St, London. Tel: 01-734-6865.

Also it is worth keeping up to date with fashion ideas and trends by regularly reading the fashion magazines that are most likely to appeal to your targeted customer groups (see Chapter 3) and watching television programmes like *The Clothes Show*.

Clothing and footwear shops – the main points

1. The trade is becoming increasingly dominated by the large retailers.
2. Real consumer expenditure on clothes and footwear has risen dramatically – by 34 per cent between 1980 and 1988.
3. Access to a good range of suppliers is required.
4. Market changes in taste and fashion (local and national) need to be monitored and acted upon quickly but with care. You can do well by reacting to market changes quickly but, at the same time, you can easily make ruinous mistakes. Seeking growth in this market can be risky.
5. Profit margins are high – between 35 and 50 per cent.
6. You will have to invest a lot of money in stock – having up to 16 weeks' worth of stock in your shop at any given time.
7. A high street location is preferable but for this you will pay a high price in terms of premises and rates.

Other non-food trades

This section very briefly covers the vast range of non food retailing operations from electrical goods to DIY retailers. Most have three things in common. First, with a few possible exceptions, they require a large volume of passing trade and therefore a 'high street' location. Second the depth and breadth of stock, sometimes of high value, to be carried makes for a relatively low rate of stock turnover and consequently a large amount of money invested in stocks. Thirdly some trades' very existence is threatened by the continued growth of the large retailer. For instance, the likes of Currys, Dixons and Comet have largely sewn up the electrical goods market; Do It All, Texas and BQ, the DIY market – not to mention the recent growth of the Large Mixed Retail Business to be found on the edge of town.

All this adds up to an area of retailing that is fraught with dangers for the small operator and if ventured into, extreme care should be taken. The small retailer cannot hope to compete on the basis of price or even stock range but can offer more in the way of personal and reliable service. For example, a number of small DIY shops have successfully set up on the basis of offering 'a complete DIY service' to customers including detailed advice and instructions of how to solve DIY problems – a service that the customer cannot currently find to a satisfactory level in most of the larger outlets.

For those entering these types of business Fig. 1.10 gives some basic

	Profit margin %	Profit mark up %	Average stock holding
Chemists:	24	32	8 weeks
Photographic goods retailers:	35	54	9 weeks
Jewellers:	39	64	23 weeks
Toy, hobby, and sports goods:	28	39	15 weeks
Florists:	37	59	not available
Carpet retailers:	31	45	8 weeks
Furniture retailers:	35	54	11 weeks
Hardware and fancy goods:	33	49	13 weeks
DIY retailers:	30	43	10 weeks

(*Source:* Based on Table 3, *Retail Business Monitor*, SDO 25, HMSO)

Fig. 1.10 Approximate profit margins, mark ups and average stock holdings for various non-food trades

information on respective approximate profit margins and average stock holdings.

One way of gaining further insights into these trades is to obtain the relevant trade paper or write to the trade association concerned – a list of relevant trade papers and associations follows.

Associations
Radio, Electrical & Television Retailers Association Ltd., Retra House, 57–61 Newington Causeway, London. Tel: 01-403-1463.
Wallpaper, Paint and Wallcovering Retailers Association, PO Box 44, Walsall. Tel: 0922-31134
National Institute of Hardware, 10 Leam Terrace, Lemington Spa. Tel: 0926-21284
British Hardware Federation, 20 Holborne Rd., Edgebaston, Birmingham. Tel: 021-454-4385.
Booksellers Association of Great Britain and Ireland, 154 Buckingham Palace Rd, London. Tel: 01-730-8214.

Trade papers
Video News
Electrical and Electronic Trader
The Bookseller
Cabinet Maker and Retail Furnisher
Drapery and Fashion Weekly
Chemist and Druggist

Furnishing World
Sports Trader
Hardware Review
Hardware Trade Journal
Pet Store Trader
Retail Jeweller
Toy Trader

What kind of shop is right for me?

The preceding sections will have given you some insight into many of the more popular retail trades and what's happening in retailing in general. Maybe as a result of your reading you have a list of ideas to explore further. Obviously, at some stage you must decide on a particular shop type to research in detail. The purpose of this section is to help you make that choice. The factors that affect your final choice from a shortlist of potential shop types can be split broadly into personal and business considerations. One way of coming to a final decision is to use your personal and business requirements as a series of sieves to weed out non starters.

Personal considerations

Your skills and interests – can you do it?

In choosing a retail trade, many people wish to capitalize on existing skills or look for a type of shop where the skill required is easily learnt. For instance specialist food shops and fast food catering require specific trade skills, clothing and fashion retailing requires an 'eye for fashion', whereas you can successfully operate a convenience store using more general retail and business skills, skills this book will help you to develop. It is worth noting that many small shops rely on a high level of personal service for success. If you intend opening a shop of this type then are you a good communicator, tactful, sensitive to peoples' needs, patient and do you enjoy meeting people?

For each retail trade that appeals to you try and identify what 'daily work activities' it will involve you in. If you don't know, find out by taking temporary or part-time work in that area or, if that is not possible, by talking to and observing people in that type of business. Remember the scale of operation can vastly alter the nature of your job in the business. If you intend to employ staff then some of the routine chores will be removed from your daily routine and be replaced with all the activities related to the management of staff, discussed later in the book.

New skills and knowledge can be obtained by a number of means. Your local Further Education College or Adult Education Centre will probably be able to offer a course in your area of need. Alternatively, or in support of joining a course, you may be able to seek temporary employment in the area of business of your choice, gaining the skills and knowledge first hand.

Your commitments

It is important not just to have the support of your family but also to take into account their wishes and needs. Are they prepared to put up with you spending evenings and weekends helping your business grow? Too many people underestimate the amount of time that running a shop takes.

Also, going into retailing can mean selling up the family home and 'living above the shop', perhaps living in an area you would not normally choose to make a home. If this means too much disruption for the family then perhaps you will have to go for a smaller lock up shop or buy leasehold instead of freehold. If, because of financial constraints and the type and scale of shop you want, you cannot afford to finance a separate home then don't make the common mistake of choosing a business on the sole consideration of where the family would like to live. Having made a decision to go into retailing the brutal fact is that business considerations must come first.

Make a list of what you personally require of a business and use it to sieve out those types of shops that don't match your requirements.

Business considerations

Is there a viable market for the type(s) of shop you are considering?

This is of paramount importance – without a sufficient market for your product or service your business is doomed before it starts. Chapters 3 and 4 deal in detail with market research but initially you must be able to roughly answer some of the following basic questions in relation to your selected shop types:

- who will buy your product or service?
- why will they buy from you instead of the competition?
- what threat is there now and in the future from large retailers?
- how big is the market?
- what will your share be?
- is the market over supplied?
- is the market growing or contracting?

Make some rough checks on the market potential for the shop types left on your list. Discard those that, in your opinion, stand little chance of attaining a viable sales level. The level of risk you are prepared to take comes into play here. High risk should equal the potential to earn high profits. High risk with low profit potential, to state the obvious, should not be considered. Some retail trades that are fast disappearing from the high street, such as fishmongers, tend to fall into this bracket. If you are interested in those types of shop, then you are best advised to look for a new slant/approach to an old idea. If you have a new and novel idea then there is bound to be uncertainty, but at the very least you should be able to identify the *who* and *why* in terms of customers. If you can't then you don't truly have a business idea.

How much capital will the business require – can you afford it?

This is obviously an important consideration. Chapter 6 will help you calculate in detail the amount you will require to start the business and Chapter 7 will tell you where you can obtain finance and how to go about raising it. At this stage, however, you need to have some idea of what business you can and cannot afford.

Calculating rough estimates of what it will cost to start up

You can very roughly estimate initial start up costs for various types of shop and scales of operation by adding together the purchase price and the stock investment. Some allowance for 'additional working capital' (see Chapter 6), to finance the business until it gets on its feet, will make the calculations more realistic. Purchase prices for various retail trades related to tenure, location and turn over are easily obtainable from your local business estate agency. Investment in stock is easily calculated by dividing the turn over by the rate of stock turn and reducing it by the percentage profit margin attributable to that particular trade (see the previous sections).

Approximating the amount of money you can raise to start up

As a rough guide most financial institutions will require you to put up nearly half the total requirement of the business venture. However, where you are buying residential property with the shop it is possible to obtain semi-commercial mortgages of up to 95 per cent of the valuation of the 'bricks and mortar'. To begin with make a list of your assets (see Fig. 1.11). How much can you raise, top end, bottom end? Now make a revised list

Assets	Cash value
● House value	How much personal capital do you have tied up in your house? Make a conservative estimate of the market value of your house and subtract the balance of your mortgage outstanding. Note: You can remortgage your house usually up to 80 per cent of its valuation.
● Life assurance policies	You can obtain a quote on their current surrender value. *Whether this is a sensible financial decision needs careful consideration.*
● Material possessions	For instance you may have a new car that you can sell and replace with a cheaper, second-hand one.
● Shares ● Premium bonds ● Savings accounts	Cash value.

Fig. 1.11   Assets list

of the shops in terms of trade, scale of operation and tenure that you can afford.

Should I buy an existing business

Having selected the retail trade you consider is right for you the question arises – should I start from scratch or buy an existing business? If you are one of the few who have a completely new retailing concept the decision, by definition, is made for you. For people wishing to open up as a newsagent or off-licence then the nature of the trade largely determines that you will have to buy an existing business. For others the choice is open.

A major appeal of buying an existing business is speed – the business is a 'going concern' and, hopefully, revenue will come in from day one. There is little inconvenience, from looking for suitable premises through choosing equipment to finding a customer base and new suppliers.

A second and important advantage is that if you have selected your business well you will have a sound base from which to expand, innovate and perhaps change direction. When starting from scratch it often takes three to six months to reach a viable sales level. But starting from scratch can be cheaper as you are not paying for 'goodwill'. Also, you can often more easily obtain exactly what you require in terms of premises, location, equipment and so on.

Buying a business is sometimes like buying a second-hand car or house – there are unseen flaws. After you take over you may find that the premises are not really as suitable as you thought. They might be in the wrong place, have the wrong equipment and there may be not sufficient room for expansion or planning permission cannot be gained for an extension.

An existing business will have a track record. You can look at past sales records and have an accountant check out the financial viability of the business. When starting from scratch the risk is greater for although market research can provide good estimates of potential revenue, it cannot guarantee it!

Buyers new to business often make the mistake of relying too heavily on the past accounts of the business for assurance that the business is a viable concern. Let the buyer beware, is a good saying to remember. The problem with records are twofold. Firstly, the records refer to what has happened in the past – there is no guarantee that the business will continue to be a success in the future. For instance, the previous owner's business may have been based on personal reputation and when he or she goes, so does the business. Also you might not run the business as well as the previous owner.

Secondly, accounts can conceal as much as they reveal and depend for their accuracy on the honesty of the owner of the business. It should also be noted that the accounts do not give the full story. For instance, they do not tell you whether double yellow lines are going to be placed outside your newly acquired newsagents or about the large store that is going to open up close by and take away all your trade.

If you plan to open a shop retailing a service, inclusive of fast food, my experience indicates you can do just as well setting up from scratch as buying an existing business provided that careful consideration is given to location.

Whether you decide to buy or start from scratch the detailed research and planning that this book deals with is equally applicable to both forms of business start up.

We will return to this topic in detail in Chapter 9.

Franchises and voluntary groups

What is a franchise – is it a good way to start in business?

An increasingly popular alternative to starting from scratch or buying an existing business is to buy a franchise. A franchise is a business relationship between a franchisor (owner of a name or method of business) and a franchisee (a local operator of that business). The franchisee agrees to pay the franchisor a certain sum of money for use of the business name or the business method or both. This payment is usually in the form of an initial fee and some agreed percentage of sales or a similar arrangement.

The main advantage of starting a business by becoming a franchisee is that you are usually buying a tried and tested method for doing a particular business. Consequently there should be a greater chance of success than with buying an existing business or starting from scratch.

The franchisor will dictate to varying degrees how the business should be run. Often this will include instructing and advising the franchisee on the product or service range, pricing policy, size and design of premises and sometimes even the style of uniform the employees should wear. A good franchisor will also provide a back-up service giving advice where applicable on such aspects of the business as management, training, merchandising, accounts, etc. Larger franchisors will usually offer advertising/sales promotion support.

The size of franchises varies considerably. The initial cost of buying a franchise ranges from a few thousand pounds upwards to half a million pounds. Franchising has now become so popular (there are now said to be in excess of 16,000 franchised units in the UK) that most of the major clearing banks have set up specialist sections to deal with finance applications from potential franchisees.

The main disadvantage of becoming a franchisee is that the business is never truly yours. As the franchisor lays down certain requirements, which can be quite comprehensive, you can never run the business exactly as you want. If the franchisor is not flexible enough to take into account the changing nature of your local business environment, this control can have adverse effects on your business. Finally, you will never be able to keep all of your profits as most franchise agreements involve some form of continuing payment related to sales or profits.

Taking up a franchise can be an attractive starting point for those entering into business for the first time. But beware: not all franchise operations are the same. As a guide to investigating a franchise, use the checklist below. If the franchise is worthwhile purchasing you must receive satisfactory answers to each question on the checklist.

Taking up a franchise – a checklist of questions

The franchise operation and operator

1. How long has the franchisor been operating in the UK?

2. How many outlets are in operation? How many have closed and why?
3. Are the present outlets successful? Does the franchise have a good name with its customers and operators?
4. Will this type of business be successful in your area? Is there a viable market in your area?
5. What is the competition in your area?
6. Is the franchise operating in an expanding or contracting market? Is it keeping pace with changes in the market?
7. Is the franchisor a member of the British Franchise Association?
8. What is the financial position of the franchisor? Is it healthy? Obtain a copy of their audited accounts.
9. Will the franchisor allow you to take up references on him?

The franchise agreement

1. What is the initial payment? What does it entitle you to?
2. What will your liability be for the payment of royalties?
3. On what conditions can/will the franchise be terminated?
4. What will the franchisor contract be able to provide?
5. Are there any minimum sales figures to be met?

If in any doubt do not proceed

Further information on franchises can be obtained from The British Franchise Association, Franchise Chambers, 75a Bell Street, Henley-on-Thames RG9 2BD; 0491 578049. The Association produces a package advising on all aspects of purchasing and operating a franchise, including a list of all franchisors registered with the Association. The fee for the pack is currently £8, obtainable at the above address by return post.

Voluntary groups

One of the reasons for the growth of the large stores and multiple chains in this country and the corresponding demise of many types of small trader was the introduction of the Resale Prices Acts of 1964 and 1976. These Acts made it illegal for suppliers, wholesalers or manufacturers to fix minimum retail prices, though a few exceptions remain relating to the sale of books, newspapers and drugs. The result was that the large retailers, in gaining larger shares of the retail market through price cutting and by dealing direct with manufacturers via their own distribution network, eroded the sales base of the more traditional wholesaler. Some wholesalers fought back by forming groups of independent retailers to trade with on a semi-exclusive basis. The wholesalers were then able to retain their sales volume, buy in from the manufacturers on the same terms as the large retail groups and pass on some of the discount to the group members. Over time these wholesalers joined together to form much larger voluntary chains.

From these beginnings the voluntary groups have become very sophisticated animals indeed. They can offer a range of services equivalent to the best franchise operations, including own brand labels, site assessment, promotional activity, staff training programmes and general guidance on store layout. Most importantly, nationally recognized voluntary groups like Spar give the small retailer an image of credibility with the shopper in terms of quality, service and, to some extent, price. For all this the small retailer does not pay the high price of losing his or her independence. The general requirement is that the trader must buy a reasonable proportion of his or her goods from the voluntary group and pay a levy on sales for additional services. The exact terms and conditions of membership vary from group to group.

Summary

If you didn't have a clear idea what type of shop to open before you started this chapter, I hope the discussions about the various retail trades and activities have helped you choose a shop type that is right for you. If you had already made a firm choice, the discussions have hopefully given you further insight into retailing and the activities have made you pause for thought to make sure that your idea matches your personal requirements and resources.

The rest of the book is about researching and planning the business venture in more detail. The next chapter will introduce you to the importance of planning, the mistakes that many new businesses make and help you to get organized for the interesting and demanding task ahead. Before you proceed use the checklist of questions overleaf. If you do this you will furnish yourself with the necessary ground base of information to tackle the more detailed research and planning that follows.

Checklist

---

1. Have you the health and stamina for your selected venture? Can you cope with the stresses and strains?
2. Are you prepared to take a calculated risk?
3. How will you cope if the going gets rough both in the planning and running of the business?
4. We all have strengths and weaknesses – what are yours?
5. How are you going to exploit your strong points?
6. What are you going to do about your weak ones?
7. Have you the necessary skills?
8. Are you a self-starter?
9. Do you have self-discipline?
10. Can you work long hours over a sustained period?
11. Have you discussed your project with your family and friends?
12. Do you have their support?
13. Have you thought long and hard and identified your reasons for opening a shop?
14. Have you contacted the relevant trade association for further information?
15. Have you consulted appropriate trade magazines/periodicals?
16. Have you identified the specific job skills (if any) you will need to acquire to operate the shop?
17. Have you some idea of what the trends are in the retail trade of your choice?
18. Have you done a 'first' rough review of the retail businesses for sale in your area of the type you are interested in?
19. Have you done a *realistic* assessment of the personal capital at your disposal?
20. If interested in franchising have you contacted the British Franchise Association?
21. Have you selected a type of shop that will meet your personal objectives?
22. Have you a degree of confidence that a viable market exists in your locality for the type of shop selected?
23. Have you discussed your responses to this checklist with somebody who knows you well?

---

2 Planning for success

The importance of planning □ The mistakes people make □ The process of planning □ Business plans □ Making a start at the business plan □ Constraints on the business plan □ Strengths, weaknesses, opportunities and threats □ Summary

This chapter discusses some of the common mistakes made by would-be entrepreneurs and, in doing so, emphasizes the importance of completing a fully detailed business plan before opening up for business. You will also be given a framework around which to build your own business plan, the detail to add to the frame being built up as you work through the second section of the book. To get you started on the plan the final sections of the chapter lead you to examine the constraints you will have to plan within and the threats and opportunities posed by the retail environment.

The importance of planning

Hopefully, you now have identified a type of shop that is matched to your personal interests, commitments, skills and financial resources. In most cases it will be a rough idea, in some, more refined. You will now need to research the idea in fine detail. Will the business idea work in practice? You will need to know the answer to this question in advance of starting your business. It is answered by thorough research and planning of your business idea.

The research and planning of the business venture is the very stuff of a business plan and is a must if the business is to have any chance of success. In fact, think of anything you have done that has been successful and the odds are that it was well thought out first – or a great deal of luck was on your side. In business, relying on luck is a luxury you cannot afford.

The pity is that many people will plan their holidays but not their business. Would you set out on your holidays not knowing where you were going, what route or transport to take, how much it will cost to get there, whether there will be accommodation at the end of your journey and how long you will spend at each place? Perhaps such a holiday may appeal to the wildly adventurous – but would you go into business in this way? It sounds absurd, but many small business people proceed exactly in this way, muddling through from one day to the next. The 'adventure' usually ends in bankruptcy and in some of the worst cases prison for fraudulent trading.

The mistakes people make

Each year thousands of businesses fail, mainly because the owners never researched and planned their business in detail. The variety of reasons for failure can be broadly summed up under the following headings. Take note and make sure you don't make the same mistakes!

The wrong location

In retailing, location is paramount. The world will not beat a path to your door simply because you have the 'right' product or service at the 'right' price. Do not be tempted, as many other small business people have been, to take premises because the rent or purchase price is low or because you like the area. Your location should be chosen carefully in relation to access to your markets.

For help in choosing the right location consult Chapter 4.

Little or no knowledge of the size of the market

Don't commit the cardinal sin of assuming that just because you think the retailing idea you have thought up is a good one that everyone else will think the same and rush to become your customers! Many new shops fail simply because the market is just not big enough to provide the necessary custom. The market you intend to serve might be contracting rapidly, be too competitive, or, for all intents and purposes, non existent. Opening a shop without researching the market is similar to taking a job without asking how much you will be paid!

See Chapters 3 and 4.

Little or no knowledge of their customers' buying motives

Many shops appear to have little idea of the type of customers they are serving. The result is the business cannot have any sales promotion/marketing strategy and may actually be unsure of what type of business it is in. For instance a business selling clothes on price, when its market holds quality and reliability as its main considerations, will not maximize sales from that market. To keep the importance of this point in the forefront of your mind *define your business in terms of its customers*.

See Chapter 3.

No systems or policy for selecting, training and managing staff

Few who enter small business for the first time have had experience of selecting, employing and managing staff, therefore, it is hardly surprising to find that many small businesses make costly mistakes in this area. One dishonest or poorly trained employee can cost you all of your profits. Remember that, in generating and keeping custom, your most valuable asset will be well-trained sales staff.

See *Hiring & Firing* by Karen Lanz, published in this series.

2

Failure to keep records

Ask any small business person questions such as, 'How do this month's sales figures compare to last month's?' or, 'How much profit did you make this month?' and the likelihood is that the majority would not be able to give you an accurate answer. The reason for this is that they have either not kept up to date with their records or don't have a proper and useful administration system. A shop founded and operated on this basis has little chance of success. Without basic accounting information, your business could be nearing failure without you recognizing the problem until it is too late. In particular, retail businesses are prone to failure through theft of stock eroding profits. A good stock control system is needed not just to closely monitor and control stock loss, but to give accurate sales information to enable you to buy in the right goods at the right time.

See Chapters 12 and 13.

Mistaking cash for profit

One of the most common errors is to mistake cash for profit. Cash and profit are two distinct items. Cash can come from a variety of sources: loans, overdrafts, retained profits, etc. Profits come from the difference between a business's revenue and its costs. Profit can be tied up in stocks and equipment and is not necessarily in the form of a growing bank balance. For instance, a business can be making a profit but be overdrawn at the bank because all of its cash is tied up in stock and debtors (people who owe it money). This position is fine if it is controlled, planned for and temporary. When it becomes uncontrolled, unplanned and permanent, disaster strikes. Cash is the life blood of a business and without it new materials, wages, stock, etc. cannot be purchased.

See Chapter 6.

Lack of cash to finance growth

If you are planning to buy empty premises and open a new shop don't make the mistake of underestimating the amount of time it will take to get the shop off the ground and reach a viable sales level. This can vary from three to six months. Failure to plan for this can lead to an early entry into the bankruptcy statistics.

Take a walk around the shopping centres in your area and you will notice that the shops that are in decline have one thing in common – poorly stocked shelves and fixtures. The sad fact is that many small shops are strangulated at birth by having far too little 'working capital' to invest in stock. The result is a vicious downward spiral with poor stock range leading to falling custom, resulting in less money to invest in stock, leading to a further drop in custom – and so on until the business fails altogether.

The opposite of this, early and fast growth, can be just as large a problem. A business that enters into a phase of unplanned rapid growth can run out of cash very quickly indeed as it has to find cash from previous smaller sales to finance such items as stock, materials and wages to meet the demands of the uncontrolled growth.

All this emphasizes the need for gaining accurate sales projections and then fully detailing and planning the cash required to finance them.

See Chapters 5 and 6.

Full costs of starting up and operating not identified

Many people start up in business without fully realizing the size and nature of the costs involved. Often, the start up costs are too high, sometimes extravagant purchases being made or certain items being purchased outright which would have been better leased.

See Chapter 5.

Lack of specialist skills & personal commitment

Many small business failures can be attributed to the lack of specialist skills on the part of the budding entrepreneur. Moreover, as can be seen from the preceding outline of the catalogue of mistakes made by small business people, many lack basic business skills. Making the transfer from employee to owner in the same line of business is not as simple as people think. For instance you can be an excellent sales assistant, butcher, clothes designer or beauty consultant but be a terrible business person!

___

If you set realistic goals in each of these areas, research each area fully and from that research decide on the best plan to fulfil your targets, there is every chance you will not make the same mistakes. Now lets turn our attention to the way ahead and examine the planning process in some detail.

The planning process

Our lives are made up of plans large and small, from how to arrive at a certain place at a certain time to getting married. A lot of our plans are designed to solve problems. In fact plans are about solving problems. Fundamentally they are about solving the problem about deciding beforehand how best to achieve what you want to do.

Effective planning in either personal or business life is matter of:

- Deciding what you want to achieve. Setting clear objectives.
- Listing your objectives in terms of importance and priority.
- Considering what you want to achieve in the light of what has happened before when attempting to attain similar objectives. Learning from your own and others' past and present experience.
- Considering the effect of fulfilling one objective on another. Sometimes the achievement of one objective will conflict with the satisfactory achievement of another.
- Collecting as much information as possible about the situation.
- Selecting possible ways of attaining your objectives.
- Considering the threats or constraints that may hinder or prevent you from attaining your objectives.
- Thinking of ways to overcome these threats and consider all the alternatives.
- Coming to an overall decision on the best way forward and listing the things (tasks) that have to be done and the order in which they are to be done, to arrive at your goal.
- Constructing your plan and taking a dry run to test for faults before implementing it. Look before you leap.

If everything 'goes according to plan' you will fulfil your objectives. If not, you may make fresh plans, perhaps revising some of your original objectives because they now, with the benefit of hindsight, appear unrealistic. For instance, you may find that the sales level you have to attain to make a profit is unrealistic, perhaps forcing you to redefine your pricing and profit margin objectives. You may even look for a different market altogether, perhaps radically altering your first conception of the business. This is quite natural. The process of planning is a fluid one of setting objectives, carrying out research, examining the objectives in the light of information obtained, making plans and reviewing progress. Don't succumb to the temptation to bend your findings to suit your original personal and business goals.

Business plans

The starting point for all business plans is the setting of business objectives, of which there will be many. All, however, will be designed to support, either directly or indirectly, the overall aim of the business which is to survive. Business survival is dependent on a number of factors, all of which have been identified by implication in our discussion of the key reasons for business failure. These can be encompassed by two overall aims, applicable to all businesses:

1. To make sufficient profit to provide the owner(s) with 'acceptable earnings', i.e. a satisfactory rate of return on the capital invested (otherwise the money would have been better placed earning interest in a savings account) and to provide sufficient monies to reinvest in the business to ensure continued growth.
2. To have adequate finance and long term positive cash flow to enable the business to meet its debts and therefore continue trading.

Subservient to these overall 'aims' are a range of more specific objectives for each part of the business plan. Your business plan can be sub-divided in many ways but it must cover the following areas.

Sales and market

Quite simply, no customers means no business! You need to collect as much information as possible about the market for your business. Some of the key questions have already been posed in Chapter 1 and the whole area will be considered in detail in Chapters 3 and 4.

The size and demands of your potential market will lay down the parameters for decision making relating to:

- Scale of operation
- Location
- The competition
- Sales targets
- Pricing and overall trading policy
- Stock range

- Additional customer services that need to be offered
- Marketing/sales promotion policies

In summation, as a small shop cannot significantly influence and change the nature of the market, you should evolve your overall business idea in response to the threats and opportunities posed by it.

Chapters 3, 4 and 14 deal with these areas in detail.

Costs

This area of the plan will detail all the costs faced in starting and running the shop for at least the first year's trading. Here care should be taken not to mistake all business expenditure for costs. *Costs* relate only to expenditure on those items that are used up in a given period of trading, such as stock sold, wages, electricity, rent, rates, insurance and so on. Expenditure on items often associated with start up such as equipment and premises are not costs. You are likely to still possess them at the end of the trading period and they are called *assets*. As each year goes by some assets will lose value through ageing and wear and tear. This loss in value is a cost and is known as depreciation.

Some costs such as electricity, rent and rates do not change regardless of how much you sell. These are known as fixed costs or, more commonly, 'overheads'. Others, most significantly stock, vary in direct proportion with the amount you sell.

A detailed investigation into the full costs of operating the shop cannot be made until decisions relating to the scale and location of the operation (derived in part from market research and financial constraints) are made. However, identification of supplies can begin almost immediately.

The formulation of objectives in this area are inextricably linked with sales targets and investment decisions.

Profit

This aspect of your planning will provide one of the acid tests for your sales and cost objectives. Will your sales bring in sufficient revenue to cover all costs and provide you with an 'acceptable profit'?

You will earn profit from the buying and selling merchandise. The difference between the prices you buy and sell at is your gross profit which will have to contribute to the payment of your overheads. What's left over is your net profit.

There are a number of factors which affect profitability:

- Sales volume
- Price
- Overheads or fixed costs
- Profit margin (i.e., the difference between the cost of stock and the price which you sell it at)

Do not make the mistake of assuming that a high profit margin will bring high overall gross profits. A low profit margin and a high volume of sales can bring in more overall gross profit than a high profit with a low volume of sales.

When you have brought together your estimates of costs and revenue, it is likely you will have to make at least minor adjustments to your sales and cost objectives. In fact, the development of your sales, cost and profit plans, because they are so closely related, will develop hand in hand.

See Chapter 4 for a full discussion of profitability and costs.

Investment and finance

The amount of money you will have to invest in the assets of the business will be determined primarily by:

- The scale of operation
- Whether you intend to buy freehold or leasehold
- The stock levels you will have to carry
- The level of credit sales

A decision to buy freehold and an increase in any of the other points will increase your investment in the business. Any decision to rent or lease instead of buying major items of equipment, ranging from vans to electronic tills, will reduce your investment.

Further, most shops experience peaks and troughs in terms of money going out (e.g. due to quarterly bills all coming at the same) and money coming in (e.g. due to seasonal fluctuations in sales). Therefore, at times there will be more money going out than coming in. This is okay over a short period of time, but over the long term you must plan your business so that a cash surplus position is reached. Full instruction, discussion and advice on cash flow forecasting and control is given in Chapter 6.

Finally, the rate of return on the money invested in the business should be in excess of what it would earn in, for instance, a savings account.

Having established *how much* is to be invested in the business and *when*, the right type of finance must be selected, applied for and secured. See Chapter 7.

Business control and administration

Once objectives have been set in the areas of the market and sales, costs, profit, investment and finance, you will need to create systems to put these plans into motion. You will need systems and policies for:

- Maintaining the security of cash and merchandise (Chapters 12 and 13)
- Recording all transactions in the business (Chapters 12 and 13)
- Monitoring sales (Chapters 13 and 14)
- Ordering goods (Chapter 13)
- Selecting, training and managing staff
- Dealing with VAT (Chapter 11)
- Handling complaints (Chapters 14 and 15)
- Conforming to legislation affecting your business (Chapter 15)

Making a start at the planning process

As you can see, the process of planning for a successful business start up is no simple matter. To begin with you will have more questions and problems than answers and solutions. Completion of the plan will be a test of your determination to succeed. Clarity in setting your objectives will certainly help. Vague objectives, or even worse no objectives at all, will lead to confusion and lack of direction. For example, 'The business will attain a minimum gross profit margin of 25 per cent and hold on average 1 week's stock' is specific and clear, whereas 'a good profit margin and low stock levels' is not. However, before getting down to setting specific objectives and formulating detailed plans you need to formulate planning guidelines. Let's make a start at this by first identifying the overall constraints within which your planning will take place and second, identifying the threats to and opportunities for your business.

Constraints on the business plan

There will be constraints you have imposed upon yourself, say to minimize risk. There will also be constraints that have been imposed upon you, for example, by the finance you can raise, the nature of the type of shop you are going to operate, local competition and customer preferences. All such factors will limit what it is feasible to achieve and, therefore, provide overall limits to your objectives and also such guidelines for more detailed planning. Use the checklist of possible constraints to define in some detail the constraints you will have to face. Some questions you may well be able to answer now whilst others will have to wait until you have gathered more detailed information. However, the important point is that you will have made a start.

Checklist for preparing planning guidelines

Financial constraints

- How much personal capital have you at your disposal?
- How much can you raise in the form of loans?
- Are you prepared to seek out partners or venture capital?

Constraints relating to personal and risk factors

- How many hours are you prepared to work in any week?
- Are you prepared to work unsocial hours and days?
- Do you or your family object to living on the premises?
- How much can you afford or are prepared to lose if the shop fails?
- Will you sacrifice a degree of security to obtain rapid growth?
- Will you minimize risk by buying an existing business or start from scratch?
- What degree of certainty will you require before you decide to open up?
- Will you want to employ and manage staff or just keep the shop as a one person or family operation?

Constraints relating to the nature of the retail trade selected

- Are there severe locational restrictions? (See Chapter 4.)
- Will you have to purchase an existing business to enter the retail tade selected?
- Will you buy a franchise or become a member of a voluntary group?
- Does the nature of your trade require a high investment in stock?
- How severe is the competition?
- How is the market for small shops in your sector of retailing changing?
- What is the minimum you will have to offer your customers in terms of location, stock range, additional services and price to trade successfully?
- Will your scale of operation limit you to certain suppliers? Will you, for instance, be precluded from dealing directly with manufacturers?
- Other?

Strengths, weaknesses, opportunities and threats

In identifying the constraints of your plan you will have largely determined what you will or can do and what you won't or can't. The next step is to examine the strengths and weaknesses of your venture in relation to the threats and opportunities posed by the environment in which it will operate. Armed with such an analysis, you will be well placed to set detailed objectives aimed at minimizing risk and maximizing opportunity.

The retail environment is made up of the larger influences of the economy: social trends, population characteristics, laws (present and pending), and developments in technology. These factors, over which you will have little or no control, will directly or indirectly impinge on your day-to-day environment of competing with other retail outlets, increasing sales, dealing with suppliers and exploiting your location to the full. Figure 2.1 summarizes the main factors. Each should be examined for the threats they can pose and the opportunities they can offer to your intended business.

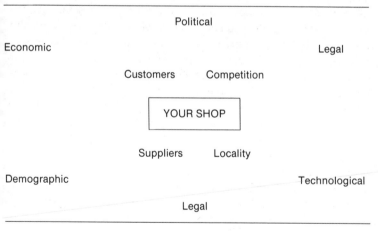

Fig. 2.1 The retail environment

Economic factors

The significant indicators to examine are:

- The rate of interest
- Unemployment trends and stability of the local economy

- Changes in disposable income
- The inflation rate

The present and future rate of interest charged on loans is important to all retailers for two principal reasons. Firstly, changes in the rate of interest will significantly alter the cost of business loans. Secondly, as a large proportion of the 1980s 'consumer boom' has been financed by credit cards and credit agreements, dramatic increases in the rate of interest can have a dampening effect on consumer demand, particularly on retail trades dealing in a high value merchandise, such as electrical goods. However, it should be noted that relatively small adjustments seem to have little effect on demand.

You should examine the local economy in general. How prosperous is it? Is it stable, growing or in decline? These factors will have some overall impact on the market you intend to serve. Trends in unemployment rates are certainly indicators. Also, if your customers depend on a few large employers for their livelihood, find out how well they are doing and, if possible, what their future plans are. A whole town and its retail trade can be decimated by just one large employer shifting production elsewhere.

Changes in real disposable income (i.e. after discounting the effect of inflation and taking taxation into account) can have a more dramatic effect on some retail trades than others. Between 1981 and 1986 real disposable income rose by 17 per cent. The most notable effects on retail sales were increases in clothes sales (up by 34 per cent) and in the purchases of TVs, VCRs, etc. (up by a colossal 97 per cent). Spending on basic needs such as food remained fairly static in the same period.

Prices of all goods and services do not go up at the same rate. The various rates of inflation for the different types of merchandise you sell and the goods and services your business consumes should be examined for their impact on costs, profits and sales. For example, a high rate of inflation on merchandise where price is an important factor can dramatically curtail sales. Further, if the price of major items of cost are rising at a greater rate than the items you sell, profits will be eroded. We will return to the subject of inflation later when we discuss the assessment of the worth and viability of shops that are for sale (see Chapter 9).

Political and legal factors

Political and legal factors are closely associated at both national and local levels. Obviously the government of the day, particularly one with a powerful majority, will largely originate and pass the legislation of its choosing. You should examine not just the impact of existing legislation on your shop (see Chapter 15) but significant legislation which is likely to be debated and passed in the future. Of special interest to retailers are changes in the law relating to such areas as hours and days of trading, credit, pricing, labelling and description of merchandise and services.

On a local level, you should try and assess whether the local authority is more or less likely to pass planning applications for large retail ventures that will dramatically effect your business. Also, what plans for housing, commercial, road/transport and other developments are in the pipeline that may effect your business?

Pressure groups and associated media reports and campaigns can have a dramatic effect on markets. For example, the anti-smoking lobby has dramatically reduced the sale of tobacco products. The drive towards healthier living and the concern over cruelty to animals led to the tremendous success of 'The Body Shop'. The concern over deaths resulting from inflammable fabrics and fillings in furniture led to a temporary boom in smoke alarms and will have longer term implications for the furniture industry as a whole. It was claimed that the widespread publicity concerning salmonella and eggs in early 1989 gave rise to a drop in national egg sales by some 40 per cent. These examples – there are many more – show social attitudes and concerns can be of immense importance to the retailer.

Social and population factors

On a national level the population has remained fairly static at around 56 million, projected to increase to only 60 million by the year 2025. This, however, masks major changes in the age, sex, economic activity and geographical distribution of the population. You must scrutinize population figures for the locality of your shop for significant changes and trends that may effect your business. How to do this is considered in detail in Chapters 3 and 4.

Overall, people are becoming more materialistic which generally is good for the retail trade as individuals are driven to possess more consumer products. However, the retailer should also be aware that the shopping public are becoming more aware of their rights through the growth of consumer associations. They are more concerned about quality than price and overall are coming to expect and demand a higher level of service from retailers. The growth in preoccupation with style and image is evident and well documented. Accordingly the retailer must take greater care to present an image that is consistent with what the consumer wants. The importance and identification of the wants and needs of your customers is the subject of Chapter 3.

Technological factors

Developments in technology can create vast new markets, as has been the case with home computers. It can also fundamentally change the way the retailer operates as is increasingly the case with the advent of bar codes on merchandise and computerized till points. The advantages and use of 'EPOS' (Electronic Point of Sale equipment) are discussed fully in Chapter 12.

Summary

The key reason for the failure of small shops is lack of planning. The mistakes that small shopkeepers make are testimony to this. How formal you make the planning process is largely up to you and the nature and scale of your business. You will, however, be well advised to conform to the general planning principles given in this chapter. In particular, you should be aware of the constraints on your overall business plan and develop objectives to minimize the threats posed and maximize the opportunities presented to your proposed shop. (A diagram of the complete planning process is given in Fig. 2.2.) In addition, you should now be aware of some of the major areas of concern, the importance of thinking through decisions, and how a decision in one area can affect decisions taken in others. The rest of the book, which can be referred to any order, will take you through the detailed planning you need.

Careful planning will:

- minimize problems and risk
- help prevent you from taking potentially ruinous action
- raise your confidence in your ability to open and operate your shop
- provide you with a framework, when your shop is up and running, for identifying and correcting problems *before* they happen.

Finally, as indicated in Fig. 2.2, planning is not a process that ends when you eventually open your shop but one that should continue throughout the life of your business.

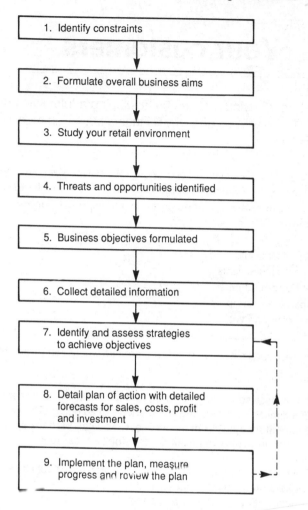

Fig. 2.2 Summary of the business planning process

3 Your customers

Customer buying motives □ Developing a total sales proposition □ Who will buy and why □ Finding out □ Summary □ Action guidelines

If the question is asked, 'Do you know what business you are entering or hoping to enter?' the commonest response would be to refer to an overall shop type or to the type of products you intend to sell. For instance, 'I am going to:

- sell records and tapes'
- open a newsagents'
- sell cards and gifts'
- open a bookshop'
- sell fruit and veg'

Such responses, if left at that level, are extremely dangerous for a number of reasons:

1. A business so blandly described lumps itself with all other shops of a similar type. Nothing will mark it out as being different from its competitors apart from its drabness. You can perhaps spot shops like this in your own locality. They don't appear to know what they are doing!
2. Defining the business simply in terms of the products it sells puts blinkers on it before it opens its doors for business. It is concentrating on what it wants to sell rather than on what its customers want. This is a form of self-centredness that must be avoided at all costs.
3. Further, the success or failure of a shop permanently locked into a merchandise range will be determined not by its owner but more by the success or failure of the products. It will not be able to adapt quickly to changes in the market and as the life cycle of the product comes to end, so will the business.

As no customers means no business, your shop must be defined not just as a broad type or solely on the basis of the merchandise it will sell, but in clear terms of how it will satisfy the needs of its customers. What is required is a full examination of your potential customers' buying motives to enable you to shape your business accordingly. The aim is to develop a trading policy, in essence a full definition of your business in terms of what will be offered to your customers in the way of merchandise, location, price and services. In doing so it is hoped that you will differentiate your shop in some positive way from the competition and provide the basis for attaining viable and expanding sales.

Customer buying motives

It can be generally said that all people buy to satisfy some goal or need. Human needs are many and varied, ranging from the basic physical needs of shelter, food and safety essential for survival, through the need to satisfy personal vanity, to intellectual and spiritual satisfaction. It is said that money can't buy you love – perhaps it can't, but florists, card shops and jewellers can make a good profit out of helping it along the way! Retailers of cosmetics sell dreams of beauty, sophistication and youth – satisfying our egos. People buy clothes to keep warm, but more are sold because people wish to project a variety of images – they need to belong and socialize. In each case the purchaser is motivated by the benefits they can derive from the purchase and less by the pure physical attributes of the merchandise. They don't buy products; they seek to acquire benefits.

It is certainly difficult to identify why people make certain purchases. Thorough examination of the needs of your customers would certainly help your understanding, but how practical would such an exercise be? Whilst noting the key importance of felt need as the driving force behind the purchase, it is easier and more practical to attempt to identify the benefits that customers seek in satisfying a need or collection of needs, rather than the needs themselves. This is perhaps the most useful and practical way of explaining customer buying motives.

To start you off on this process try to identify the benefits you sought when making purchases. The first thing you will probably find is that the decision to buy was not influenced solely by benefits attached to the product itself, but equally or even more so by other benefits derived, for example, from the price, the image, location, reputation of the shop, the existence of additional services and so on.

The reality is, successful shops and stores integrate their products' benefits into a more comprehensive benefits package. They attempt to build a trading image that differentiates them in a positive way from the competition. If they are successful, then the customer will always identify the store first before going on to make decisions appertaining to the product and/or the brand. It is not that the product is ignored, but rather that the benefits which are associated with it become inseparable from the

overall store image. It is in this way that the success of such retailers as
'Next' can be explained. Next's phenomenal growth is attributable not just
to the fact that it offers more sophisticated fashion to men and women
who are seeking new images, but more importantly, that it does so in the
context of an overall store image consistent with its customers' perception
of the fashion and life style they wish to aspire to.

The implications for you are clear. Whilst emphasising the benefits
attached to the merchandise you sell you must try to focus the
customer's mind foremost on the benefits of shopping at your
particular store. The question now is what package of benefits will be
effective in relation to your shop?

Developing a total sales proposition

From the foregoing we have seen that the successful shop owner must
look beyond the narrow bounds of his or her merchandise. Customers seek
a *total proposition* which includes benefits derived from a *marketing mix*
of:

- The Merchandise
- The Place in which it is sold
- The Price
- The Service that they receive

All this must be promoted in a way that they can relate to and perceive the
total importance of the whole package being offered to them.

Let's consider each aspect in turn and also attempt to do some initial
ground work on your 'total sales proposition'. As one of the main purposes
of developing a positive trading policy is to differentiate you from the
competition, you will be encouraged to examine in some detail the varying
package of benefits offered by your potential competitors and other
similar businesses. However, you will not be able to arrive at a 'total sales
proposition' without full reference to exactly *who* your customers will be.
It is only then that the benefits different groups of customers are seeking
can be fully identified and acted upon. After completing this introduction
you will move on to identifying your customers in some detail.

The merchandise

As we have already discussed the merchandise is much more than a physical item offered for sale. The merchandise as a range of items or as a single product offers a collection of benefits to the customer. These may be directly associated with its use, for instance a washing machine may bought because it offers the benefit of an economy wash enabling the user to save on electricity bills. Alternatively, the sale may be attributable to the fact that the customer is offered a full range of brands to choose from in one store, making for the benefit of ease of shopping.

What will your customers be looking for in your merchandise package? Consider the following then complete the action plan guidelines.

3

Merchandise range

What depth and breadth range will you have to offer to prevent customers from going elsewhere? Considerations will have to be given to colour, size, and brand name range. Principally you are offering the benefits of choice and convenience.

Full consideration to ranging policy will be given in Chapter 13.

Quality, design and style

Benefits associated with such factors are diverse and subject to differing customer needs and perception. For instance, quality might be sought for the benefits of long life and reliability or, on the other hand, because the buyer wishes to project an image of affluence. Similarly, design might be an important feature because it offers ease of use but perhaps more so because it matches existing possessions.

Display and layout

The way you display your merchandise should aim to enhance the inherent benefits of your merchandise. For instance furnishings should be displayed in room settings to emphasize their design, quality and image. Display and overall layout creating a store atmosphere should appeal to the customer's self-image and perception of the product. A customer visiting a shop selling expensive high quality fashions would expect the merchandise to be displayed with care, the fixtures to be of high quality and the lighting and decor to be tasteful.

Full discussion of store layout and merchandising is found in Chapter 8.

Merchandise policy action guidelines

1. What key ranges of merchandise do similar businesses stock?
2. Which do they seem to feature the most (i.e. through allocation of sales space, display areas, or advertising)?
3. What key benefits do they point out with some force to their customers? Consider:

   - The way they display it
   - The way they advertise it (look for the benefits in the wording of the advertising 'blurb')

4. In order of importance what brand names do they stock?
5. For their major merchandise ranges, how comprehensive are their stocks in terms of colour, style, brands, models, etc. as appropriate?

The place

The importance of location cannot be understated and the next chapter deals with this subject in depth. Here, it is important to note benefits the customer seeks that are attributable to location.

The needs of the group or group(s) of customers you intend to serve will be the major determinants of location. The prime consideration for most customer groups is convenience. However, what constitutes convenience may vary from one customer group to another and according to the type of merchandise required. A neighbourhood location is perhaps convenient for residents to make the forgotten grocery purchase but is far from convenient for the larger full week's shopping trip because of the lack of sufficient car parking space and good access. Further, but less tangible, the customer will not equate such a location with benefits normally derived from a visit to the supermarket. So even if you operated a convenience store in a neighbourhood location with prices and a merchandise range equal to that of local supermarkets, it is still unlikely that you would attract even the local market in significant numbers to do their main grocery shopping at your store. As customers, we are educated to associate certain shop types with particular locations. To some extent this has led to certain types of shops, such as shoe shops, to cluster together. The customer benefits from the convenience of being able to assess what is on offer on one shopping trip – the cluster of shops has such a powerful pull that it is unlikely that the customer will visit shops that are located elsewhere.

For some types of shop convenience is a less important factor. For example, a retailer of designer clothes would lack credibility trading in a run down inner-city area no matter how convenient the location might be to his customers. Here the overall ambience of the area would be much more important.

Location action guidelines

By surveying similar shop types, to what extent do the following seem to be important locational attributes?

Attribute	Number of times observed	Total score
1. Car park		
2. Nearby car parking facilities		
3. Close to good transport facilities		
4. Residential area		
5. Industrial area		
0. High street location with a high volume of pedestrian passing trade		
7. Main road site with a high volume of car traffic		
8. Clustered together with other shops of a similar type		
9. Found in proximity to:		

....

Shops of this type are predominantly located in areas characterized by:

_____

_____

_____

Price

The first thing to note is that the price policy you adopt will have to meet your financial as well as your market goals. The effect of price on profits will be fully discussed in Chapter 5. Here, however, we are more concerned with the effect of price on the customer's decision to buy.

It is a pity that many owners of small shops consider price to be the greatest single influence on customer buying motives. Often the search for other benefits comes first. This doesn't dispute the fact that price is a very important means of communication between your business and its potential customers; on the contrary, it is a significant part of your marketing/sales promotion strategy. Rather it means that you don't *have* to adopt a policy of pricing cheap to attract custom.

Certainly, low price may be an important buying motivator in relation to some merchandise, but not in all cases. For instance, it is commonly known that in the case of high-quality merchandise such as jewellery, designer fashions, quality or exotic foods, a low price can have an adverse effect on sales. A low price in such cases may lead the customer to question the quality of the merchandise – 'Why is it so cheap?' The lesson to be learnt is that all the various aspects of your 'total sales propoposition' should be consistent with each other.

So how do you begin to shape your pricing policy? Like all aspects of planning for your business, your decision must be based on sound objectives. The long-term objective will be to adopt a pricing policy that will result in the best combination of sales volume, price and costs, while at the same time conforming to the shop's overall image. No firm decisions regarding pricing policy should be taken until you have completed the work related to the discussion in Chapter 5: 'Will my shop be profitable?' However, at this stage you must address yourself to benefits sought by your customers from price. To do this, complete the following action plan.

Pricing policy action guidelines

1. For your major merchandise ranges, find out and list the current prices being charged by your potential competitors.

Merchandise range   **Competitor**

	A	B	C	D	E	F

1. _____

2. _____

3. _____

4. _____

5. _____

2. You may find that the price difference between competitors may vary from one merchandise range to another. What is the difference when all the merchandise ranges are considered together?

3. To what extent is there an accepted market price that the majority of the competition adheres to?

4. To what extent do the shops surveyed use price in sales promotions? How important do you think price features in their overall sales proposition to the customer?

The service

There are two main considerations here:

- The selling method you choose to adopt
- The additional service levels you offer

Selling methods

As customers, most of us are familiar with the three main selling methods used by retailers:namely personal service, self-selection and self-service. There is no strict dividing level between the three; rather they are on a service continuum.

Personal service	Self-selection	Self-service

←————————————————————————————————→

Sales assistant service throughout the sale.	Impersonal service. Customer makes the choice from merchandise on display.

Personal service is characterized by counter service. Counter service is to be found in retailing mainly where:

- Shops are 'old' and long established
- The merchandise does not lend itself to open displays, as with specialist food shops such as bakers and butchers
- There are security concerns as in the case of jewellers

Self-selection is a mid way point between personal and self-service. The actual level of service will vary from shop to shop. A good example of this type of method practised on a large scale is 'Marks and Spencer'. The merchandise is left on open display but assistance is available if the customer requires help.

Self-service in the extreme is where the customer's only point of contact with the store personnel is at the payment point, typified in food retailing by discount operations which focus primarily on price to attract custom.

Having read so far you may think the decision in this area is made for you by custom and practice. Not so. To offer a different approach to selling than is traditionally given can, if planned with care, offer the customer the excitement of a new shopping experience. Also many customers, whilst welcoming the coming of the large mixed retailer and their gigantic stores, still moan about poor levels of customer service. There is nothing to stop you offering a high level of personal service while at the same time adopting a modern and bright self-selection store layout (see Chapter 9).

Customer services

This is the part of the overall sales proposition that can often be used effectively to successfully differentiate your shop from the competition. Careful selection and the provision of additional services often costs little but achieves a lot.

Consideration should be given to whether any of the following will significantly influence your customers' decision to buy from you:

- **Credit facilities**
- **Extended opening hours**
- **Home delivery services**
- **Installation service**
- **Merchandise demonstrations**
- **Merchandise wrapping or gift packaging service**
- **Alteration and repair service**
- **Full advice on use and care of the merchandise**
- **Additional merchandise guarantees**

3

Credit facilities

More and more people are using credit facilities to finance both major and minor purchases. Consumer debt, in pure cash terms, more than doubled between 1982 and 1987! The majority of this vast increase is attributable to the growing use of credit cards such as Visa and Access. In 1986, collectively Visa and Access had over 21 million cards in issue. This is a dramatic increase on 1975 levels when collectively there were only around six and half million in use. Consequently, there has been a corresponding increase in the number of shops, both large and small, offering to accept such forms of payment. In addition, of course, shops offer a range of credit facilities to customers from hire purchase and credit sale agreements on major items to short term credit allowed for example on newspaper deliveries. As a small retailer the forms of selling on credit open to you are:

- Become a member of a credit card scheme(s) such as Visa or Access – applicable to all retailers. Such schemes work along similar lines. First, the retailer applies to become a member, on acceptance paying a fixed joining fee. This membership allows him or her to accept customer payment using the scheme card. The retailer then presents the credit sale vouchers to the credit card company (through the bank) who then immediately credit the retailer's account to the total value of the vouchers. For this service the retailer pays approximately two per cent of the value of the credit sales to the credit card company. The advantages of joining such a scheme are:
  1. As the majority of the shopping public possess, and increasingly use, either Access or Visa cards to obtain a range of goods and services,

failure to accept such cards may deter a large percentage of potential customers.

2. You do not finance or administer your customer's debt and therefore there is little, if any, effect on your cash reserves of offering such a service.

- To offer to arrange finance facilities for the purchase of large items by becoming an agent for a finance company. In such circumstances you sell the item, say a video recorder, to the finance company who in turn sells it to your customer on credit. If you decide to do this you, in effect, become a credit brokerage and as such you will be required under the Consumer Credit Act 1974 to apply for and obtain a credit licence from the Office of Fair Trading.

- To offer your customers weekly or monthly accounts or short term low cost credit facilities. Accounts settled monthly or agreements where the rate of interest is not in excess of one per cent above the clearing banks' base rate or thirteen per cent whichever is higher, are termed 'exempt' by the Consumer Credit Act. However, offering credit on such a basis, that is financing it out of your own pocket rather than getting an outside agency to finance the customer's debt, can severely affect your cash flow (see Chapter 5).

Whether or not you should offer credit facilities depends on whether any subsequent increase in sales and profits will more than cover the cost of offering and operating the facilities. If you intend to sell large value items such as electrical goods, furniture and clothing, then careful consideration of Fig. 3.1 will probably make your mind up for you!

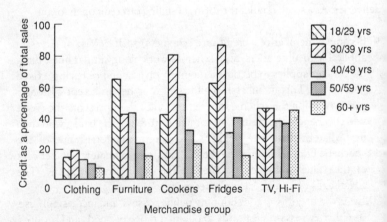

Fig. 3.1 Credit expenditure as a percentage of total household expenditure by age

Retailers of low value items though should seriously consider becoming a member of at least one of the popular credit card schemes. For instance, it cannot have escaped your notice that of late even supermarkets are offering the customer the benefit of using their Visa and Access cards to buy their weekly shopping. Obviously, careful consideration needs to be given to the type of credit facilit which would appeal most to the customer group you intend to serve.

Of course, if the existence of credit facilities does not figure highly in your customers' decision to buy, then, because there is always some cost attached to offering them, they should be avoided.

Customer services policy action guidelines

3

1. What do similar shops, including prospective competitors, offer in the way of additional services to the customer?

Service	Number of times observed	Total score
1. Visa		
2 Access		
3. American Express		
4. Hire purchase		
5. Monthly accounts		
6. Personal service		
7. Self-selection		
8. Delivery service		
9. Installation service		
10. Extended opening hours		
11. Merchandise demonstrations		

12. **Wrapping or gift packaging service**

13. **Alteration and repair service**

14. **Full advice on use and care of the merchandise**

15. **Additional merchandise guarantees**

2. **Which service or package of services seems to equate with busy trading?**
3. **Is it within your capability to provide such services?**
4. **Do additional services seem to figure highly in similar businesses' overall sales propositions?**

Promotion

Once merchandise, pricing, location and service policies have been devised you will need to shape effective sales promotion strategies. To put it simply, your customers will need telling and convincing that the total sales proposition you are offering is what they want! For a full discussion on sales promotion strategies turn to Chapter 14: 'Forecasting, maintaining and expanding sales'.

Who will buy and why

We have gone some way in identifying the benefits that your customers *might* be looking for. However, the total sales proposition should be specifically designed with particular customer groups in mind. To this end we will now focus our attention – to identify in some detail who will be your customers and what package of benefits they will be looking for.

Firstly, we will explore ways in which you can describe your customers. Secondly, we will identify their needs or the benefits they are seeking. Finally, we will try to match what you can offer with what they want and, in doing so, eventually define a sales proposition that will be unique to you.

Customer profiles

Many shop owners if asked, 'Who are your customers?', would probably respond with such statements as: 'Everybody', 'Locals', 'Mainly women', 'Passing trade', 'Oh, some come in cars and ...'. Such 'descriptions' are symptomatic of little, if any, thinking about their customers. They say very little about where they may be found, how can they be reached, or how they can be satisfied. Such shops simply beg to fail. What is required is a complete profile of your major customer groups. A detailed description of what differentiates them from other customer groups in terms of the benefits they are seeking is required. It must also be compiled in such a way that, as a group, they can be measured, reached, communicated with and sold to.

3

Customers and consumers

In trying to determine who your customers are, you must not lose sight of the influences (the why) on customer buying behaviour. It is important that in profiling customers you also determine who the consumer is. Yes, there is a difference between customer and consumer! The consumer is the end user of the merchandise, who is not necessarily the customer. The parents buy toys for children, the wife buys clothes for her husband, the housewife buys food for her family and so on. What is worthy of consideration here is to what degree do the needs of the end user influence the customer's decision to buy? Clearly it varies from one type of purchase to another and often takes into account both parties' needs. For instance, a child may encourage her parents to buy a certain toy because her friends have it or she has seen it advertised on TV. To the child, price, suitability to age group, educational value, or availability locally, may have little meaning but to her parents they may be important.

Making a start

The task of identifying viable customer groups can be approached in many different ways. Many start from an armchair analysis of their proposed shop, thinking about the benefits it can offer and trying to decipher, using intuition and experience, customer groups to match. We all do this to some extent; however, it is useful to take this approach further by having a structured 'brain storming' session with the family or friends. Simply collect together about four to six people, sit round a table, take a large sheet of paper, divide it in two and on one side write down 'Who?' and on the other 'Why?' Then get each

person in turn to voice their ideas in response to the two questions. If somebody gets stuck for an idea quickly move on to the next person. Don't stop to examine any of the ideas, this will spoil the flow, just keep going round until everybody 'runs out of ideas'. When you reach that point you can then go back and examine each idea in some detail. You will probably find that some you will discard as being 'silly' or 'unrealistic'; however, don't be too quick to jump to conclusions. Some you may be able to group together and warrant as worthy of further investigation. It is more than likely that this process will help clarify woolly thinking and perhaps produce some potentially different and profitable ways of looking at possible customers.

To help you make a start at profiling your customers consider some of the following ways in which they can be described.

Age

This can be relatively obvious where your shop is aimed, by its nature, at a specific age group, for example toys and babywear outlets. However, to reiterate, never stop at such surface observations. Always ask who is the customer, who is the consumer and who influences the decision to buy.

As a general rule people of different ages have different needs. For instance, a retired couple may have a greater need for durability and reliability and have a strong fear of getting into debt. Conversely, a young couple with a family and a tight budget may have low cost and availability of credit facilities as priorities. Refinement of such generalizations can often be made by reference to published statistics such as the *Household Survey, Social Trends* and the *Family Expenditure Survey* as Fig. 3.1, earlier in this chapter, confirms.

Is the age of your customers a significant factor in your locality and type of business? For instance does a predominance of senior citizens indicate that your convenience store should offer a range of small pack sizes, a delivery service and high profile courteous service?

Sex

Will your customers be mainly women or men? Again, this may seem obvious if your merchandise is aimed at a specific sex, for example male or female fashions. But, once again, pause for thought. In the clothing trade it is fairly common knowledge that thirty per cent of mens' clothing is purchased by women buying for their husbands, sons or boyfriends.

Location

Of great importance to retailers is in some way to describe all of their customer groups by where they can be found. This is, obviously, essential information when deciding where to open up. You can often define your customers by where they live, work, where they go and how they get there.

For retailers who by definition and custom, such as convenience stores and newsagents, serve a local, usually residential, market, then clear definition of the limits of the geographical catchment area of the shop is crucial. This will be considered in detail in Chapter 4, 'Choosing a location and assessing a site'.

Social and economic groupings

Research has shown that there are varying degrees of correlation between a person's occupation, social background, education and income grouping and their tastes/attitudes and expectations – and thus their shopping habits and buying behaviour. Much can be gleaned about the characteristics of various socio-economic groupings by reference to published statistics (see later 'Market research'). Relevant customers can be described by one or a combination of the following factors:

- Income
- Social class (largely based on occupation – see Fig. 3.2)
- Education
- Occupation
- Household size

Segmentation of customer groups using such criteria can prove useful. For instance, a TV and VCR retailer will find in the *General Household Survey* (HMSO), amongst other pertinent facts, that ownership of VCRs in 1985 varied significantly with occupation and social class, i.e. 42 per cent of managers and employers had use of or owned a VCR compared with only 18 per cent ownership or use amongst unskilled manual workers.

Not many shops appeal to all ranges of income. Obviously, if your shop is going to focus on high-quality merchandise your customers are more than likely to be in a high income bracket. Refinement of such generalizations can be made by reference to published statistics. The *Family Expenditure Survey* (HMSO) will enable you to identify high spending groups in terms of merchandise groups relevant to you by:

1. Income groupings of head of household (16 sub-divisions ranging from less than £45 per week to more than £550 per week).
2. Combined sex, age and income.
3. Households with and without children, sub-divided by kind of household, i.e.:
   One adult and one child
   One adult, two or more children
   One man, one woman and one child
   One man, one woman and two children
   One man, one woman and three children
   Retired households mainly dependent on state pensions
   Other retired households
   One man, one woman (non retired)
   Two men or two women
   Three adults
   Four plus adults
   Each grouping is further sub-divided into four income groupings.
4. Occupation of head of the household (broad patterns of expenditure).
5. Employment status of the head of the household (e.g., employed, unemployed).
6. Region of the UK.

Class A: Higher managerial, administrative, or professional
Class B: Intermediate managerial, administrative, or professional
Class C1: Supervisory or clerical and junior managerial, administrative or professional.
Class C2: Skilled manual workers
Class D: Semi and unskilled manual workers
Class E: State pensioners or widows (no other earners), casual or lowest grade workers or long-term unemployed.

Source: Social Trends, 1988, p. 204. (HMSO)

Fig. 3.2   Social class: Institute of Practitioners in Advertising (IPA) definition

Benefits sought and usage

No matter how you choose to describe your customers, it is important that for the customer profile to be fully useful to you, it must include in the description the benefits they are seeking. Analysis of each customer group should be undertaken to pin-point the principal benefit being sought.

A useful way of defining customer groups is to identify groups according to the way that your merchandise or shop is used by customers. For instance, a DIY shop might find that its customers are made up of a number of different users: an infrequent user (e.g. chef); a high skill frequent user (perfectionist/DIY enthusiast); and a high skill large quantity user (trade customers). Each of the three customer groups may have different characteristics and seek different benefits in terms of price, merchandise, place and service. Similarly a convenience store may find it useful to categorize its customers by the number of times and for what reasons they visit the store.

Customer profile action guidelines

Whatever characteristics you use to define your customer groups they must be able to pass the following tests:

1. **Can the group be measured? Will you be able to estimate the number of customers in each segment? This is necessary to enable you to calculate the total value of trade each group may generate for your store (see Chapter 4). If you have used any kind of demographic characteristics in your customer profile, such as age, sex, location, etc., this should be relatively easy. Measuring a segment becomes much more difficult if it is *solely* defined by intangible criteria such as life style or taste in fashion. This is not to say that such criteria are not important; on the contrary, they can lead to effective shaping of the shop's trading policies. As we noted earlier, 'Next' was built on the basis of appealing to customer groups who follow a particular life style and have a need to project a certain self-image. Where a market is identified using such sociological and psychological criteria, as perhaps would be the case with a fashion store, you should endeavour to identify further descriptors that are directly measurable.**
2. **Is the customer group of a significant size in relation to the scale of your proposed venture? It is possible to become over enthusiastic and define too many target markets, resulting in confusion.**
3. **Is the customer group a potentially profitable one? There is little point in identifying a large group of people as potential customers if they have little ability to pay. The definition of customer need in commercial terms must include the ability and the will to pay.**
4. **Will you be able to reach, communicate and sell to the customer groups identified? Can you provide the benefits they are seeking?**

Finding out

We have discussed the principal reasons why people buy, the importance of offering a unique selling proposition and the way we might usefully describe different customer groups. In addition, along the way I have encouraged you to speculate in some detail who will be your customers and why. Now is the time to come up with some hard facts about your customers so that you can, with a degree of confidence, define a sales proposition that will be both successful and unique to you. You can conduct your own surveys – which is highly recommended – and/or refer to secondary information in the form of government statistics such as the *Family Expenditure Survey* and by reference to appropriate books.

Finding out for yourself

As we have already noted, careful surveying of the competition can provide a useful guide to who their customers are. Your research can be enhanced if you serve a simple questionnaire on a sample of customers using such outlets to find out more about them. A simple technique I have used on many occasions is reproduced below. You can use it as it stands or adapt it to your own needs. Care needs to be taken in designing the questionnaire, deciding who and how many to interview, to obtain any meaningful results. Each concern we will consider in some detail as we go along.

Action guide lines

- **Find out where the competition is by using *Yellow Pages*, and tour by car around likely areas to discover shops not listed.**
- **Observe and question the customers using each shop on selected days of the week and different times of the day: mid-morning, early afternoon, late afternoon and evening. Use a simple questionnaire as produced below or construct your own following the guidelines given later. The questionnaire reproduced in Fig. 3.4 is intended for exploring the needs of customers using a convenience store.**

Survey sheet for each batch of questionnaires

Date: _____   Time: _____

Name of shop: _____

Brief description of the shop (image, selling method, services, etc.)

_____

_____

Brief description of the site (main road, other shops, parking space, etc.)

_____

_____

_____

Brief description of the neighbourhood (housing type, schools and amenities, proximity to other shopping areas, signs of affluence or decay, etc.)

3

_____

_____

_____

Number of customers questioned: _____

The questionnaire

Hello. I am carrying out a market research survey with the aim of improving customer service. Would you like to participate?

1. Age: Teenager   18–29   30–39   40–49   50–59   60+
2. Sex: Male   Female
3. Are you making this shopping trip:
   From home ☐   On the way home from work ☐
   On the way to work ☐   Other ☐
4. How did you get here:
   on foot ☐   by car ☐   by bus ☐   by taxi ☐
5. Could you roughly estimate how far you have travelled:
   ½ mile ☐   1 mile ☐   2 miles ☐   3 miles ☐
   4 miles ☐   5 miles ☐   6 miles ☐   7 miles ☐
6. What area do you live in (estate or road)

   ....

7. What is the main reason for making this shopping trip:
   (a) Weekly shopping trip ☐
   (b) Forgotten items from your visit to the supermarket ☐

(c) Because you have run out of something ☐
(d) Impulse, just passing ☐
(e) Other ☐ ....

....

If (d), what attracted you to stop and buy

....

....

8. What type of goods do you normally buy here:
General grocery ☐   Frozen food ☐   Greengrocery ☐
Confectionery ☐   Cigarettes ☐   Beer & Lager ☐
Spirits ☐   Wine ☐   Other ☐

9. (a) Which type of goods would never or rarely buy here:
General grocery ☐   Frozen Food ☐   Greengrocery ☐
Confectionnery ☐   Cigarettes ☐   Beer & lager ☐
Spirits ☐   Wine ☐   Other ☐

(b) Why not:
Too dear ☐   Poor range ☐   Poor quality ☐
Do no stock the brands that I like ☐
Prefer to do with my main shopping ☐
Other ☐ ....

....

10. How often do you shop here:
Daily ☐   More than twice a week ☐   Weekly ☐
Rarely ☐

11. How much do you usually spend on each trip to this type of shop?
Less than £1.00 ☐
£1 to £3 ☐
£3 to £4 ☐
£4 to £6 ☐
£6 to £8 ☐
£8 to £10 ☐
More than £10 ☐

12. What would you say sums this shop up best:
Friendly and helpful service ☐   Poor service ☐
Clean ☐   Dirty ☐   Reasonable prices ☐
Expensive ☐   Cheap service ☐   Wide choice ☐
Poor choice ☐   Convenient ☐   Bright and modern ☐
Other ☐ ....

....

13. How could the shop be improved?

    ....

    ....

    ....

14. Where do you do your main shopping of this type?

    ....

    ....

    ....

15. Why? (Tick as many boxes as appropriate.)

Car parking facilities	☐	1	2	3	4	5
Good transport, ease of getting there	☐	1	2	3	4	5
Good product range	☐	1	2	3	4	5
Special offers	☐	1	2	3	4	5
Cheap	☐	1	2	3	4	5
Friendly service	☐	1	2	3	4	5
Speedy service	☐	1	2	3	4	5
Delivery service	☐	1	2	3	4	5
Quality merchandise	☐	1	2	3	4	5
Credit facilities	☐	1	2	3	4	5
I like the atmosphere/image	☐	1	2	3	4	5

which I would describe as:

    ....

    ....

Other ☐ ....

How important to you, on a scale of 1 to 5, is each of the above: 1 being unimportant and 5 being an essential requirement.

16. Finally, to assist in sorting the information it would be helpful if you could tell me your:

    occupation ....

    occupation of wife/husband ....

    Thank you for your co-operation.

From the use of such a questionnaire you can proceed to identify customer groups on the basis of the benefits they seek and the usage of the shop type. Each group can then be further described by such measurable criteria as age, sex, occupation, place of residence (or area), method of transport used to carry out shopping of this type, and place of work.

Questions 1, 2, 3, 6 and 16 give you basic information to allow you to describe the respondents in some tangible and measurable way.

Quetion 3 allows you to separate local shoppers from others and linked with questions 4, 5 and 6 gives a fairly good indication of where various customer groups are to be found geographically.

Question 4 linked with question 15 (b) will indicate whether parking or good transport facilities are required.

Question 7 will allow you to group customers according to the way they use the shop type.

Questions 7, 8, 10 and 11 will allow you to identify existing profitable customer groupings.

Question 8 will give you some indication as to merchandise preference in relation to this type of shop. Note that a more detailed questionnaire can be compiled to identify brand preferences.

Questions 9 and 14 allow you to identify potentially profitable customer groups not yet reached or tapped by this shop type. Questions 12, 13 and 15 should show which benefits have to be offered (if possible) to attract such custom.

Question 15 (b) allows you to identify and rank the benefits sought by each customer group.

Designing the questionnaire

The framework given above can be adapted for use with different types of shops. In designing a questionnaire adhere to the following guidelines.

- Many make the mistake writing the questions without being clear about what they want to find out. Questions are written down because they sound good, not because they will find out what the researcher wants to know. Take time first to detail *exactly* what you want to find out.
- The questionnaire must include a means of identifying customer groups by some tangible and measurable factors such as age and sex.
- The questionnaire should be kept short. I would recommend that it not exceed the length of the one given on pages 63–5. The problem with over-long questionnaires is that the respondent can become bored and irritated, therefore giving inaccurate information.
- Keep the questions short, clear and unambiguous. Never ask two questions in one. Always test the questionnaire on friends to see if any questions are misleading, confusing, likely to have two meanings, suggest an answer, etc.
- When the questionnaire is complete go over it again and query each question: 'Why am I asking this question? What useful information will it give me?' Modify or discard any questions that don't pass this test.

- In constructing the questionnaire always remember that the information collected will later have to be collated and analysed. Therefore, where it is appropriate, given the respondent a range of responses to choose from (as in the example). This makes it easier to analyse the questionnaires.
- Many avoid questions that relate to factors such as income, occupation and expenditure as being too personal. However, where you consider this information important, do include it in your questionnaire. If the interview is conducted in a 'professional' and cordial manner most people will answer such questions.

Deciding on who to sample, and how

Designing the questionnaire is one thing, knowing who to interview is another. It is obviously impractical to survey all people who might be potential customers. This would involve taking a complete census. The time needed and the cost would be enormous. You must select a small manageable group (a sample) from the entire population of customers. The findings from the sample are then extended to the total population of which the sample is representative by expressing the responses in the sample as a percentage of those interviewed and extending that percentage to the total population. For example, if:

(a) from your sample 80 per cent of all households interviewed within one mile of your shop said they will buy from your shop once a week; and

(b) there are 250 households within one mile of your shop (total 'population'); then

(c) by extending the percentage to the total population it is probable that you will have 200 customers from within one mile of your business, per week (250 × [80/100] = 200).

Whether or not such findings would prove true depends on two factors:

- To what degree did the design and implementation of the questionnaire elicit honest/accurate answers?
- How representative of the total population was the sample? For instance, it could have been that a large proportion of the households surveyed were wholly untypical of the neighbourhood.

To prevent unwanted bias creeping into the sample you should endeavour to make sure that your sample is representative of the entire population you want to know about. Bias can be easily and unwittingly built into a sample. An extreme example would be to use a telephone directory to select at random a number of households to interview, when the people you wish to survey do not all possess telephones!

In all sampling procedures the underlying method used is random selection of respondents from the entire population. The idea is to remove as much unwanted bias as possible by giving each member of the population an equal chance of being interviewed. There are two main ways of constructing a random sample – by use of random numbers or by what is known as quasi-random sampling.

- The first method is rather time consuming and requires the use of random number tables or access to a computer to generate random numbers. It is only applicable when you can identify each member of the entire population by a number, as is the case with electoral roles. For instance, if you wanted to take a random sample of an electoral ward, the 'population' being all those over 18 entitled to vote in that ward, you could use a series of random numbers to select a representative sample.
- A much simpler method is 'quasi-random', sometimes known as 'systematic sampling'. This is where you chose every 'n'th person from an entire population. For example, if the entire population is made up of 500 individuals and you wished to take a sample of 50 you would interview every tenth person on the list (i.e., 500/50 = 10).

So far we have been discussing samples by assuming we are dealing with groups of people who have only one characteristic (i.e., of the same sex, live in the same area, etc.) when of course in practice they will have many characteristics. To refer back to the earlier example at the beginning of this section, to sample households solely on the basis of distance from a proposed site for a shop may be very misleading if the housing stock, income of the householders, tastes, and habits are different. It is possible, by say taking every fifth street and every fifth house, that all the detached properties in the area have missed being sampled, making any predictions about the neighbourhood from the sample taken highly dubious. A much more accurate way forward is to first stratify the sample according to known characteristics of the neighbourhood. For instance, if the neighbourhood consists of 30 per cent detached bungalows, 10 per cent detached houses, 20 per cent semi-detached houses and 40 per cent town houses then the sample should be stratified accordingly. Proportionate random sized samples should then be taken in each stratum (i.e., 30 per cent random sample of detached bungalows, 10 per cent random sample of detached houses, and so on).

The main problem with the random sampling procedures just described is that they require you to first stratify the population and also to know the total size of the population. This is often not practical and, in many cases, neither the size nor the characteristics of the population are known, as when exploring customer groups for the first time. In such cases you are advised to take a quota sample. Simply, this is where you interview members of the public passing by in the high street or using a particular kind of shop (stopping, for example every tenth person to minimize personal bias) up to a certain predetermined number. The sample is then stratified after, rather than before being interviewed. The results of the survey can then lead to the identification of customer groups worthy of more precise sampling. This procedure would certainly be applicable to the questionnaire on pages 63–5 and is considered in the next section.

Before we proceed, some mention needs to be made as to the number you should interview. Statistically techniques can actually be used to calculate the sample size needed to give a desired degree of accuracy; however, such attention to detail is not really required. When you consider that the majority of the surveys of the total adult population of the UK rarely exceed 2,000 respondents then samples of 50 to 100 are more than adequate for local surveys.

Making sense of the information

Once the survey has been completed then the questionnaires will have to be collated and made sense of. The basic method is to construct a series of sieves to sort the responses and isolate groups of customers who share something in common. However, this must have some meaning, therefore, the selection criteria should be related to your original list of what you wanted to find out. For instance, if one of the key reasons for the survey was to identify customers who use the shop type frequently and spend In excess of three pounds, then you would search your questionnaires and select on those two criteria. From that point you can then proceed to search the selected batch for common denominators that might suggest a distinct customer grouping. Principally you will be looking for some commonality in the benefits they are seeking, plus other descriptors which will enable you to identify, reach and sell to them. As you sieve through the selected batch you may find that there is not just one distinct group but two or three, or, that there is nothing to say a distinct group of customers exists. The chances are that you will have to sieve and re-sort the data many times using different combinations of criteria to select on before any meaningful conclusions can be drawn. Because of the hundreds of possible combinations of questions, it is advisable that, if you have the required skills and knowledge, you use a computer database or spreadsheet (with a database facility built in, such as SuperCalc 3 or 4) to sort and select the responses from the questionnaire.

Using secondary data

A most under-used repository of vast amounts of information relevant to small business people is your central reference library! There you will find many of the publications discussed below.

Central and local government statistics give information such as family expenditure on different goods and services (as discussed earlier) and population statistics (age, income groups, geographical distribution, etc.). Some local government offices also publish monthly or quarterly reviews of different sectors of business. Of key interest to you will be:

- *Family Expenditure Survey*, HMSO (discussed earlier in the section, 'Customer profiles'). The *FES* is published every year but unfortunately because of the time it takes to carry out the survey and interpret the results, the information contained in the current edition relates to expenditure as it was approximately two years ago. Its main use to you, other than enabling identification of 'profitable' customer groups, is, in connection with official population figures, to calculate the sales potential of a site. This, including how to update FES figures, will be tackled in the next chapter.
- *Social Trends* (HMSO) which gives a wealth of information ranging from household characteristics, through expenditure patterns to leisure activities of the population of the UK. Of course, not all the information given is relevant to retailers but I do strongly recommend you take a good 'browse' through its contents – I would be surprised if you did not find something useful. It is published every year and is currently priced at over £20, but it is commonly found in the reference section of your local library.
- *The Census County Report* gives a detailed analysis, down to town level, of the characteristics of the local population. The tables include the following information:

1. Total population
2. Male/female break down
3. Distribution of the population by age
4. Distribution of the population by social class
5. Percentage of the population with higher educational qualifications
6. Percentage of employed residents working in various industries
7. Average number of persons per household and other household characteristics
8. The method of transport used to travel to work

- The *Retail Business Monitor*, published every year, should be consulted by all shop owners. You are, however, unlikely to find it in your local reference library, but invariably central reference libraries will stock it. It is packed full of information about the retail trade. You will find such information as average sales and profit margins by type and scale of retail outlet. It also shows what percentage of your total sales is likely to be derived from various groups of merchandise. It unfortunately gives little information to help profile customer groups. We will be using this publication later in the book when we assess your sales and profit. Note that much of the information given in Chapter 1 is derived from this source. Re-read Chapter 1, which demonstrates some of the uses the information can be put to.
- Other publications of value include:

> *General Household Surveys*
> *Economic Trends*
> *Regional Trends*
> *Annual and Monthly digest of statistics*

A note of caution: some care must be taken when drawing conclusions from all published statistics. For example, with reference to census statistics, these can be anywhere between one and ten years out of date (though it is sometimes possible to get up to date projections from your local authority). This means, for instance, that the 10,000 children being listed as under five years old in 1981 will be buying pop records and teenage fashion in 1990 and will have little use for baby clothes and push chairs! Mistakes like this are easily made. When using such statistical information read the title and notes accompanying the tables with great care. Be sure that you understand precisely what the information relates to and if you are not clear, ask the librarian.

Larger reference libraries carry directories of business associations (many are already listed for you in Chapter 1). In these you will find literally thousands of trade and special interest associations, some of which may be worth contacting to find out if they can help. Further to this, many trade associations publish periodicals and year books (again some of which are listed in Chapter 1) that may provide useful information. Many large libraries stock these in their periodicals section.

The marketing, business and social science sections of the library will be worth a scan. A search in these sections may reveal some interesting research work relating to your particular kind of shop. If you have a university or college library nearby, pay it a visit since it is not that uncommon to find that members of the teaching staff or students have carried out local research into the retail market – most of the hard work could have been done for you. Nearly all university and college libraries are open for the use of reference facilities by the general public – it is a pity that only a few people seem to realize this.

The prospect of so much information to look through to find what you want can be daunting – like looking for a needle in haystack. Clear research objectives certainly help, so before you start list clearly what you are trying to find out. In any case don't be put off; there is help at hand. Most library assistants are only too pleased to help; they are professionals and know how to track down information. If you approach them in a polite manner they will usually go to great lengths to help you find the information. However, be prepared to spend the equivalent of a full day at the library and do not be too disappointed if you don't find exactly what you are looking for.

The main advantage of using secondary data is that it is obviously quicker and easier than the do-it-yourself methods of market research. However, there are many problems. Firstly, the data is, to varying degrees, always dated. Secondly, there are many problems in finding appropriate data. Thirdly, the data is not compiled for the specific purpose you want to put it to. It will, therefore, have to be further manipulated and interpreted to make it useful with the attendant possibility of making mistakes in judgement, leading to false and dangerous conclusions. Fourthly, the total populations to which they refer are often far in excess of the size of the local markets the small shop proprietor is interested in. For instance, what degree of confidence can you have that the average household expenditure figure for the UK on general groceries is typical for your locality? None the less you would be foolish not to make use of such sources of information. They can be used before and after your own customer and broader market research. Reference to secondary data can be a starting point to enable you to identify possible market segments, allowing you to target your customer survey more precisely. After you have finished your survey you can compare your findings with relevant published statistics. Any large discrepancies may be due to local factors or to a fault or flaw in your survey. If it is due to local factors you should attempt to identify what marks your locale as being different from say the region as a whole; such information may be useful.

Summary

The importance of having the most complete possible picture of your customers in terms of what influences them to buy and who they are, cannot be overstated. Without such knowledge you will not be able to shape your business to make the most effective use of potential custom. A shop that does not understand its customers cannot really know what it is selling. The starting point for your business plan is your customers. Let their needs, within the constraints of what you can profitably offer, shape your trading policy. If you do this first task well then you will develop a 'selling proposition' that is unique to you, by which your future customers will positively and strongly identify you. If there is a secret of success in retailing, then this is it.

3

Checklist

The plan

1. What are your market research objectives?
2. What techniques/methods are you going to use to research the information?
3. Are they valid? Will they find out what you want?
4. Are they reliable?
5. How will you attempt to verify the results?
6. How will you use the results to modify your business idea?

The questions

1. Why will people buy from my shop?
2. Who could be my customers?
3. What benefits will they seek in terms of merchandise, price, location and services?
4. What constraints are there to prevent me from wholly or partly offering these benefits?
5. What package of benefits do the competition offer?
6. How can I satisfy my customers' wants in a way that differentiates me from the competition?

7. How can I most usefully group and describe my customers?
8. For each customer grouping:

- Who makes the decision to buy?
- Where are your potential customers?
- What will they buy?
- How much will they buy?
- How often will they buy?
- What will they use the product or service for?
- What are their major needs?
- What other major influences are there on their buying behaviour?
- How important is price to them?
- What services will they look for?
- What store image do they most favourably react to?

The techniques

1. Questionnaire – what will be its objectives?
2. How will it be implemented (telephone, door to door, etc.)?
3. What are the characteristics of the sample interviewed?
4. Have you made sure that the sample has the same characteristics as your envisaged target market?
5. How will you make sense of the information collected?
6. Will you have some method of observation (e.g., customer count, etc.)?
7. Have you identified the competition?
8. What have you learned from detailed observation of the competition?
9. Have you checked out the usefulness of the statistics on population and consumer expenditure?
10. Have you spoken to any local business people?
11. Have you checked and read any trade publications in your area of business?

For each targeted group of customers:

1. **The following factors mark this group of customers as different from the wider market** ....

2. **This group's value to my business, if reached and sold to, is rated at** ....

3. **The Total Sales Proposition sought by this group of customers in terms of the mix of retail variables is profiled against what the principal competition can offer and contrasted with what my constraints allow me to provide:**

Benefits sought by customer group	Relative importance to customer group					Degree to which principal competitor provides					Degree to which your constraints will allow you to provide				
Merchandise															
	1	2	3	4	5	1	2	3	4	5	1	2	3	4	5
	1	2	3	4	5	1	2	3	4	5	1	2	3	4	5
	1	2	3	4	5	1	2	3	4	5	1	2	3	4	5
	1	2	3	4	5	1	2	3	4	5	1	2	3	4	5
The price															
	1	2	3	4	5	1	2	3	4	5	1	2	3	4	5
	1	2	3	4	5	1	2	3	4	5	1	2	3	4	5
	1	2	3	4	5	1	2	3	4	5	1	2	3	4	5
	1	2	3	4	5	1	2	3	4	5	1	2	3	4	5
The place															
	1	2	3	4	5	1	2	3	4	5	1	2	3	4	5
	1	2	3	4	5	1	2	3	4	5	1	2	3	4	5
	1	2	3	4	5	1	2	3	4	5	1	2	3	4	5
	1	2	3	4	5	1	2	3	4	5	1	2	3	4	5
The service															
	1	2	3	4	5	1	2	3	4	5	1	2	3	4	5
	1	2	3	4	5	1	2	3	4	5	1	2	3	4	5
	1	2	3	4	5	1	2	3	4	5	1	2	3	4	5
	1	2	3	4	5	1	2	3	4	5	1	2	3	4	5

4. The comparative profile suggests that my areas of strength in satisfying this group are .... ; and my areas of weakness are .... The probability of competing successfully for this group of customers is assessed as ....

5. The customer groups identified as the most viable to compete for are ....

6. My Unique Selling Proposition offered to these targeted groups can be best summed up as (not more than 50 words) ....

● THIS IS MY BUSINESS

4   Choosing a location and assessing a site

The importance of location □ Choosing a general area in which to locate □ Determining and measuring catchment areas □ Assessing the sales potential □ Calculating the sales potential for an individual shop □ Factors to consider when choosing a site □ Summary

The importance of location

If you get your pricing policy wrong, find you are stocking the wrong merchandise and not offering the right service, speedy action can be taken to correct things. However, choose the wrong location and you are likely to be stuck with it until you go bankrupt. In fact, many experienced retailers would go so far as to say that choosing the right location is the key to success. Certainly a great deal of care must be taken in choosing both an overall location and a particular site within that general area.

From the previous chapter we have seen that location is part of the Unique Sales Proposition you will offer to your customers. As such your location and site choice should be determined, as far as availability and cost of suitable premises allows, by the needs and shopping behaviour of the customers you wish to serve. Two questions of key concern will be:

● Where can targeted customer groups be found in sufficient numbers?
● What constitutes an ideal store location for them?

Choosing a general area in which to locate

Before individual sites can be selected and assessed, choice of a general area in which to locate needs to be made. For many who have no wish to move large distances, that choice may be limited to the comparison of neighbourhoods, villages, towns and cities within around a thirty mile radius of home. Obviously for others the choice is wide open and will perhaps begin with consideration of various trends for their type of retail operation in different regions of the UK. No matter which, all will be concerned with comparing the potential of different neighbourhoods or shopping centres. Your final decision will be arrived at by a full analysis of each area, including how well it will fit the characteristics of your targeted group of customers and its sales potential.

Customers and types of location

To some extent the combination of the type of shop you intend to operate and the traditional shopping habits of its associated customers broadly determines the type and size of areas you are likely to consider. For instance, the would-be operator of a convenience store would locate in close proximity to the desired targeted group of customers, whereas a neighbourhood location would not be consistent with the image of, for example, a fashion store, or the shopping habits of its customers. Whether or not your shop should be located in a main shopping district, in a smaller cluster of shops such as a local shopping precinct, or more isolated in a main road position, relying mainly on passing car borne shoppers, or in a neighbourhood location, depends very much on what you have found out about your targeted customer groups (discussed in Chapter 3).

Shopping centres

Many types of shop require the pull of a shopping centre to attract customers in sufficient numbers. Also, some retail outlets, as discussed in the previous chapter, would lack credibility if located anywhere else than in a prestigious and prosperous shopping area. Centres may be classified as follows:

- City centre The advantages of such locations are obvious but the enormous cost of locating in such areas will be prohibitive to most of you. Often a better sales level can be obtained by taking a prime site in a smaller town or district centre than settling for a poor site in a city centre at a much higher cost.
- Town centres. The size of the catchment areas can vary widely, from as little as 10,000 to in excess of 50,000 customers. In the more successful centres, one would expect to find the presence of nationally recognized names (though not large department stores), a wide range of choice in both shops and merchandise and the presence of banking and some leisure facilities.
- Neighbourhood centres and village centres. These are usually composed of anything between half dozen to twenty shops. Such centres are found in many different contexts and are consequently very difficult to generalize about. In the main they largely cater for convenience

shopping, although in some larger centres some forms of specialist retailing is viable. They can be fairly prosperous where the established retailers have developed a good reputation with their customers and there are problems of access to the larger nearby town centres. The presence of vacant shops and outdated shops in such small shopping centres should be taken for what they are, signs of decay and decline.

- Even smaller clusters of shops can be found within residential areas, most typically groupings of newsagents, convenience stores, 'sweet shops', off-licences and small video shops.

Of principal interest in comparing shopping centres is their relative attractiveness to customer groups who are likely to use a shop of your intended type. There are two main ways of assessing the relative customer pull of various shopping centres.

- By appraising the customer attractions of the centre.
- By analysing and calculating the limits of its trading or catchment area.

Customer attractors

In the larger shopping centre the presence of a number of well-known, successful multiples is always a good indicator of prosperity. Such outlets act as a magnet, pulling customers in. Other such attractors of customers to a centre are:

- A good range of retail outlets offering a comprehensive range and choice in merchandise and services
- Banking facilities
- Plentiful car parking facilities
- Good access in terms of uncongested roads and good public transport
- Leisure facilities
- A pleasant shopping environment, i.e., clean modern shops, litter free, lack of vandalism and grafitti, good pedestrian access between shops and parking and transport facilities.

Further, your research related to Chapter 3 should have provided you with a list of benefits attributable to location that your targeted customers are seeking. Use this to access the value of various shopping centre locations (see Fig. 4.2 and associated discussion later in this chapter).

Determining and measuring catchment areas

The geographical area from which a shopping centre draws the majority of its customers is known as its catchment area. Obviously, one cannot say that customers further than a certain distance from a centre will not visit it; rather the catchment area really indicates the area over which the shopping centre has significant influence. If this area can be geographically identified, then an estimate of the centre's market in £s turnover can be made. On this very tangible and meaningful basis shopping centres can be compared.

Just as shops compete with each other, so do shopping centres. Of interest is to determine the distance between two or more shopping centres where the influence of one shopping centre grows and the other wanes; that is the break even point. To compare shopping centres in proximity to each other, on the basis of size of catchment area, adaptations of the now famous (in retailing circles at least!) *Riley's Law of Retail Gravitation* can be used. The original 'law' argued that the dominance of one centre over another depends on the relative sizes of the populations immediately surrounding each of the centres and the distance between the two centres. The approximate limits to the catchment area of one shopping centre in miles relative to another can be calculated using this formula:

$$\text{Limit to the catchment area of centre A (in miles from centre A)} = \frac{\text{Distance A to B}}{1 + \sqrt{\dfrac{\text{Population of B}}{\text{Population of A}}}}$$

(Note: The calculation is easy if a calculator with a square root function is used.)

To illustrate, if the distance between town A and town B along principal transport routes is 8 miles and their respective populations are, town A 38,000 and town B 62,000, then the break even point where neither town predominates:

$$= \frac{8 \text{ miles}}{1 + \sqrt{\dfrac{62,000}{38,000}}}$$

$$= \frac{8 \text{ miles}}{1 + \sqrt{1.63}}$$

$$= \frac{8 \text{ miles}}{1 + (1.3)}$$

$$= \frac{8 \text{ miles}}{2.3}$$

= 3.5 miles from town A or 4.5 miles from town B
(NB: all figures rounded to 1 decimal place)

By calculating the break even points for town A relative ot other nearby towns the catchment area boundary for town A can be drawn, as illustrated in Fig. 4.1.

How true a picture the use of this method produces depends on how much influence a town's population has on the size, quality and, hence, pulling power of its shopping centre. It may be that the town's population, in itself, may not be directly related to the customer pulling power of the shopping centre. Also, no account is taken of the relative access to each centre and availability of public transport. Further, a very practical problem encountered when using this method is being able to isolate and quantify the town to which the shopping centre relates. With small towns and villages that are not part of a larger urban area this is not usually a problem and this is the ideal context for its use. The town or village can be isolated and population figures obtained from the local planning department or county census of population. However, if you wish to draw the catchment areas for two shopping centres in the same urban area (i.e., not physically separated by 'green fields', etc.), the method becomes unworkable in its present form. The alternatives are either to adapt the model by substituting other more significant criteria for population, as each situation indicates, or to use the method of 'customer spotting' which is discussed later in the chapter.

One possibility is to substitute some measure of the pull of customer attractors in each centre for population. You could simply take some estimate of the number and size of the retail outlets in a shopping centre, on the basis that a centre with sixty shops would have greater customer pulling power than one with only twenty (although allowance would have to be made for the quality, size and range of outlets). Alternatively, you could go for a more sophisticated and, hopefully, more accurate measure that would take into account the relative importance of various attractors to your potential customers. This would have the obvious advantage of

Town	Population	Miles from A	Break even points in miles from A
A	38,000	–	–
B	62,000	8	3.5
C	140,000	6	2.0
D	50,000	10	4.7
E	18,000	12	7.1

Catchment area boundary – – – – – – –

Break even points   ●

Principal transport routes ——————

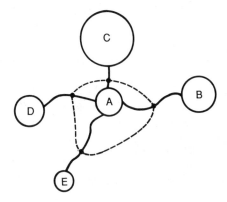

Fig. 4.1 Drawing a catchment area boundary using population and distance

making the method more specific to the customer groups you are interested in.

● **The process, although time consuming, is quite simple:**

1. **Identify the attributes that your potential customers seek from a shopping area (as discussed in Chapter 3).**
2. **Rate each attribute on how important it is to the customer group, using a scale of say 1 to 5 – 1 being not very important, 5 being essential.**
3. **Award points to each shopping centre on the basis of the existence, scale and quality of each attribute (as appropriate). For example, 0 does not exist; 5 meets customers requirements exactly.**
4. **Each shopping centre can now be scored on how well it does on each attribute by multiplying the importance weighting by the points scored.**

5. **A total measure of customer attractiveness can then be arrived at for each centre by simply adding the scores for each attribute.**

An example is given in Fig. 4.2 for your guidance using the same towns A and B as in the previous example. Adapt it as is appropriate to your customers and the shopping centres to be assessed. As with all such methods that require you to make subjective evaluations try to be as objective and consistent as you can. To improve objectivity, try and select attributes that can be assessed on some quantifiable basis. For instance, if it is important to customers that there should be a wide ranging choice of shops in a centre, develop some scoring system such as: 1 to 3 shops of same type = 1 point, 4 to 6 = 2 points, and so on.

Attributes	Importance	Centre A Points score		Centre B Points score	
Wide range of shops	5	2	10	4	20
Banking facilities	1	1	1	4	4
Good parking facilities	4	4	16	2	8
Good access	3	5	15	1	3
Measure of attractors:			42		35

Fig. 4.2 Attributes of towns/customer attractiveness

Although centre B is apparently larger than centre A, as is evidenced by its greater range and number of shops and banking facilities, centre A is more attractive to the customer group because of its superior access and parking facilities.

● The break even point between A and B in miles from A using an adapted Riley's formula would be calculated as follows:

$$\frac{\text{Distance A to B}}{1 + \sqrt{\dfrac{\text{Attractiveness of B}}{\text{Attractiveness of A}}}}$$

$$\frac{8 \text{ miles}}{1 + \sqrt{\dfrac{35}{42}}}$$

= 4.2 miles from A, an improvement in A's sphere of influence of nearly a mile by using customer attractors instead of population.

A different but complementary method is to take a random sample (see Chapter 3) of the customers using a shopping centre and simply ask them their place of residence. The results of the survey can then be spotted on to a large scale map of the area, a mark being made on the map for each customer interviewed. A further helpful refinement is to use a different colour for each customer group. From such a map you can identify concentrations of specific customer groups (very useful, for instance, for targeting advertising – see Chapter 14), and the break even point in the sphere of influence between competing shopping centres. This method should prove to be very accurate and particularly suitable for the analysis of shopping centres with small catchment areas.

With all of these approaches to catchment area analysis, good judgement must be used in assessing the use of each in terms of your type of shop and the nature of the area you are dealing with. In all cases you should seek to identify and assess both physical and psychological limits to a centre's catchment area. For instance, congested roads cutting physically through an area slow down traffic wishing to cross from one part of town to another but, even more importantly, they can also create a psychological barrier in the customer's mind, a feeling that the journey causes too much frustration and stress.

Catchment area characteristics, trends and stability

Once the limits to the catchment area have been identified, you should become concerned with the population characteristics (as discussed in Chapter 3) and the trends within the area, in particular its stability (see Chapter 2).

The following questions should be asked:

1. What plans do the local authority have for the area? Visit the local authority Planning Department where they will have 'Structure Plans' and written statements, including future plans for local shopping centres, road networks, etc. You can usually buy copies or, alternatively, they can be viewed at the planning office. Local libraries are also likely to have copies. Also try and assess whether the local authority is more or less likely to pass plans for large superstores. Has it been responsive to pressure from local small traders in the past? To find out:

- Visit the 'Clerk's Office' to see if you are able to consult the minutes of relevant past planning committee meetings;
- Contact the local chamber of trade and commerce;
- Check with the local newspaper.

2. How stable is the area? Is it over-reliant on just a few large employers? If so, what are their prospects?
3. How prosperous is the shopping centre. Find out by:

- Visiting the rating office. Valuation registers show the addresses and rateable value of all properties in the authority's area.
- Visiting a local commercial estate agents. Try and get some indication of how often various shops change ownership and which types are taking a long time to sell.

4. What are the characteristics of the population in the catchment area? (Discussed at length in Chapter 3.)
5. What is the total size of the population in the catchment area? The Census County Population report (produced every 10 years) will give figures down to town level. The OPCS monitor (Office of Population, Censuses and Surveys) gives up-to-date forecasts, but for more up-to-date counts and analysis of smaller areas, visit the Electoral office of the local authority. Here you will be able to gain access to electoral roles. These are detailed lists of registered voters listed by their place of normal residence and grouped according to electoral ward. With the aid of ward maps you can make very detailed population counts for very small areas. If you wish to include under 18 year olds in your population counts, you will have to adjust the figures by use of 'average number per household' from census information.

Assessing the sales potential

Having identified the limits to the catchment area and the number of customers it will produce, you will need to establish its sales potential. Obviously, to know how many potential customers there are in a catchment area is not the same as knowing how much they will buy. The sales potential of any given catchment area is the product of the actual number of customers, multiplied by their expenditure on the type of merchandise you intend to retail. The key information required is:

- Number of potential customers in the catchment area
- Average expenditure per customer or household over an appropriate and meaningful period of time (a week, month or year).

This information may come from either published data (principally the *Family Expenditure Survey*), your own research (see Chapter 3), or a combination of both.

Using the Family Expenditure Survey

The *Family Expenditure Survey* (FES), published each year, provides a very detailed breakdown of weekly household expenditure. However, as the data is produced from a comprehensive and complex set of surveys, the information in the current edition relates to expenditure as it was two years before – so the 1988 report refers to 1986 expenditure. Obviously in the intervening period there will have been price rises, in rare cases even price decreases and, probably, some change in expenditure patterns. To adjust an *FES* figure to allow for inflation you must first calculate the percentage increase in prices in the given period from the General Index of Retail Prices.

The general index of retail prices can be found in either the *Annual* or *Monthly Digest of Statistics* (the *Monthly Digest* is more up to date). It is constructed to show how the prices of groups of merchandise and services have changed over time. You will find that the table is sub-divided into broad groups with columns representing changing price levels for: all items, food, alcoholic drink, tobacco, durable household goods, clothing and footwear. The price level for a given date is given as a percentage of some reference point in the past, called the base date or year 1. The base date level is given as 100 and the actual year of the base date is to be found at the top of the table. The figure 100 is chosen to represent the base price level because later levels can then be easily expressed as a percentage of it. For example, if the base year is 1980, the base level is 100 and the index for 1988 is 390, then prices have risen by 290 per cent between 1980 and 1988. To calculate the price increase in food between two dates, say 1984 and 1986, is simply a matter of taking the difference between the RPI numbers for 1984 and 1986 (food column) and expressing it as a percentage of the 1984 index number:

$$\frac{1986 \text{ RPI number} - 1984 \text{ RPI number}}{1984 \text{ RPI number}} \times 100 = \text{Average percentage increase in food prices from 84 to 86}$$

$$\frac{347.3 - 326.1}{326.1} \times 100 = 6.5\% \text{ average increase in food prices from 84 to 86}$$

Once the percentage increase in prices for the given period has been calculated, then it is a simple matter of increasing the *FES* expenditure figure by that percentage. The updated weekly household expenditure survey figure can then be multiplied by the number of households in the catchment area to give the area's average weekly sales potential.

If you have detailed population characteristics for the catchment area that correspond to *FES* classifications, then it is possible to make a more detailed profile of the sales potential of the catchment area. (Note, some census of population information is classified using similar criteria to that of the *FES*.) Such a profile could usefully include a mapping of the location of various customer groupings within the catchment and area and their individual sales potential.

- **Note of caution**. When calculating approximations of sales potential for catchment areas using statistics compiled for larger areas than your envisaged trading area, you should always attempt to use an alternative method, preferably first hand market research, to verify your results. Your local area may be wholly untypical of regional and national spending patterns/trends. Does the average household expenditure (adjusted for inflation) on your merchandise groups for your customer groupings as quoted in the *FES* roughly correspond to information you have derived from other market research sources/techniques? If not, why not? What are the reasons? Which is the more valid and reliable source?

Calculating the sales potential for an individual shop

The market value of a catchment area for a range of merchandise is not, on its own, a direct measure of the value of that location. The potential custom in the catchment may be already adequately supplied and the addition of another similar retail outlet may result in the market becoming saturated. To prevent you locating in an area that is already over supplied, assess each catchment area in the following way:

- By carrying out a detailed visual survey of the centre, firstly sharpening your skills of estimating length and breadth. Estimate the total square footage devoted by all retailers to selling the merchandise you intend to sell.
- Add to this figure, the approximate square footage of selling space you would add to the centre if you chose this location.

- Divide the sales potential for the merchandise range by the total square footage that would be devoted to it.

The result will give you an approximation to average sales that would be earned per square foot of selling space in the centre with the addition of your shop. If this figure is below what you require (see Chapter 5: 'Will my shop be profitable?') then the location is unsatisfactory. For example, if the sales potential of a small shopping centre for women's clothing is £50,000 per week, the sales space already devoted to such sales is estimated at 40,000 square feet and the addition of your shop would bring that total to 41,200 square feet, then the average weekly sales potential per square foot would be £1.21 (£50,000/41,200). This would give you an average weekly sales figure of £1,452 (your selling space, 1,200 sq. ft. × £1.21 average sales per sq. ft.). If you require £1,500 per week just to cover costs then, obviously, this location would be far from satisfactory.

A shop's ability to capture a share of the market is, of course, not based solely on its size. The percentage of the market you are likely to capture, as discussed in Chapter 3, is likely to be equal to or at least in rough proportion to your ability (relative to that of the competition) to satisfy the needs of your customers. To estimate market share on this basis we can use a similar method to that used earlier in the chapter for assessing the attractiveness of a shopping centre. Work through the action guidelines.

4

From your work with Chapter 3 you should be able to complete the following exercise to estimate your potential market share.

1. **List the features that potential customers are looking for in a shop of your type.**
2. **Give each feature a weighting from 1 to 5, to signify its importance to the customers.**
3. **Award points, on a scale of 1 to 5, to each shop in the centre or catchment area (including your own if it were to exist there) on how strong they are in providing each feature.**
4. **Multiply the importance weighting by the points awarded for each shop to obtain its score.**
5. **Finally, total each shop's score and analyse the results.**

Features	Importance	Your shop Points score	Competitor Points score	Competitor Points score
Totals:		_____	_____	_____
		_____	_____	_____

Once the analysis is complete, it is possible to quantify your market share. For example, if the results of your analysis revealed the scores as listed in Fig. 4.3, then it could be estimated that your shop has the potential to capture 23.1 per cent of the sales potential of the catchment area based on its ability, in relation to its competitors, to satisfy that market (i.e., appeal to customer buying motives). With the total sales potential of the catchment area being currently £30,000 per week, you can expect to eventually achieve a turnover of £6,930 per week. Put another way, there is probably potential for you to gain three times the market share of competitor 1, but only three quarters of the turnover of competitor 2, and so on.

Sales potential of catchment area: £30,000

	Score	Share %	in £s
Your shop:	30	23.1	6,930
Competitor 1:	10	7.7	2,310
Competitor 2:	40	30.7	9,210
Competitor 3:	30	23.1	6,930
Competitor 4:	20	15.4	4,620
Total:	130	100.00	30,000

Fig. 4.3   Calculating the market share based on proportionate ability, in relation to competitors, to satisfy customer need

Unfortunately, there is no mathematical certainty about this method. However, it is much better than taking a stab in the dark. Its accuracy will depend on the following factors:

- How accurate you have been in identifying and ranking needs (buying motives) of your customers.
- How accurate you have been in your assessment of your business and its competitors.

In trying to estimate the sales potential for your shop it is often worthwhile to further sub-divide the sales potential of a catchment area not just into merchandise groups, but into scale of operation. To illustrate, if you wanted to buy a convenience store situated in a residential neighbourhood with a clearly defined catchment area of 800 households, each spending on average £40.00 per week on the merchandise you intend to sell, then to state the catchment area sales potential as £32,000 would be slightly absurd. It should be obvious that a large proportion of that expenditure on food will be spent during the main grocery trips to the supermarket. Therefore, the true sales potential of the catchment area is the percentage of the main food bill that is attributable to convenience shopping. Without doing detailed, 'on the ground' research, that figure can be estimated from published statistics. By using Tables 7 and 10 (see Chapter 1, Fig. 1.2) of *The Retail Business Monitor* you will be able to decipher that the small retailer is, at best, likely to capture only 20 per cent of the grocery market. Providing the convenience store does not have any competition on a similar scale in the catchment area, this will make the shop's maximum sales potential £5,400 (i.e., 20/100 × £32,000).

Factors to consider when choosing a site

4

Once the location has been chosen the search must be on for a suitable site. Obviously, there will be constraints in terms of what's for sale and the price you can afford. In assessing and comparing available sites, consideration must be given to the following factors.

Traffic flow

The first question to ask is: do the targeted customer groupings pass the site? Certainly this should be investigated by:

- Conducting customer interviews in the vicinity of the site, taking quota samples of around thirty or forty customers at three distinct times of day. For example, 9 am to 12 am, 12 am to 2 pm and 2 pm to 5 pm.
- Taking hourly customer counts on half past the hour starting at 9.30 am. The reason for taking them at half past the hour is that the counts taking place between the hours of 12 am and 2 pm will measure the traffic flow during the middle, rather than the ends and beginnings, of the two principal dinner hours and are therefore likely to be more accurate.

The customer counts should be taken in the same spots and for the same length of time; a period of between five and ten minutes is optimum. Factors that may affect the count, such as whether it is raining, or is colder/ hotter than usual, should be noted. The results of each customer count can then be extended to estimate the total number of people passing the site in the hour in which the count took place. For example, if 50 people were counted on the 10.30 am count and it lasted for 5 minutes, it can then be estimated that 600 people passed the site between 10 am and 11 am (i.e.,

$60/5 \times 50$). The percentages of the total passing population deemed to be potential customers, for each of the three times of day selected, can then be estimated from the three samples of customers interviewed, as in Fig. 4.4.

Time	Estimated number passing	
9am to 10am	300	From the sample interviewed from 9am to 12am, 3% met the characteristics of the targeted group of customers, therefore 39 customers are estimated in this time period.
10am to 11am	600	
11am to 12am	400	
Total:	1,300	
12am to 1pm	650	From the sample interviewed from 12am to 2pm, 2% met the characteristics of the targeted group of customers, therefore 20 customers are estimated in this time period.
1pm to 2pm	350	
	1,000	
2pm to 3pm	700	From the sample interviewed from 2pm to 5pm, 4% met the characteristics of the targeted group of customers, therefore 55 customers are estimated in this time period.
3pm to 4pm	380	
4pm to 5pm	300	
Total:	1,380	

Total customers estimated for the day = 114

NB: If the average expenditure per customer is known, then this is an additional way of assessing the sales potential of a site.

Fig. 4.4 Analysis of a customer count

Similar counts can be made of car borne customers. This could be of significance when assessing out-of-centre, main road sites for say an off-licence, convenience or CTN store. The process is basically the same except that, instead of counting pedestrian traffic, you would count passing cars. Also, as a sample of the occupants of the cars cannot be taken, then the number of car borne customers stopping at the site to buy should be noted. For example, if 50 cars are counted in a 5 minute period and five stopped to make a purchase, then it could be estimated that 10 per cent of passing car traffic is potential custom.

How complex and comprehensive you wish to make your customer count depends on the degree of accuracy you wish. For a full picture of customer flow and estimates of potential custom, because trading patterns invariably fluctuate throughout the trading week, a detailed count and survey should be undertaken on each day.

Parking and transport facilities

For most shops, other than those that are primarily visited on foot, close proximity to such facilities is usually important. Parking facilities are invariably a problem in shopping centres but may be compensated for by the benefits derived from being sited close to other busy shops and facilities used by your customers. Certainly, the appearance of double yellow lines outside a small shop, particularly on a main road site, has been the death knell for many small traders. As checks should be made not just on the present parking facilities but also on the possibility of future restrictions, check with the police and the local authority on the likelihood of parking restrictions being imposed. Do your customers travel by bus? Where is the bus stop, both in and out of town?

Site conditions: magnets and distractors

Aspect

An important consideration that is often overlooked is whether the customers can clearly see the store. For example, a particular main road site may, at first sight, appear good for a convenience store but, view it from a car approaching at thirty or forty miles per hour, does the potential customer see it in time to feel the desire to buy and then stop? Similarly, in high street locations, some shops are less noticeable than others because of the structural clutter of surrounding buildings. The only way to test for such obstructions to the customer's view is to view the site yourself, from as many angles and distances possible.

Atmosphere

Vacant shops and buildings should be noted. Empty shops generate no customer flow and cast an air of depression over the site. Further, they may indicate that the site area is in decay. The area around the site should also be checked for any smells that are not conducive to the merchandise you sell. For instance, locating a baker's backing onto a Chinese take-away would certainly not be a good idea!

More important than people think, particularly in winter months, is which side is the sunny side of the street? Similarly, where are the sheltered spots from the cold and biting winter winds?

Poor access and congestion

Lack of adequate pavement areas can cause congestion. In such circumstances customers will be too intent on working their way through the crowds to stop and browse through your displays. In this way it is possible for a site to be too busy! Also note where the pedestrian crossings are. These can work both to your advantage and disadvantage. A store sited opposite a pedestrian crossing will have the advantage of customers walking directly towards their shop. Good use of an attractive store front and displays can then be used to entice them in while you have their attention for a few seconds as they cross the road. However, a pedestrian crossing can also feed customers away from your shop if there are no further attractors on your side of the street.

Hours of operation of the shops in proximity to the site

If you are planning on acquiring a shopping centre site then don't throw away one of the main reasons for locating in such an area, namely the pull of other shops. Will the opening hours of the shops in proximity to the site match your proposed opening hours? Is there a traditional early closing day? An off-licence in a small shopping precinct may do well during the day, but in the evening the precinct may become a very lonely and sinister place indeed where groups of young people may 'hang about', deterring potential custom.

Types of shops in proximity to the site

Will the surrounding shops:

- help generate further trade because they sell complementary goods to yours (e.g., clothing, cosmetics, footwear)?
- force you to compete for the same customers and spending on the same merchandise (e.g., licenced convenience store, off-licence)?
- distract in some way from the image of your business (e.g., jewellers, butchers)?

When carrying out such assessments, take care in identifying competitors. For instance, to open up a women's fashion store in proximity to Marks and Spencers is an advantage (if you can afford such a site) for you would not be projecting the same overall selling proposition, therefore, you would not be in the same business. In any case the sheer customer pulling power of such a retail outlet would far outweigh any disadvantages of sharing custom for a group of merchandise. Further, for some types of shops (shoe shops being a classic example) customer expectations make locating in an area of heavy competition beneficial.

Summary

The choice of location for your shop is perhaps the most critical decision you will ever have to take in relation to your business. Once made, the decision, in the short term at least, is irrevocable.

To make the right choice, consideration needs to be given first to choice of the general area in which to locate and secondly to identification of the factors that will make a good site. In choosing the location, the size and characteristics of the catchment area, including its sales potential, needs to be identified and calculated.

Assessment of each location must be made on the basis of what realistic market share can be expected. The sales potential then needs to be quantified for your shop and compared with the sales figure you need to attain to make your business viable. Once the location is decided upon, the site must be selected via careful examination of customer concentrations and flows, and full consideration of factors that may attract and deter customers from the site.

Finally, it is unlikely that you will find a perfect location – there will always be strengths and weaknesses to be found in any site. In the end the decision will be yours but it should be remembered that, as in most things, whilst recognizing the inevitable financial constraints, the needs and subsequent requirements of the customer groups you intend to serve are of paramount importance.

4

5 Will my shop be profitable?

Not as simple as you might think! □ Your costs □ Gross profit and stock cost □ Costs and sales volume □ The break even point: sales volume, costs, selling price and profit □ Price changes: their effect on sales and profits □ Multi-product break even □ The break even profit point □ Estimating your target profit □ Margins and mark ups □ The projected profit and loss account □ Summary □ Checklist

Not as simple as you might think!

From the previous chapter we have seen that the sales of a shop can be forecast. The next step is to establish whether the costs involved in attaining such a sales level will result in a large enough profit to warrant further consideration of a particular site.

The solution to the problem at first seems simple. Reasonably, you may think it is a matter of deducting all the costs involved in operating the business from the monies earned from expected sales. To see whether this is true, let's take an imaginary example of a shop just selling one kind of merchandise, 'Wondermix' (a revolutionary new product that will clean and fix literally anything!). To keep the example simple we will assume the business only has to meet the costs of rent, electricity and stock. Rent and electricity work out at £10,000 per annum and the cost price of each bottle of 'Wondermix' bought from the wholesalers is £i.00. The business has estimated it will sell a total of 20,000 bottles of 'Wondermix' in its first year's trading. With a prevailing market price of £2.00 it sets out to estimate its profit:

Sales volume revenue (20,000 × £2.00):		£40,000
Rent and equipment costs:	£10,000	
Raw materials costs (20,000 × £1.00):	£20,000	
Total costs:		£30,000
Profit:		£10,000

The shop will be profitable, or will it? What will happen if the sales drop by half? Will this result in the profits being halved to £5,000? The answer is no, because not all of the costs have the same characteristics. Logically the cost of stock will be reduced by half in proportion with the drop in sales. But what about the other costs? The business will still have to pay rent on the premises and maintain its equipment. Regardless of how much it sells, these costs will remain the same. The business will not be profitable:

Sales revenue (10,000 × £2.00):		£20,000
Rent and equipment costs:	£10,000	
Raw materials costs (10,000 × £1.00):	£10,000	
Total costs:		£20,000
Profit:		ZERO!

You should be able to see that for this shop to operate at a profit it would have to do one, or a combination, of the following:

- Increase its sales volume
- Increase the selling price
- Reduce its costs

However, attempts to change one factor to the advantage of the business may, inadvertently, bring about a disastrous change in another. For example, if the selling price of 'Wondermix' is increased to £2.50 in an attempt to offset the effect of the fall in sales, customers may go else where to seek cheaper prices, possibly cutting the already reduced sales volume by half. This would put the business in an even worse position:

Sales revenue (5,000 × £2.50):		£12,500
Rent and equipment costs:	£10,000	
Raw materials costs 5,000 × £1.00):	£5,000	
Total costs:		£15,000
Loss		£2,500

This very simple example clearly shows that the task of estimating profit is not as simple as it first appears. The factors that determine profit – costs, sales volume and selling price – are all intertwined. Altering one factor can have a marked effect on one or all of the others.

To be able to predict the profit or loss your shop could make we need some method or model capable of clearly calculating and showing the impact of changes in any one of these factors on the profitability of your intended business. We require a model that will answer all those 'if then what questions', such as: If I fail to meet my sales target by ten per cent what will my total profits be? If my stock costs rise by fifteen per cent, how many more do I need to sell to maintain my profits? etc. To build up this model we will have to examine all of its components: cost, selling price, and sales volume, in much more detail.

Your costs

- Not all expenditure is a cost!
Before we can proceed to examine the characteristics and structure of costs in detail it is important for you to understand what is and what isn't a cost to a business. Otherwise you may fall into the trap of classifying all the expenditure you make in relation to your business as a cost.

Money going into a business is soaked up into two distinct areas, the costs the business incurs and its capital requirements (for a full discussion of the characteristics of capital, see Chapter 6). To be able to easily distinguish between expenditure on costs and capital (acquisition of assets) you would be well advised to remember the following working definitions:

- Cost is the value of something the business has used.
- Capital (assets) is the value of something the business has.

To illustrate, if a shop buys in £20,000 worth of stock at the beginning of the month and has £5,000 worth of stock left from the delivery at the end of the month, then £15,000 of stock will have been sold (discounting the possibility of theft and wastage) This stock, having been used up in the business, will be a cost and the £5,000 of stock left on the shelves, being something the business still has, will be capital.

Try to determine which items from the following list of expenditure, made by a shop proprietor in his first year, represent capital investment in the business and which are definitely costs.

	£s
Van for visiting the cash & carry:	5,500
Shop fittings and electronic till:	10,000

Expenditure on maintenance, petrol and oil:	1,000
Closing stock (not sold):	4,000
Expenditure on stock sold during the year:	80,000
Capital repayments on business loan used to buy the van, fixtures and fittings:	5,150
Interest charges on the loan:	1,550
Drawings out of the business by the owner:	10,000

You would be right to identify the expenditure on stock sold (but not the unsold closing stock), maintenance charges, petrol and the oil as costs, for those items will have been used up by the business in the course of the year. On the other hand you cannot count all of the expenditure on the van, shop fittings and electronic till as a cost because the shop proprietor will still possess both items at the end of the year. However, it is obvious that the van, fixtures and the till, through their use in the business, will have lost value – they will have depreciated. The amount by which they have depreciated can be counted as a cost.

The important thing to remember is that the cost of major capital purchases (known as fixed assets) are spread out over their working life. So that, for example, a van costing £8,000 with an expected working life of four years, could be depreciated at £2,000 per annum.

To determine what depreciation costs your business will incur you will need to identify what your major purchases will be (see Chapter 6) and then adopt a suitable method of providing for depreciation. You may refer to Appendix 5 (at the rear of the book) to select a method, or decide that this is best left to your accountant.

Now let's turn our attention to the last three items on the list. First, the loan repayments and interest charges. The total interest charges for the year are definitely costs: the expenditure has been used up servicing the loan for that trading period. The total repaid on the business loan, however, is neither expenditure on an asset nor a cost, but quite simply a repayment of capital and, as such, it must come out of profits. The use to which the loan monies have been put will have already been classified as asset or cost expenditure and, therefore, to count the repayments as either would result in double counting. For example, if £1,000 has been borrowed to buy a till, £1,000 will be spent on the till and £1,000 will be eventually repaid to the lender, but to say that £2,000 'costs' had been incurred has a result of these transactions would be absurd!

Finally, the £10,000 drawn out of the business by the owner may cause some confusion. Certainly it cannot be an asset for the monies have permanently left the business. Having discounted this possibility, you may have reasonably assumed it to be a cost, defining the payment as wages to the owner. I am afraid this is not the case. Unless the shop is a limited company (more about this in Chapter 11: 'Opening up as ...') the owner is not paid wages but earns the profit the business makes. This profit may be left in or drawn out of the business. Therefore, the £10,000 drawn by the proprietor is termed 'drawings on profit'. If the business only made £8,000 profit the owner would have overdrawn by £2,000. The overdrawn monies would have to be paid out of the assets of the business.

● So far we have identified what defines a cost and looked briefly at one kind of cost depreciation. There are of course many other costs involved in operating a business and, as discussed at the beginning of the chapter, certain costs react in different ways to changes in sales volume. We must now turn our attention to classifying the costs involved in running your shop. They fall broadly into two groups: those that don't change with sales and those that do.

Fixed costs

These are the costs you will have to pay whether your business is going well or badly. A good test to apply to determine whether an item is a fixed cost is to ask the question: 'If I don't sell anything at all, will I still have to pay out for this item?' If you will, then it is definitely a fixed cost. For example, you will still have to pay for such items as rent, electricity and permanent staff wages even if no customers come into your shop! Over short periods of time, say less than a year, these costs will change very little with how much you sell – they are 'fixed' and not affected by changes in sales volume. Obviously, over a longer period they may change, for example, you may set up an additional till point and take on more sales staff.

We can now start to build our model of how costs, sales volume, selling price and profit interact together by drawing up a simple chart to show how fixed costs behave in relation to sales volume (Fig.5.1).

Forecasting fixed costs

The size of your fixed costs will largely depend on the type and scale of the retail operation you plan to run. Here is a rough guide to help you construct a forecast of your fixed costs.

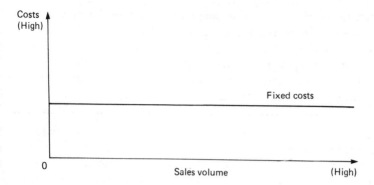

Fig. 5.1 Sales volume and fixed costs

- Depreciation. First you will have to list and cost the fixed assets you will need. To do this, consult Chapter 6 and then refer to Appendix 5 to calculate the depreciation on the assets. To begin with rough estimates can be made.

- Accountancy and legal fees. Certainly you will incur legal fees in purchasing the shop. Accountancy fees will vary depending on how much you want your accountant to do. Contact a range of solicitors and accountants to find out their fees.

- Sales promotion/advertising. To compile detailed estimates consult Chapter 14. Again rough estimates can be made at this point.

- Utilities. Gas and/or electricity can be estimated from general experience. For detailed estimates contact British Gas or the Electricity Board for information – both run small business advisory services. Similarly, contact British Telecom to obtain rates for business users.

- Rent and rates. These are, of course, specific to the premises you wish to acquire and as such will be supplied by the vendor. You should check out any figures given to you. In the case of rates, check with the local authority rating office. With the rent, check with your solicitor what possibility there is of rent increases. Further, see Chapter 9: 'Buying the Shop'.

- Wages and salaries. Depend obviously on the quality and number of staff you intend to employ. Check out wage rates for sales assistants in the area. In particular, check what additional costs you will have to incur through employing staff, for instance provision of dinner or break facilities, cover for sickness, employers' National Insurance contribution, etc.

- Interest charges. Interest will be payable on overdrafts and business loans. To estimate these see Chapter 6 and, when you have a rough estimate of your loan requirements, obtain literature on loan costs from the banks to refine your estimate.

- Miscellaneous. There will be many small costs such as cleaning materials, repairs to equipment, wrapping materials, till rolls, pricing/ marking materials, stationery, coffee. Some liberal estimate of these costs must be built into your forecast.

To enable you to make some initial profit calculations, rough fixed costs forecasts can be made by reviewing the accounts of businesses that are for sale (visit your local commercial estate agent), similar to the type you wish to open or buy. In particular the Profit and Loss account will provide you with a clear listing of the expenses incurred on fixed costs over the previous year. After studying enough of these you will have a good idea of the type and scale of costs you are likely to face in running the type of shop you intend to set up or buy.

One final and important point that needs to be made is that, in estimating your costs, you need to be precise and clear in terms of the time period to which they relate. Many newcomers to business tend to make the mistake of counting all the monies that will be paid out in costs in say a twelve month period as costs relating to that period. This is not necessarily the case. For example, rental payments on premises are often made quarterly, in advance, so that in the first year there will be five payments, but the last one will relate to costs incurred in the first quarter of the second year's trading, and not to the costs of the first year of trading. Similarly with electricity bills; these are payed in arrears so that there will only be three payments in the first year, with the final one relating to first year costs falling due for payment in the second year. The timing of these payments is certainly important to your cash flow (considered at length in the next chapter), but should be ignored in terms of calculating profit or loss for a given period of time.

Lastly, all costs and sales figures should be estimated excluding VAT. (See Chapter 10, section on VAT.)

Variable costs

These are costs that vary with changes in sales volume – hence their name. Their key characteristic is that they will rise or fall in direct proportion to rises or falls in sales volume.

For almost all retail businesses the most significant variable cost will be that of stock. It can be easily seen that the cost of stock will vary in direct proportion to how much is sold. If sales double, so will the cost of stock. This relationship is illustrated in Fig. 5.2.

Other costs, such as casual labour costs for Saturday staff and petrol for your delivery van, will vary with your sales, but not in direct proportion. An increase in sales from £1,000 to £1,500 per week may entail the employment of an extra part-timer but this will probably suffice for any further increase in sales, say up to £2,000 per week. Such costs jump in steps rather than increasing smoothly with sales. They are termed semi-variable costs, neither wholly fixed or wholly variable. The problem of

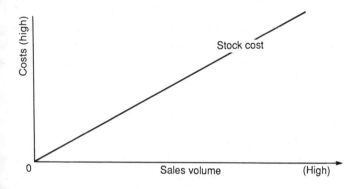

Fig. 5.2   Sales volume and variable (stock) costs

how to most usefully classify these costs is answered when one considers their scale in relation to your stock costs. To illustrate, for a small convenience shop the petrol and casual wages bill is not likely to exceed a couple of thousand pounds in any one year whereas the stock costs will be measured in terms of tens of thousands of pounds. Therefore, for practical reasons, it is best to classify such semi variable costs as fixed costs for the purpose of profit forecasting, leaving stock as the single variable cost.

Forecasting variable costs

If you were to sell just one item of merchandise as in the simple example at the beginning of the chapter, then forecasting and plotting stock costs would be straightforward. All you would have to do is find out the cost price of the merchandise from the wholesaler or manufacturer. However, in running even a small shop, you could be selling hundreds if not thousands of different items. How can you forecast the cost of stock in such circumstances? The answer is perhaps simpler than you think, but first you must understand the meaning of profit in a retail business.

Gross profit and stock cost

In retailing (and business in general) there are two types of profit, gross and net. Gross profit is the difference between the sales and the cost of stock to make those sales or, to put it another way, the difference between the cost price of an item of merchandise and its selling price. Out of the gross profit, payment for fixed costs has to be made. The remainder (if there is any!) is the net profit. That is the amount that, after it has been taxed, you can do with as you please!

Gross profit in retailing is often expressed as a percentage of the selling price. When gross profit is given in this way it is known as the gross profit percentage margin, or just simply as the profit margin. The calculation is simple:

$$\text{Profit margin} = \frac{\text{Gross profit}}{\text{Selling price}} \times 100$$

To give an example, if the cost price of a skirt is £3.00 and it sells for £4.00, the gross profit will be £1.00 and the profit margin will be 25 per cent (i.e., $\frac{1}{4} \times 100$). Similarly, if the sales of a shop are £3,000 and the cost price of the goods sold to make those sales is £1,500 then the margin will be 50 per cent.

Retail businesses common to a particular type (i.e., newsagents, off-licences, female fashion shops, greengrocers, etc.) tend to operate to a set gross profit margin (see information given in Chapter 1 relevant to your kind of shop). This is because they tend to sell at similar market prices and buy in stock at similar cost prices. The ability to be able to predict the probable profit margin you will operate on, with a reasonable degree of accuracy, is very useful. For if the margin is known it is then relatively simple to calculate the percentage of sales that is represented by cost of stock sold and consequently the actual cost of stock to attain any given sales level. To illustrate, as Fig. 5.3 clearly shows, if the profit margin is 20 per cent then the percentage of the value of sales which is attributable to stock costs must logically be 80 per cent, a 30 per cent margin would result in 70 per cent stock costs, a margin of 40 per cent in 60 per cent stock costs, and so on. The actual cost of stock for a given sales level is then just a simple percentage calculation from that sales level. For example, if the margin is 25 per cent and the expected sales for a year are £100,000, then the actual stock costs will be £75,000 (i.e.: 75/100 × £100,000).

Gross profit	20%
Stock costs	80%

Selling price (100%)

Fig. 5.3 Structure of a price or sales

Costs and sales volume

Now we can bring both types of cost together and see how the cost of producing each £1.00 'unit of sale' is affected by sales volume. Let's take a simple example to illustrate the effect.

Quick Shop is an imaginary small convenience store. Its fixed costs for one year of trading are estimated at £10,000 and the profit margin is expected to accord with that given for the trade as a whole (see Fig. 1.1) at 20 per cent, giving stock costs at 80 per cent of sales. Quick Shop's total variable costs will of course vary for different levels of sales; £100,000 sales

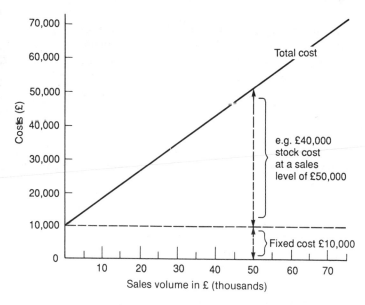

Fig. 5.4 Sales volume, fixed and variable costs

will result in £80,000 variable costs (i.e., 80/100 × £100,000), £50,000 sales will cost £40,000 and so on. Figure 5.4 shows the relationship between its fixed and variable costs over a range of sales levels.

The total cost of producing each one pound sale can easily be calculated from this graph by dividing total costs for the number of £1.00 sales achieved (i.e., total costs/Total sales in £s). Figure 5.5 shows the relationship between its fixed and variable costs over a range of sales:

Sales in £s	Fixed cost	Stock cost	Total cost	Cost to make each £1.00 unit of sale	Profit/Loss per each £1.00 unit of sale
10,000	10,000	8,000	18,000	1.80	(0.80)
50,000	10,000	40,000	50,000	1.00	0.00
90,000	10,000	72,000	92,000	0.91	0.09

You can see that for higher sales levels the cost of selling each item is reduced. The variable stock cost per unit will remain the same but the fixed costs per unit are reduced as they are spread out over a greater output (i.e., total fixed costs divided by sales = unit fixed costs).

Fig. 5.5   The relationship between fixed and variable costs over a range of sales

Operating on a 20 per cent profit margin, Quick Shop would certainly make a net profit at a sales level of £90,000 per annum, a net return of £8,100, but quite a loss, of £8,000, if it only attained sales of £10,000 per annum. At a turnover of £50,000 it would neither make a loss or a profit. This is known as its break even point. It is critical for any business to know this point, when sales revenue will begin to overtake costs and produce a profit.

The break even point: sales volume, costs, selling price and profit

Having investigated how sales volume affects costs, we can now fully integrate gross profit into our model to show how all the factors, sales volume, costs and selling price, interact together to affect net profit.

We can proceed by simply adding a sales revenue line to the graph as in Fig. 5.6. This is done by graphing the revenue that will be earned at different sales levels, a simple enough task seeing that a sales level of say £80,000 will earn a revenue of £80,000! The point where the sales revenue line intersects the total cost line is where the business will just be making sufficient revenue to cover all costs, this is the BEP (break even point). Below that sales volume, the business will make a loss; above it, it will make a profit. Drawing the graph helps you to quickly see and read off the various profits or losses you could make at any given level of sales. However, this way forward is a trifle clumsy for our purposes and does not allow you to quickly examine the effect of changes in price on profitability.

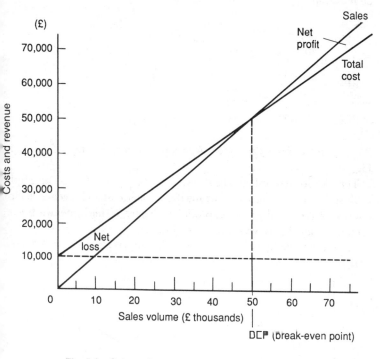

Fig. 5.6 Sales volume, costs, selling price and profit

The alternative is to dispense with the variable cost and revenue lines and simply plot gross profit against fixed costs. There is no need to plot the variable cost if gross profit is used, because, as we have already discussed, the gross profit is that amount left after payment for stock costs have been made. The break even point is reached when enough gross profit has been earned to fully contribute to the cost of overheads. After that point, any addition to gross profits will be able to contribute directly to net profits. This can be shown either in graph form or by a simple formula.

Due to the fact that the gross profit on each £1.00 sale has to contribute to the payment of fixed costs, to break even enough individual gross profits have to be made to cover fixed costs. This gives the formula:

$$\text{Break even sales point} = \frac{\text{Fixed costs}}{\text{Gross profit margin}}$$

Let's substitute some figures from our Quick Shop example to demonstrate.

$$\text{BEP} = \frac{£10,000}{20\% \text{ (ie., } 20/100)}$$

$$\text{BEP} = \frac{£10,000}{0.2}$$

$$\text{BEP} = £50,000$$

As you can see this is the same conclusion we came to using the graph in Fig. 5.6.

The BEP formula can also be shown to work in graph form. The graph is constructed as before, but this time the variable cost and revenue line is omitted and replaced by a gross profit line. Figure 5.7 illustrates the break even point for the convenience store example.

The gross profit line is drawn by first selecting a sales volume (£100,000

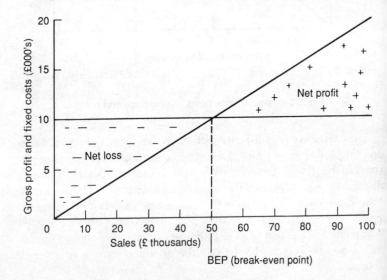

Fig. 5.7 Constructing a break even chart using a gross profit margin

in the example), then calculating how much gross profit the volume of sales will produce with a given margin (20 per cent in the example) – in this case it will be 20 per cent of £100,000 which is £20,000 gross profit – and marking the profit against the level of sales on the graph. The gross profit line is then drawn with a ruler from zero gross profit/zero sales (obviously, zero sales will result in zero profit) through the marked point on the graph. You can see that the graph gives the same sales £50,000 to break even as the formula method does.

You can turn the graph into a more dynamic model by adding different profit margins to gauge the effect of different selling prices on the break even sales figure, to attain desired net profit levels. As we shall see in the next section, price changes can have a dramatic effect on sales and the profit margins and, consequently, overall profitability.

- **Try constructing your graph. The shop may not be able to achieve the break even sales figure. What sales figure would it have to achieve if it charged a slightly higher level of prices and operated on a 25 per cent margin?**
- **To give you some more practice, let's assume the shop faces severe competition and has to drop its prices and so operate on a 15 per cent margin. With a 15 per cent margin. What is the new BEP? What sales level must be achieved to make a net profit of £100,000?**

  Note: **You can either construct a graph and plot all the different gross profit lines (i.e., 15 per cent, 20 per cent and 25 per cent), or use the BEP formula. Work with the method you prefer.**

Price changes: their effect on sales and profit

The pricing policy you adopt, as discussed in Chapter 3, must be appropriate to your targeted customer groups and consistent with your overall mix of place, merchandise, place and promotion. The pricing level you adopt is also subject to financial considerations. Your goal must be to select a price level that will give the best combination of sales revenue and profit margin to maximize total gross profits.

Any change in price will have two effects:

- To either increase or decrease sales revenue
- To raise or lower the profit margin

Attempts to assess the effects on both must be made.

Prices and sales volume: the price sensitivity of demand

Whether or not changes in your pricing level will have a dramatic effect on the amount of merchandise sold depends on how important price is to your customers. It is common knowledge that, for most merchandise, a drop in prices will bring about an increase in the quantity purchased. There are of course exceptions to the rule where low price may convey an image of poor quality or lack of exclusivity, such as is the case with 'high class fashions'.

A decrease in price may lead to an increase in the quantity of merchandise bought, but will it be sufficient to raise sales revenue? For instance, a drop in the price of sweatshirts from £10 to £8 may result in an increase in weekly sales from 80 to 100 but, when the full picture is examined, the increase in sales revenue is zero!

Price	×	Quantity sold	=	Total revenue
£10		80		£800
£8		100		£800

Clearly, for a price reduction to be effective in increasing total revenue the increase in quantity sold must be of such a magnitude to offset the loss of revenue on each item sold. Use of the following calculation will give the minimum number that will have to be sold just to maintain sales revenue at the same level.

p^1 = present price
p^2 = price after reduction or increase
q^1 = the present quantity sold or expected to be sold

$$\frac{p^1 \times q^1}{p^2} = \text{Revenue break even quantity}$$

To illustrate, a further reduction in the price of sweatshirts from £8 to £5 would have to result in an increase in sales from 100 to at least 160 per week (i.e., [£8 × 100]/£5). Similarly, looked at from the point of view of price increase, an increase from £5 to £8 would not be viable if customer demand fell off by more than 60 per week.

The calculation can also be performed for a merchandise range where the prices are all different but a flat price percentage reduction is being considered. For example an off-licence, with present canned beer sales of 400 per week, may wish to assess how many cans of beer will have to be sold to maintain present sales revenue if all canned beer prices are reduced by five per cent. If the price level on the merchandise group is taken as

100 per cent and the new price as 95 per cent (i.e., present price, less 5 per cent), then the calculation is:

$$\text{Quantity required to break even on sales revenue} = \frac{\text{Present sales volume}}{\text{New price level}}$$

$$= \frac{400}{0.95 \ (\text{i.e., } 95\%)}$$

$$= 421 \text{ cans per week.}$$

This would be true if the mix of total beer sales remains the same. However, the likelihood is that the price reduction may have more effect on one line than another. Accordingly, the percentage increase in sales that each line must surpass should be calculated:

$$\frac{\text{Increase in sales required}}{\text{Present sales level}} \times 100$$

In this case, for the price reduction to viable, each brand of beer would have to increase its sales in excess of 5.25 per cent (i.e., $21/400 \times 100$). Any that failed to show such an increase would demonstrate the demand for the line to be unsensitive to changes in price of this magnitude.

The owner of the off-licence will want to do more than just 'stand still'. Let's assume that he or she wishes to increase sales revenue by 25 per cent by making this price cut. What new sales target would have to be reached? The answer is obtained by simply adding the desired increase in sales revenue to the calculation, thus:

$$\frac{400 \times 1.25}{0.95} = \text{a new sales level of 526 cans per week}$$

or, a targeted increase of 31.5 per cent per brand.

Prices and gross profit

Total gross profit earned is the result of:

Price × Number sold × Profit margin

or, similarly:

Sales revenue × Profit margin

Price changes and profit margins

Increasing the number sold, even if it results in an increase in sales revenue, will not necessarily bring about an increase in the total gross profit earned. This is because the price reduction will have an adverse effect on the profit margin. For example, assuming that cost prices remain unchanged, a price reduction of 10 per cent on a 20 per cent profit margin will have the following effect. Taking the price level before the decrease as 100, a reduction of 10 per cent will reduce the price level to 90 and the profit from 20 to 10, so, remembering that the profit margin is Profit/ Price × 100, the new margin will be 11.1 per cent (i.e., 10/90 × 100 = 11.11 per cent). In this situation, an increase in sales revenue from say £3,000 to £3,500 would result in actual decrease in gross profits:

£3,000 × 0.2 (i.e., 20 per cent margin)   = £600 gross profit
£3,500 × 0.11 (i.e., 11.1 per cent margin) = £389 gross profit

A price increase will have the effect of inflating the profit margin. For example, again assuming that cost prices remain unchanged, a price increase of 10 per cent on a 20 per cent profit margin will have the following effect. Taking the price level before the increase as 100, an increase of 10 per cent will inflate the price level to 110 and the profit from 20 to 30, giving a new profit margin of 27 per cent (30/110 × 100 = 27.3 per cent).

To avoid making disastrous pricing decisions you need to be able to quickly determine for any contemplated price increase or decrease either:

- the percentage sales volume increase,
or
- the percentage sales revenue increase,
to break even on gross profit.

Price decreases: calculating the sales volume increase to break even

A price reduction will decrease the gross profit earned on each item sold by the amount of the reduction. For example, with a selling price of £1 and a profit of twenty pence, a ten pence price reduction will reduce gross profit by exactly a half. Therefore, to make the same gross profit that would have been previously earned from the sale of one item, two have to be sold – sales volume will have to increase by 100 per cent. The loss in gross profit per item sold (i.e., the price reduction) divided by the gross profit remaining on each item multiplied by 100 will give the percentage increase in number sold that must be surpassed to increase overall gross profits:

Percentage increase in sales volume required to break even on gross profit $= \dfrac{\text{Price decrease (i.e., lost profit on each item)}}{\text{Gross profit − Price decrease (i.e., increased profit on each item)}} \times 100$

For example, a contemplated price decrease of 10 per cent, when operating on a 15 per cent profit margin, will require a 200 per cent increase in sales volume to break even, that is make the same gross profit as before.

$$\frac{10}{15-10} \times 100 = 200 \text{ per cent}$$

5

This would mean that, with present sales of 500 per week, for the price decrease of 10 per cent to work (i.e., increase gross profits) more than 1,500 per week would have to be sold.

To help you quickly determine the increase in sales volume that has to be surpassed to increase overall gross profits with given price decreases and profit margins consult the table in Appendix 1.

Price increases: calculating the sales volume decrease to break even

It is equally important to know the percentage decrease in sales volume that can be supported by a price increase without having an adverse effect on gross profit. In this case, gross profit on each item of sale is added to rather than being reduced by the price change. With these appropriate changes, the same calculation will give the percentage decrease in sales revenue that can be supported by the price increase:

Percentage decrease in sales volume that can be supported by a price increase $= \dfrac{\text{Price increase (i.e., addition to gross profit on each item)}}{\text{Gross profit + Price increase (i.e., increased profit on each item)}} \times 100$

For example, a contemplated price increase of 10 per cent, when operating on a 15 per cent profit margin, will support up to a 40 per cent decrease in sales volume:

$$\frac{10}{15 + 10} \times 100 - 100 = 40 \text{ per cent}$$

To help you quickly determine the percentage decrease in sales volume that a percentage price increase will support, consult the table in Appendix 2.

Price decreases: calculating the sales revenue increase to break even on gross profit

To check what level of sales revenue in £s is required to break even on a price reduction is simply a matter of dividing the current gross profit by the new margin after the price reduction:

$$\frac{\substack{\text{Sales revenue at price level} \\ \text{before the price reduction}} \times \substack{\text{Profit margin before the price} \\ \text{reduction}}}{\text{(Profit − Price reduction)/Price − Price reduction)}}$$

(i.e., gross profit level before the price reduction)

(i.e., profit margin after the price reduction)

For example, a shop with a turnover of £2,000 per week operating on a 20 per cent profit margin considering a 10 per cent reduction in prices would have to increase its sales to £3,600 per week, just to maintain present gross profit levels – a net increase in turnover of 80 per cent.

$$\frac{£2,000 \times .2}{(20 - 10)/(100 - 10)} = £3,600$$

Dividing the profit margin before price reduction by the profit margin after price reduction will give the number of times sales revenue will have to increase to make up the loss. Reducing a profit margin from 50 per cent to 25 per cent will require a twofold increase in sales revenue to maintain gross profits. This gives the following calculation:

Increase in Sales revenue required to maintain gross profit $= \left(\dfrac{\text{Profit margin}}{\text{New profit margin}} \times 100 \right) - 100$

To illustrate, using the figures given in the previous example:

$$\left(\frac{20/100}{10/90} \times 100 \right) - 100 = 80 \text{ per cent increase in revenue required.}$$

To help you quickly determine the percentage increase in sales revenue that has to be surpassed to increase total gross profits with a price increase consult the table in Appendix 3.

Price increases: calculating the sales revenue decrease to break even on gross profit

As before, it is equally important to know the percentage decrease in sales revenue that can be supported by a price increase without having an adverse effect on gross profit. In this case the gross profit margin is increased instead of being decreased by the price change. The calculation is as before. For example, a shop operating on a 20 per cent profit margin, considering a 10 per cent increase in prices, could support a decrease in sales revenue of 26.7 per cent:

$$100 - \left(\frac{20/100}{30/110} \times 100 \right) = 26.7\%$$

Therefore, with a present turnover of £2,000, a reduction in sales level in the range £2,000 to £1,466 could be tolerated, i.e.:

£2,000 × 0.2 (i.e. 20 per cent margin) = £400 gross profit
£1,466 × 0.273 (i.e. 27.3 per cent margin after
increase) = £400 gross profit

To help you quickly determine the percentage decrease in sales revenue that a percentage price reduction will support consult the table in Appendix 4.

Measuring the price sensitivity of demand for merchandise

Measuring the price sensitivity of demand for your intended shop can be achieved by surveying your customers, using a suitable sample and questionnaire. Designing a suitable questionnaire to achieve these ends is fraught with problems and it is suggested that, to attain some degree of accuracy, only high demand merchandise is selected.

Firstly you must be clear about what you seeking to measure. Will you be intending to assess whether customers will buy more on each visit, or the same amounts but more frequently, or whether new customer groups will be attracted as a result of a lower pricing policy being adopted? For example, the prospective owner of a convenience store might want to find out if his or her targeted customer groups will spend a higher percentage of their grocery bill at the store if he or she adopted supermarket prices. Secondly, in interviewing customers you will be asking them to predict what their behaviour will be in a hypothetical situation. Consequently, although the replies may be truthful, they may not be accurate. However, once in business, if detailed sales records are kept, measuring the elasticity of demand for various ranges of merchandise is relatively simple. The responsiveness of sales to fluctuations in price can then be measured accurately because actual, rather than predicted, behaviour is being monitored. The information will be very valuable in planning such things as price promotions. The optimum price, in terms of generating sales revenue, can then be determined for individual ranges of merchandise.

Further information on the effect of price on customer demand and, consequently, sales volume can be obtained by:

- **Consulting state produced publications; for instance the recently published, *The Future of the High Street* produced by the Distributive Trades Economic Development Committee and published by HMSO, gives some details on price sensitivity of certain merchandise groups.**
- **Consulting appropriate trade journals.**
- **Talking to people in the trade.**
- **Surveying the competition and identifying the merchandise they select to promote on the basis of price. This indicates the merchandise ranges that are possibly more sensitive to price fluctuations.**

The effects of various pricing levels on net profit can be compared by plotting alternative operating profit margins on the break even chart, as described in the previous section.

Multi-product break even

We have now created the model we started at the beginning of the chapter. The model, as it stands, makes use of a single profit margin for the shop as a whole. It has already been recommended that the margin for your type of business can be taken from published statistics. The results will be fairly accurate if your shop is going to be 'typical' of its kind. It may be the case, however, that you will sell different merchandise groups than those that are common for your type of shop, or operate on a lower pricing level than is the norm for selected ranges, and so on. The net result will be a different sales and profit mix and consequently a different operating margin than is usual. Also, it is helpful to take the break even model further to allow you to calculate break even sales figures for different merchandise groups, or even individual items of merchandise. All this can be achieved by modifications to the original break even formula.

The way forward is to decide on some method of apportioning the fixed costs to each product or product group. There are a number of ways of doing this. One common approach adopted in retailing is to divide the total overheads by the square footage of selling space and allocate overheads on the basis of how much selling space is occupied by each merchandise group. The break even figure for each range is then worked out using the standard calculation. Another, not unreasonable, method is to allocate fixed costs to each product on the basis of the percentage of total gross profits each is expected to generate. Simply, an item of merchandise or merchandise group that generates more gross profit than another will be called upon to 'pay' a larger share of the overheads. However, as discussed previously, do not mistake a large profit margin on a product as an indicator that it will produce the largest gross profit. It is the number of times that profit margin is earned (Sales × Profit margin) that is important.

Although in the planning stage you cannot fully forecast the sales of each product, you can estimate the percentage of total sales that might relate to each product. Such estimates can come from first hand market research (see Chapters 3 and 4) and/or published statistics. The *Retail Business Monitor* (HMSO) gives the average proportion of total sales that are to be found in up to 40 different merchandise groups over thirty different types of retail operation. For example, on average an off-licences's total sales are made up, not surprisingly, as follows: 72.5 per cent alcoholic drinks, 17.7 per cent tobacco products, with the balance being made up mainly by confectionery and soft drinks (source: *Retail Business Monitor* SDO 25, Table 9).

The average gross profit margins for each merchandise range can also be determined by consulting published statistics. However, it is much more accurate to assess them yourself by obtaining cost prices from manufacturers, wholesalers and cash and carrys. Simply, spot check a number of high demand items in the merchandise group for cost price and selling price, calculate the margin, and take the most frequently recurring margins as the average for the group. In most cases this will give a reasonable degree of accuracy. Further, most manufacturers' representatives will be only too pleased to indicate the profit margin you are likely to realize on their ranges.

Having collected this information you are now in a position to allocate overheads on the basis of the proportion of total profits each product is expected to produce. For example, you sell two merchandise ranges A and B, with respective profit margins of 30 and 40 per cent. Merchandise range A is expected to sell three times as much as merchandise range B, so that A will generate 75 per cent of the sales and B 25 per cent. Fixed costs would, therefore, be allocated to each product by calculating the ratio (proportion) of A:B in providing total gross profit as follows:

	Sales	×	Margin	=	Rated gross profit
A:	75	×	30	=	2,250
B:	25	×	40	=	1,000

This gives a ratio of 2,250:1,000 simplified, by cancelling down, to 9:4. Therefore fixed costs will be apportioned:

$9/13 \times 100 = 69.23\%$ to product A
$4/13 \times 100 = 30.77\%$ to product B

With overheads of £1,000, £692 will be allocated to A and £308 to B. The break even point can then be calculated using the standard formula: BEP = Fixed costs/Gross margin. This would be £2,306 for product A and £770 for product B, giving a total break even sales figure for the business of £3,076. The same result can be achieved by modifying the standard break even formula to include the above information:

$$BEP = \frac{\text{Fixed costs}}{\underset{(\%S \times P)}{\text{merchandise A}} + \underset{(\%S \times P)}{\text{merchandise B}}}$$

$$BEP = \frac{\text{£1,000}}{(0.75 \times 0.3) + (0.25 \times 0.4)}$$

$$BEP = \frac{£1,000}{0.225 + 0.1}$$

$$BEP = \frac{£1,000}{0.325}$$

$$BEP = £3,076$$

- Let's take a more realistic example to explore the process in more detail. A newsagents, 'Paper Stop' (an imaginary business), has researched the market and costs for their principal merchandise ranges. The percentage of sales in each merchandise range and their respective profit margins have been found to be roughly the norm for this kind of business, and are as follows:

Range	Sales %	Profit margin %
A Newspapers & periodicals	22	27
B Tobacco products	38	8
C Confectionery	20	25
D Soft drinks	5	30
E General grocery & misc.	15	20
Total sales	100	

Paper Stop's fixed costs are estimated at £10,000 per annum.

To calculate the total sales needed to break even Paper Stop use an extended version of the break even formula:

$$BEP = \frac{\text{Fixed costs}}{\underset{(\%S \times P)}{\text{Range A}} + \underset{(\%S \times P)}{\text{Range B}} + \underset{(\%S \times P)}{\text{Range C}} + \underset{(\%S \times P)}{\text{Range D}} + \underset{(\%S \times P)}{\text{Range E}}}$$

$\%S$ = percentage of £ total sales in each product.
P = gross profit margin (contribution) produced by the product.

- The sales percentage can be represented as physical units of sale but, if this is done, then the gross profit must be expressed as a money figure. Accordingly, the break even sales figure will be in physical units. This variation may be suitable for businesses which are selling high price items in low volume, where the break even sales figure is required in terms of sales volume (e.g., number of TV sets, dish washers, etc.).

• In the version we are currently using the sales percentage represents £ sales and the gross profit is, therefore, expressed as a percentage margin. Accordingly, the break even sales figure will be in pounds.

Using the formula we can obtain the total sales in money Paper Stop needs to break even:

$$\text{BEP £s} = \frac{£10,000}{(0.22 \times 0.27) + (0.38 \times 0.08) + (0.2 \times 0.25) + (0.05 \times 0.3) + (0.15 \times 0.2)}$$

$$= \frac{£10,000}{0.0594 + 0.0304 + 0.05 + 0.015 + 0.03}$$

$$= \frac{£10,000}{0.1848}$$

$$= £54,112.55$$

As we already know what percentage of total sales will be in each product, we can easily calculate the break even £ sales for each product. In addition, to prove the 'extended formula' works, let's calculate the gross profit each product will contribute to fixed costs to see whether it is sufficient:

Product	% of total sales	Break even sales £	% Margin	Gross profit £
Newspapers	22	11,904.76	27	3,214.28
Tobacco	38	20,562.77	8	1,645.02
Confect.	20	10,822.51	25	2,705.63
Drinks	5	2,705.63	30	811.69
General	15	8,116.88	20	1,623.38
Totals:	100	54,112.55		10,000.00

The calculations involved to achieve the break even figure for this example seem tedious but with practice can be done quite quickly. If you build this multi-product break even model using a computer spreadsheet (one is duplicated in Appendix 6 for guidance) you can substitute a range of profit margins, prices and costs and recalculate the BEP with ease – this will greatly help decisions relating to prices, costs and sales mix.

When this calculation has been done once, you can easily obtain an overall percentage gross profit margin for the sales mix and transfer the information to a graph to study the effect on profits over a range of sales volumes. Paper Stop's expected gross margin from its sales mix is easily calculated by dividing BEP gross profit by BEP total sales and multiplying the result by 100, i.e., £10,000/£54,112.55 × 100 = 18.48 per cent gross profit margin on sales.

The break-even profit point (BEPP)

We have already used the model to identify the profits that will be earned with varying combinations of sales volumes, costs and selling prices. However, it would be advantageous to start with a desired profit and proceed directly to calculate the level of sales required to achieve it. Calculation of the break-even profit point is simply a matter of adding your profit objective to fixed costs and dividing the result by the gross profit/contribution per unit of sale:

$$\text{BEPP} = \frac{\text{Fixed costs} + \text{Desired profits}}{\text{Unit gross profit}}$$

In other words, you are asking the question, 'how many individual contributions of gross profit will have to be made to cover both fixed costs and my desired profit?'

Suppose in our previous example the owners of Paper Stop had to meet a profit objective of £15,000, then the break-even profit point would be:

$$\text{BEPP} = \frac{£10,000 + £15,000}{18.48 \% \text{ (i.e. } 18.48/100 = 0.1848)}$$

$$\text{BEPP} = \frac{£25,000}{0.1848}$$

$$\text{BEPP} = £135,281$$

As we already know the percentage of total sales in each product, you may like to work out BEPP for each product.

Estimating your target profit

As we have seen, if your estimates and classification of costs are accurate, you can use the break even model to readily identify the sales volume necessary to generate a desired net profit. The unanswered question is what target profits should you be aiming for. The answer, 'enough to live on' is not good enough and neither is some figure off the top of your head. Out of net profits you will have to provide for:

1. What you consider to be sufficient living expenses for yourself. You may use your present annual wage plus an allowance for inflation, but you must add on the non-wage benefits associated with employment, such as sick pay and pension schemes, which you will only receive at additional cost when you become self-employed.
2. Repayment of capital loans less interest.
3. Allowance for retaining some profits in the business to finance future capital requirements (see Chapter 6). Although the replacement of fixed assets is partly allowed for in the cost of depreciation, you would be well advised to remember that the replacement cost may be well in excess of original purchase price – you will have to find the difference out of profits or take on another capital loan. Many businesses face bankruptcy after their first year's trading because they failed to allow for sufficient profits to be retained in the business to finance future expansion.

Further you should be seeking a profit that represents a satisfactory return on the money invested in the business. The profits earned by your business should be greater than the return you would get if the money (yours or borrowed) was invested elsewhere, say a savings account. With a prevailing interest rate of 10 per cent offered on savings accounts, £100,000 invested in a business should produce net profits well in excess of £10,000 p.a. otherwise the owner might as well stay in bed and put the money in the bank! Further, as there is virtually no risk of not getting your money plus interest back from a savings account, and investment in a small business is fraught with risk, you should be aiming for profits that will represent a far higher return on capital invested than offered by a savings account. The riskier your business, the higher the rate of return on capital invested should be.

Calculate what your minimum profits per annum should be to represent a satisfactory return on your investment by:

- Finding out the current rate of interest (before tax) on savings accounts.
- Adding on a percentage for the element of risk involved. For an entirely new product this will be high (say 30 per cent), for a tried and tested business this will be low (say 10 per cent).
- Calculating the capital that will, on average, be employed in the business over its trading year (see Chapter 6).
- Then using the following calculation:
  Profit = Capital employed × Target percentage return
  For example:

Capital to be employed:	£50,000
Current rate of interest:	10%
Provision for element of risk:	20%
Target rate of return on capital employed:	30%

Therefore, minimum profits per annum required to provide a satisfactory return on capital employed in the business: £50,000 × 30% (30/100) = £15,000.

Mark ups and margins: Cost plus profit mark up

Before we leave the topic of profitability, it is important that you should understand another way of expressing gross profit, other than as a percentage margin. The alternative is to take the gross profit as a percentage of the cost price. This percentage is known as the mark up. It should not be confused with the percentage profit margin. Although both refer to the same profit in money terms, in the case of *profit margin*, the profit is expressed as a percentage of *sales* whereas, in the case of *mark up*, profit is expressed as a percentage of the *stock cost*. Its main use is in pricing up stock to obtain a desired profit margin.

Using mark ups and margins in calculating profit and pricing stock

When you have decided on an acceptable percentage gross margin on sales, you will need to convert this to its equivalent percentage mark up to enable you to arrive at a selling price for each item of stock. The process is as follows:

- As profit can be expressed as:

$$\text{Profit margin} = \frac{\text{Profit}}{\text{Price}} \quad \text{and Profit mark up} = \frac{\text{Profit}}{\text{V. cost}}$$

Then the percentage mark up can be derived from the percentage margin by:

$$\text{Profit mark up} = \frac{\text{Profit}}{\underset{\text{(i.e., V. cost)}}{\text{Price} - \text{Profit}}} \times 100 \quad \text{(to turn the fraction into a percentage)}$$

- The process can be easily reversed to derive a percentage margin from a percentage mark up:

$$\text{Profit margin} = \frac{\text{Profit}}{\underset{\text{(i.e., Price)}}{\text{V. cost} + \text{Profit}}} \times 100 \quad \text{(to turn the fraction into a percentage)}$$

For example, if you intend to make an average margin on confectionery of 20 per cent you would have to mark your stocks on average by:

$$\text{Profit mark up} = \frac{20 \text{ (profit)}}{100 \text{ (price)} - 20 \text{ (profit)}} \times 100$$

$$= \frac{20 \text{ (profit)}}{80 \text{ (cost)}} \times 100$$

$$= 25\%$$

To help you check your calculations refer to the conversion chart in Fig. 5.8.

The last step before deciding on a final price for the merchandise is to assess whether such a mark up will give a competitive price. If not, you will have to review your margin for this item. If forced into competitive pricing you may still find you are able to maintain the overall margin on the merchandise range by greater mark ups on other items in the same range.

Margin	Markup	Margin	Markup	Margin	Markup	Margin	Markup
1.00%	1.01%	26.00%	35.14%	51.00%	104.08%	76.00%	316.67%
2.00%	2.04%	27.00%	36.99%	52.00%	108.33%	77.00%	334.78%
3.00%	3.09%	28.00%	38.89%	53.00%	112.77%	78.00%	354.55%
4.00%	4.17%	29.00%	40.85%	54.00%	117.39%	79.00%	376.19%
5.00%	5.26%	30.00%	42.86%	55.00%	122.22%	80.00%	400.00%
6.00%	6.38%	31.00%	44.93%	56.00%	127.27%	81.00%	426.32%
7.00%	7.53%	32.00%	47.06%	57.00%	132.56%	82.00%	455.56%
8.00%	8.70%	33.00%	49.25%	58.00%	138.10%	83.00%	488.24%
9.00%	9.89%	34.00%	51.52%	59.00%	143.90%	84.00%	525.00%
10.00%	11.11%	35.00%	53.85%	60.00%	150.00%	85.00%	566.67%
11.00%	12.36%	36.00%	56.25%	61.00%	156.41%	86.00%	614.29%
12.00%	13.64%	37.00%	58.73%	62.00%	163.16%	87.00%	669.23%
13.00%	14.94%	38.00%	61.29%	63.00%	170.27%	88.00%	733.33%
14.00%	16.28%	39.00%	63.93%	64.00%	177.78%	89.00%	809.09%
15.00%	17.65%	40.00%	66.67%	65.00%	185.71%	90.00%	900.00%
16.00%	19.05%	41.00%	69.49%	66.00%	194.12%	91.00%	1011.11%
17.00%	20.48%	42.00%	72.41%	67.00%	203.03%	92.00%	1150.00%
18.00%	21.95%	43.00%	75.44%	68.00%	212.50%	93.00%	1328.57%
19.00%	23.46%	44.00%	78.57%	69.00%	222.58%	94.00%	1566.67%
20.00%	25.00%	45.00%	81.82%	70.00%	233.33%	95.00%	1900.00%
21.00%	26.58%	46.00%	85.19%	71.00%	244.83%	96.00%	2400.00%
22.00%	28.21%	47.00%	88.68%	72.00%	257.14%	97.00%	3233.33%
23.00%	29.87%	48.00%	92.31%	73.00%	270.37%	98.00%	4900.00%
24.00%	31.58%	49.00%	96.08%	74.00%	284.62%	99.00%	9900.00%
25.00%	33.33%	50.00%	100.00%	75.00%	300.00%	100.00%	

Fig. 5.8 Conversion chart

The overall profit margin for a shop is dependent on the mix of sales and margins on the various ranges sold; the same is true for the merchandise ranges themselves. This can be seen by doing the same shopping at different supermarkets. The likelihood is that the total bill will be very similar in them all, but when the prices of individual items are studied, you will often find that there is quite a variation between stores.

The projected profit and loss account

Having detailed and classified all of your costs, decided on a selling price(s) and arrived at a break even profit point to give you the necessary sales volume to achieve your net profit objective, you are ready to compile a summary of the expected profit position of your business at the end of its first year's trading. This summary is known as a profit and loss account. In its simplest form it shows the expected sales revenue and details of total costs which have been incurred within the trading year. The costs are subtracted from the sales revenue to give the gross and net profits. It is laid out as shown in the example given in Fig.5.9.

The sales revenue is taken directly from the BEPP. If your BEPP is physical units of production then obviously sales volume will have to be multiplied by selling price to obtain sales revenue.

The cost of stock sold is the variable cost in this case. If variable costs have been plotted on a break even chart the figure is simply read off the chart. If a percentage margin as been used to arrive at BEPP, then the percentage of sales revenue that is variable cost will be 100 (sales revenue or selling price) minus the profit margin. For example, if the profit margin is 25 per cent then the cost of goods must be 75 per cent of the sales revenue.

The fixed costs are simply entered from your estimates.

● Important note on VAT and profit and loss projections. VAT should not be included in any of your profit and loss projections. That is, all costings and sales receipts should be estimated *exclusive* of VAT. The reason for this, as we shall see later, is that VAT has no effect on profits.

	£	£
Sales:		100,000
Stock costs (net of closing stock):	75,000	
Gross Profit:		25,000
Overheads		
Rent:	4,000	
Utilities:	2,000	
Advertising:	3,000	
Professional fees:	1,500	
General expenses:	1,500	
		12,000
Net profit before tax:		13,000

Fig. 5.9   Projecting and compiling a profit and loss account

Summary

Detailing and classifying the costs of your business and examining the way in which they interact with sales volume and selling price is the key to establishing the profit or loss your business may make. It is a major part of the planning process for any new retail venture (including buying an existing shop) and should be carried out with as much accuracy as possible. Once completed it should be referred to constantly as the business grows; comparison of projected and actual costs should be monitored closely and acted on as necessary.

The results of your costing exercise may require you to carry out further market research or even to revise the nature of your business venture. Do not become disheartened by this for the costing will have served its purpose in preventing you from making costly if not ruinous mistakes!

If the conclusion of your work with this chapter is that your shop will make a profit, do not automatically assume the business is viable, for you might not be able to finance its overall capital requirements.

5

Checklist

1. Do you know the difference between cost and capital?
2. Have you made a full assessment of all of your fixed costs including:
   - depreciation
   - interest charges
   - administration
   - selling (including advertising budget)
   - maintenance and repairs
   - utilities: telephone, electricity, gas and water
   - transport
   - miscellaneous budget
   - full cost of permanent staff
   - professional fees (accountant/solicitor)?
3. Can any of your fixed costs be reduced by:
   - delaying purchases
   - buying second-hand?

4. Are all of your fixed costs necessary?
5. Have you compared the cost of leasing fixed assets to outright purchase?
6. Have you made a full assessment of your variable costs?
7. Have you fully researched suppliers of stock, equipment and services?
8. Have you chosen your suppliers of stock, equipment and services on some objective basis as:
    - delivery times
    - price
    - discount terms on bulk purchases
    - delivery cost
    - payment terms
    - quality and reliability?
9. Have you estimated your target profit?
10. Does it allow for a satisfactory rate of return on the capital employed in your business?
11. Does it allow for retaining profits in the business to finance future trading?
12. What is your break even sales figure – best and worst estimate?
13. What is your break even profit sales figure – best and worst estimate?
14. Does your market research information confirm that your break even figures are achievable?
15. What margin of safety have you allowed?
16. Are your costings too optimistic?
17. Do you know the difference between a percentage margin and a percentage mark up?
18. Have you compiled a projected profit and loss account to show the expected position at the end of your first year's trading?

6 How much money will I need?

Investment in equipment and premises: your fixed assets □ Investment in stock and the concept of working capital □ How much cash will your shop need? □ A cashflow example □ Summary □ Checklist

One of the most common mistakes made by potential new businesses is getting the total money/capital requirements for efficiently starting up and operating their new venture wrong – you can't afford to make such a mistake.

The actual amount you need will of course vary with the scale and nature of your business but all businesses will have to find capital for two specific purposes:

- The acquisition of items which the business expects to keep for a long period of time (i.e. for periods greater than a year) such as premises and equipment. These are known as *fixed assets* and, accordingly, the capital necessary to acquire them is known as *fixed capital.*
- The provision of sufficient monies to operate the shop on a day-to-day basis. This is known as *working capital* and is needed to cover payments for such items as stock, materials and wages which have to be paid for on a regular basis throughout the trading year. This capital is constantly 'working' to keep the business alive.

Together the capital requirements in each of these areas will represent the total amount of money you will need to invest in the business at any one time. The best way forward is to examine each broad area of capital requirements in turn.

Investment in equipment and premises: your fixed assets

Nearly all businesses will require a certain amount of fixed capital. For most, the acquisition of premises will represent the largest fixed capital investment they will make. An example of a possible fixed asset requirement schedule for a small retail business is given in Fig. 6.1 (not to be taken as the norm for this type of shop).

	Investment £s
Premises (leasehold, 2,000 sq. ft.)	18,000
Shop frontage, sign and decor	2,500
Display stands and shelving	3,000
Freezer display units	1,750
Chiller display units	1,750
Cold storage	1,000
Pricing guns (2)	120
Trolleys and baskets	300
Miscellaneous equipment	200
Electronic till	700
Microcomputer (accounts/stock control)	1,200
Small delivery van	7,500
	38,020

Fig. 6.1 Fixed asset schedule for a small food store

A number of factors will influence your decisions as to what items you should acquire and on what scale. These can be roughly listed under the following headings:

- The market for your business – you will have to acquire assets that are consistent in their attributes with the needs of your customers.
- The type of shop and range of merchandise sold – obviously, specialist food retailers will require different equipment from say a fashion shop.
- The goals/objectives of your business – your 'shopping list' for fixed assets must be consistent with what you intend your business to achieve in terms of its markets, profitability and organization. It is certainly a good idea to list your business's objectives along with their separate resource/asset requirements. For example, the objective of reducing shop lifting to one per cent of sales, would require an effective surveillance and security system possibly implying the necessity of such assets as closed circuit TV surveillance and security mirrors.
- The scale of finance at your disposal – most small shops have limited finance available with which to purchase assets. In effect there will be competition between various investment proposals for this limited finance. In deciding whether or not to acquire any fixed asset you should ask yourself the following questions:
  - What will it do for my business?
  - Is it really needed?
  - Will the acquisition of the asset prevent the business from acquiring other assets? If so, what effect would that have on the business?

- Is there an alternative item available that will achieve similar ends? If so, which will represent the most cost-effective purchase?

Carefully consider the effect these factors will have on your requirements and compile your fixed asset list.

Investment in stock and the concept of working capital

The circulation of working capital

We have seen that fixed capital will stay 'locked up' in fixed assets for a long time. Working capital is more 'liquid' in that it changes its form more rapidly. To illustrate this, look at the way working capital circulates in a small retail business, 'Kerrys', shown in Fig. 6.2. Money goes out to buy stock, services and labour needed to provide the overall service and sell the merchandise, and eventually money comes back as customers pay cash. Following the cycle through: working capital changes from money into stocks of merchandise, then into thirty-day loans made to customers who have bought merchandise under such payment terms and, finally, back into cash as the customers settle their accounts. In our example, on any given day there will be money in the bank (or they should be if the business is to remain solvent!) to meet payments for supplies, wages and other expenses, stocks of unsold merchandise, some services such as the rent payed for in advance, cash coming in from sales and money owing to the business from customers who have not yet settled their accounts. All these items represent things that the business possesses – they are its current assets, being differentiated from its fixed assets in that they will be turned back into cash (hopefully!) in the near future.

With each turn of the cycle profit is produced.

Gross working capital and current assets

For an existing business, if you add up the total value of its current assets on any one day you will have calculated its total gross working capital. To illustrate, the calculation of Kerrys' gross working capital on 3 August 1989 is shown in Fig. 6.3. However, what is very important to note is that the total gross working capital requirements for 3 August 1989 are just that, and that more working capital may be required a day, a week or a month later. For instance, if Kerrys plan to increase sales, then it is obvious that more working capital will have to be invested in the full range of its

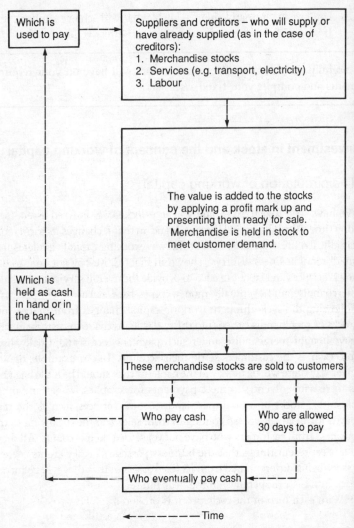

Fig. 6.2 Flow of working capital

current assets to make those sales possible. The additional working capital may come from loans or by increased retention of profits.

Net working capital

In case you were beginning to worry that you will have to fund all the gross working capital requirements of your business, take relief, as that is not the case. Just as businesses have things that they possess, assets, they also have

	£s	
Cash in hand –	1,500	(ready to pay suppliers and expenses)
Finished products –	5,500	
Debtors –	700	(total value of customer accounts outstanding on 3.8.89)
Gross working capital:	7,700	

Fig. 6.3   Total gross working capital of Kerrys on 3.8.89

things that they owe, liabilities. Short term liabilities such as trade credit and overdrafts, known as *current liabilities*, reduce the working capital that has to be found from the internal resources of the business (or, if you prefer the term, 'from your own pocket'). The difference between current assets and current liabilities is the amount your business will have to contribute to gross working capital – it is known as net working capital.

Obtaining interest-free trade credit (usually 30 days) is the best method of reducing net working capital requirements. For example, imagine a business with no current asset requirements other than stock, that can obtain 30-day credit from its supplier and sell all that stock within 28 days of receipt. It would have net working capital requirements of nil! In effect the supplier of the goods would be funding all the gross working capital requirements for free!

Calculating your working capital requirements

The working capital your business will require at any one time is dependent on:

- The length of time it will take for the working capital to complete the cycle from cash to stocks and back into cash again; and
- The level of sales it has to support.

The longer it takes to complete the cycle and the higher your level of sales, the more gross working capital you will need to run the business.

The largest current asset you will have to finance is stock. For retail businesses that offer monthly settlement terms to some customer groups, the other significant current asset will be debtors. Let's examine these two components in some detail, including how to establish/calculate their individual working capital requirements. The other major current asset all businesses require is cash – this warrants lengthy discussion and will be dealt with separately.

Stock investment

The two main factors which will affect the size of your stocks are as follows:

- The usage rate of the stock – the daily, weekly or monthly rate at which merchandise is sold.
- The lead time between placing an order and receiving the goods or the time lapse between deliveries.

The weekly time lapse between deliveries multiplied by the weekly usage rate, plus a margin of safety, will determine the necessary maximum stock level to maintain the business. The shorter the time lapse between deliveries, the lower the maximum working capital that is required for stock. The example in Fig. 6.4 clearly shows this relationship.

	ABC Ltd	XYZ Ltd
Weekly sales @ cost: (i.e., usage rate of stock)	£2,000	£2,000
Lead time in weeks	4 ×	2 ×
Value of reorder to maintain stocks:	£8,000	£4,000
	+	+
Minimum safety stocks held:	£1,000	£1,000
Maximum stock level:	£9,000	£5,000

Fig. 6.4   The effect of different lead times on stock level

When stocks are at a maximum just after delivery, XYZ enjoys the benefit of operating with £4,000 less working capital than ABC due to the simple fact that they have secured more frequent supplies. Effectively this means that XYZ have a faster cycle of working capital. ABC have to wait four weeks to realize the full return on the capital they have invested, whereas XYZ only have to wait two weeks.

It is impossible to make any general rules about the minimum stock levels you must hold; each retail operation will have its own peculiarities. Suffice it to say when compiling an estimate you should carefully assess customer demand. For instance, what breadth and depth of stocks will they demand you to have on hand or display? The greater your stock range, the greater your minimum stock level will have to be (see Chapter 13 for a discussion of stock plans).

An alternative or complementary way to estimate your average stock equirements is to refer to the average rate of stock-turn for your type and ize of business in *The Retail Business Monitor*. (Information is given in Chapter 1 on stock holding levels for most types of shop.) The rate of tock-turn figure is the number of times the average holding of stock has peen sold in a given period of time (usually one year). It is obtained by the imple formula shown in Fig. 6.5.

$$\text{Rate of stock turn} = \frac{\text{Value of the volume of sales for the period}}{\text{Value of average stock level}}$$

Note: both sales and stock should be at the same valuation. For example, if he stock level is valued at cost price so must the sales volume.)

Fig. 6.5 Calculation of rate of stock-turn

The rate of stock-turn is in effect a measure of how long stocks are held nd, consequently, the speed of the circulation of working capital in the pusiness – the more frequently stock is turned over (bought and sold), the ess working capital is required to finance stocks. An RST of 52 per annum means that one week's stock is on hand, an RST of 12 per annum means hat one month's stock is held, and so on.

If you know what rate of stock-turn you can reasonably expect for your ype and size of shop (from Chapter 1, published statistics, or first hand esearch) and your estimated sales for your first year's trading (see Chapters 3 and 4), then it is a relatively easy matter to calculate/estimate he amount of working capital you will have tied up in stocks and for how ong. For instance, if you were planning to open a newsagents with an stimated RST of 5.6 and projected sales of £120,000 per annum, then you ould reasonably expect that:

- On average you will have to hold 65 days' worth of stock, because there are 365 days in a year and the stock is expected to be turned over 5.6 times in that period – 365/5.6 = 65.
- The retail value of that stock will be £21,370 – (65/365) × £120,000 = £21,370 (on average).
- If the margin of profit on that stock is 36 per cent, then the valuation of it at cost will be £13,677, because 100% = retail value, 36% = profit, cost = 100% – 36%, therefore 64% of £21,370 (64/100 × 21,370) = £13,677.

The method to estimate how much working capital (on average) you will have tied up in stock is simplified in Fig. 6.6.

The method to calculate a day's stock held is simplified in Fig. 6.7.

$$\text{Average stock level} = \frac{\text{Value of the volume of sales for period}}{\text{Rate of stock-turn}}$$

Note: If you use a sales estimate valued at selling price then the value of average stock level value you obtain will also be at selling price. Thus, to revalue the stock at cost price (i.e., what you will pay for it), you have to reduce its value by your expected gross profit percentage margin. (For a full discussion of gross profit and the calculation of percentage margins see Chapter 5.)

Fig. 6.6 Calculation of average stock requirements for a given level of sales using annual rate of stock-turn

If you expect to secure trade credit it is useful to compare the number of days credit given (on average) by your suppliers with the number of days stock is held (on average), to estimate your average net working capital requirements for stock. If the newsagents in the previous example could secure 30-day trade credit then it would effectively reduce the amount of time average stocks are held from 65 days to 35 days. The business would only have to finance 35 days worth of stock instead of 65. Hence, the net working capital required to finance its average stock-holding would decrease from £13,677 to £7,365, i.e., (35/65) × £13,677:

Assets:
    Stock: £13,677

Liabilities:
    Creditor: £ 6,312

Net Working Capital: £ 7,365

To gain further information on average stock holdings obtain copies of final accounts of businesses for sale, similar to the type you intend to se

$$\text{Days stock held} = \frac{\text{Value average stock level}}{\text{Value of volume of sales per annum}} \times 365 \text{ (days in period)}$$

Note: Both sales and stock should be at the same valuation, either cost or selling price. If you want to compare day's stock held to day's credit given by your supplier you should value both sales and stock at cost.

Fig. 6.7 Calculation of day's stock held

up. The accounts should contain the necessary information, sales and stock figures, for you to use the formula given in Fig. 6.5 to calculate the business's rate of stock-turn (To find out how to 'read' and interpret final accounts refer to Chapters 9 and 12.) Calculate the RST for a number of businesses, take an average and apply it to your venture.

Debtors

Selling on credit lengthens the working capital cycle and thereby increases the amount of working capital required to operate the business. For instance, if a shop with sales of £90,000 per annum were to extend thirty days settlement terms to all its customers, it would increase its gross working capital requirements (on average) by £7,397 (30/365 days × £90,000). However, allowing for slow payers, the actual length of credit taken would probably be 45 days, an increase of £11,096 (45/365 days × £90,000)!

If you plan to sell on credit, work out the greatest and least demands credit sales will make on working capital. As a general guide to working out the length of credit your customers will take, increase the days' credit allowed to your customers by at least a half to account for slow payers. If you are going to sell to other businesses (for instance, a butchers may supply local hotels) find out how fast they usually settle their accounts; you will probably discover that many companies (in particular the larger ones) will think nothing of taking up to three months to pay! Failure now to investigate the days' credit your potential customers may take will probably spell disaster for you in the future. (For a fuller discussion of credit control, see Chapter 12.)

How much cash will your shop need?

Cash, profit and capital

It is not uncommon for newcomers to retailing to mistake cash for profit. Cash and profit are two distinct items. Cash can come from a variety of sources: loans, overdrafts, retained profits, etc. Profits come from the difference between a business's revenue and its costs.

If a shop is under-capitalized (i.e. not enough finance has been placed in the business to finance fixed assets and working capital), then part or all of the profits will have to be retained in the business to make up the shortfall. Profits will then be tied up financing such items as equipment, stocks, bills that have to be paid in advance, debtors to the business, etc. It can be easily seen that profit is not necessarily in the form of a growing bank balance. Consequently a shop can be making a healthy profit, but be overdrawn at the bank. This position is fine if it is controlled, planned for and temporary – it is when it becomes unncontrolled, unplanned and permanent that disaster strikes. Cash is the life blood of a business and without it new materials, wages, stock, etc. cannot be purchased.

Cash flows

You should now be fully familiar with the idea that working capital circulates in the business, changing its form as it circulates (e.g. cash → stock → debtors → cash). Cash, as part of the cycle, flows into and out of the business. For a shop to continue trading, there must be more cash coming in (from whatever source) than going out, otherwise the business will be unable to meet its liabilities (debts) – it will become insolvent. If the owner of such a business continues to trade knowing that such a situation exists, then he or she will be liable for prosecution for fraudulent trading. At the very least, creditors will make claims in law against such a business which could lead to bankruptcy.

To minimize the risk of insolvency, you should forecast your cash needs. Before you start your business you must prepare what is known as a cash flow forecast for your first year's trading. This is a month-by-month or week-by-week forecast of how much cash will be coming in and how much will be going out. To some extent you probably already do this with your own personal finances but in a less formal way:

> 'If Bob pays me back that money he owes me on time and I get that tax rebate, I should be able to cover the electricity bill at the end of the month ... but how am I going to find enough cash for the holidays the following month ... I wonder if I will get that pay rise?'

To draw up a cash flow forecast you will need to know:

- How much cash is coming in, when and from where.
- How much cash is going out, when and where to.

Forecasting personal and family cash needs

But before you attempt to do this for your business idea, compile a cash flow forecast for your own personal or family finances – this will help you understand the process involved. First, prepare a list of cash in and cash out, as in the example in Fig. 6.8 and then use this information to compile a cash flow forecast, as in Fig. 6.9.

Cash in:

Item	When received	Comments
David's wages	monthly	£600 net, increases to £650 in September
Sue's wages	weekly	part-time shop worker/gains extra hours in the summer and Christmas periods

Cash out:

Item	When paid	Comments
Mortgage	monthly	£175 per month
Life assurance	monthly	£40 per month
Loan	monthly	£38 per month
Gas	quarterly	use previous year's bills and allow for price increases and extra appliances
Electricity	quarterly	as above
Telephone	quarterly	previous bills show little change over the year
Water rates	½ yr	£53 in October & £63 in April
House insurance	quarterly	£28 per quarter
TV licence	per annum	£55
Car tax	½ yr	£55
Car insurance	per annum	£100
Petrol	–	£48 per month
Clothes	–	New clothes for holidays and school clothes for children in Sept.
Food	–	£180 per month
Miscellaneous	–	£100 per month – general expenses
Holiday	–	£280
Christmas	–	£300 presents etc.

Fig. 6.8 Cash in/cash out, family example

The top of the cash flow forecast shows the cash coming in, in our example David's and Sue's wages; the middle section shows the cash going out each month; and the bottom half shows the all important monthly cash balances. The first balance shows the surplus (or deficit in brackets) for each month (total cash in minus total cash out); the second is the opening balance for the month (the closing balance from the previous month

	July	Aug	Sept	Oct	Nov	Dec
Cash in:						
Wages 1	600	600	650	650	650	650
Wages 2	200	200	100	100	100	320
	800	800	750	750	750	970
Cash out:						
Mortgage:	175	175	175	175	175	175
Life ins:	40	40	40	40	40	40
Credit cards:	28	28	28	28	28	28
Rates:	42	42	42	42	42	42
Bank loan:	38	38	38	38	38	38
Gas:			30			50
Electric:			60			90
Telephone:		47			47	
Water rates:				53		
House ins:		28			28	
TV lic:						
Car tax:				55		
Car ins:				100		
Petrol:	48	48	48	48	48	48
Clothes:		100				100
Food:	180	180	180	180	180	180
Miscellaneous:	40	40	40	40	40	40
Misc:		20	20	20	20	20
Holiday:		280				
Christmas:						300
Tot. Exp.:	591	1,066	701	819	686	1,151
Inc. – Exp.:	209	(266)	49	(69)	64	(181)
Opening bal:	0	209	(57)	(8)	(77)	(13)
Closing bal:	209	(57)	(8)	(77)	(13)	(194)

Fig. 6.9 Cash flow forecast

Jan	Feb	Mar	April	May	Jun		Totals:
650	650	650	650	650	650		7,700
80	80	80	80	80	130		1,550
730	730	730	730	730	780		9,250
175	175	175	175	175	175		2,100
40	40	40	40	40	40		480
28	28	28	28	28	28		336
42	42	42	42	42	42		504
38	38	38	38	38	38		456
		50			40		170
		90			60		300
	47			47			188
			63				116
	28			28			112
55							55
			55				110
							100
48	48	48	48	48	48		576
							200
180	180	180	180	180	180		2,160
40	40	40	40	40	40		480
20	20	20	20	20	20		220
							280
							300
660	686	751	729	686	711		9,243
64	44	(21)	1	44	69		7
(194)	(130)	(86)	(107)	(106)	(62)		
(130)	(86)	(107)	(106)	(62)	7		

brought forward); and the third is the closing balance (the cumulative cash position, calculated by adding the monthly cash surplus or deficit to the opening balance for the month).

David's and Sue's cash flow forecast shows that they will need to obtain an overdraft from the bank for the greater part of the year, or attempt to reduce expenditure on some items if possible. The main cause of their shortage of cash is the planned expenditure on a holiday in August. As their total cash flows in only exceed total cash flows out by £6 over the course of the year, it would be perhaps wise for them to forego the holiday this year. Whatever they decide, they now have useful information and a good method at their disposal to look into the future, know when problems are on the way and be able to take action to prevent them.

Forecasting cash needs for a business start up

Compiling a cash flow forecast for a new business is similar to the exercise you have just carried out for your personal or family cash needs. The differences will be in where the cash comes from and where it goes to. There will also be a greater degree of difficulty in estimating the timing and volume of the cash inflows and outflows. Let's look at cash in and cash out in turn and then consider a fully worked example.

Cash in

Cash coming into a business comes from a number of sources: sales, owner's capital and loan capital.

Sales

Ideally any retailer would like to see his or her sales evenly spread out over the year (as in Fig. 6.10 (a)). Clearly this would make the business easier to plan and operate. However, depending on the nature of the market for your shop (see Chapters 3 and 4) your sales pattern will probably look more like that shown in Fig. 6.10(b)).

The first task then is to translate your sales pattern into an estimate of monthly sales. How you do this will depend on the nature of the information gained from your market research and its detail. Some initial guidance can be obtained from published statistics. Certainly, the quarterly pattern of expenditure on broad ranges of merchandise can be obtained from most state-produced consumer expenditure tables. More detailed must be added by your own market research. (A method of 'flexing' your

(a) Ideal sales pattern

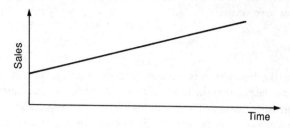

(b) Actual sales pattern

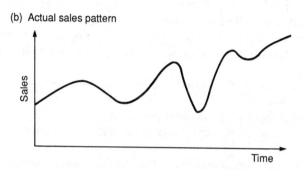

Fig. 6.10 Sales pattern: ideal and actual

year's sales target to take into account seasonal fluctuations in demand is discussed in Chapter 14.)

If all of your sales are on a cash basis then the pattern of your cash inflows from sales will be the same as your sales pattern. However, if your business will sell all or part of its products/services on a credit basis, then the cash from those sales will lag behind the actual sales by the average days' credit taken by your customers. For example, if you are offering one month's settlement terms then the cash from sales made in January will not come in until February, perhaps even later when you account for slow payers (as noted earlier in the chapter).

How accurate your sales projections will be depends on the number and nature of assumptions you will have to make. Obviously, nobody can predict the future with 100 per cent accuracy so, therefore, the golden rule in compiling a cash flow projection is to:

● underestimate cash coming in from sales; and
● overestimate cash going out.

It is better to be pleasantly surprised by having more cash than expected, rather than having to face an unexpected cash crisis six months after you have started.

Capital

To start the business it is obvious that a certain amount of money is required to be put into the business to make a variety of purchases so that sales can be generated. There will be injections of capital. It will either come from your own personal funds or from long- or short-term loans (see Chapter 7). You can obtain an approximation of the amount of capital you will have to find by adding together your estimates of fixed and average working capital requirements for your first year. However, this will not be entirely accurate because it will not take into account or include:

- variations in working capital requirements associated with fluctuating sales over time;
- the timing of your fixed asset purchases;
- the size and timings of your own personal drawings from the business.

You can, of course, calculate your exact working capital requirements for each monthly or weekly period; however, this can prove rather tedious. The compilation of the cashflow will help you to decide the actual size, timing and nature of the capital injections you will have to put into the business. A simple method is to draw up a 'first' cashflow forecast without any capital input, then substitute different scales and timings of capital injections until a satisfactory cumulative cash flow position is reached. As this indicates, the cash flow forecast is an ideal tool for solving 'if, then what' type problems, e.g., 'If I increase the initial capital input by £2,000, what effect will that have on my cumulative cash flow in month four?'

Cash out

Cash outflows will result from expenditure on:

- Fixed costs (overheads), e.g. rent, rates, electricity, etc.
- Variable or direct costs – for most this will be mainly stock.
- Fixed asset purchases, e.g. premises and equipment.
- Personal drawings.
- Loan repayments (net of interest).
- Taxation payments.

Overheads

These are the easiest to predict because, by definition, they are not affected by short-term fluctuations in sales (see Chapter 5). You will have to research in detail the timing of such payments. Here is a rough guide:

- Utilities such as electricity and gas are paid quarterly in arrears. However, it is possible you may have to pay connection charges or a deposit if you are a new customer. If you wish to spread the costs more evenly over time you can have your future bills estimated and arrange for monthly payments to be made direct from your bank account.
- Rent is usually paid in advance. The terms of leases vary but it is not uncommon to pay quarterly or six-monthly in advance.
- Buildings and contents insurance is usually paid for in advance. However, most insurance companies will usually arrange monthly payments.
- Wages/salaries are usually paid a week or a month in arrears. It is obviously better to pay monthly rather than weekly as this shortens the net working capital cycle. PAYE and NI deductions from wages will be paid monthly in arrears. Therefore, net wages (i.e. after deductions) should be shown separately on the cash flow forecast.
- Advertising budget – if you plan to promote your business effectively you will have to compile a sales promotion plan (Chapter 14 tells you how to do it). Such a plan should also contain the size and timing of the costs involved.
- Motor vehicle expenses – road tax and insurance can be readily estimated, petrol with a little more difficulty. The main problem is with unexpected expenditure on such items as repairs, etc. One way to account for the unexpected is to allocate a sum to a contingency fund for such eventualities. Another, is to lease the vehicle (the lease to cover repairs etc.) or to take out a maintenance contract which includes regular servicing and breakdowns – this is equally applicable to other forms of equipment and machinery.
- Professional fees. Expenditure on legal and accountancy services will undoubtedly be erratic. You will perhaps make more use of such services in the initial start up period and at the end of your trading year as your final accounts are drawn up.
- Miscellaneous items. This will include expenditure on numerous minor items such as coffee, stationery, cleaning materials, etc. For cashflow purposes it is better to put the same amount down each month.

6

Variable costs

These, by definition, will vary with sales. Therefore in the first instance, the accuracy of predicted cash outflows related to variable costs will directly depend on the accuracy of monthly sales estimates. The largest single item representing continuous cash outflows is stock purchase. Much has already been said about stocks – detailed consideration must also be given to:

- the size of initial stock
- the frequency at which stocks will be replaced
- the payment terms

1. Initial stocks: Calculating the size of the initial stock level can prove to be a problem. The simplest method is use the annual rate of stock turn to calculate initial stocks (as discussed earlier). For example, if the expected rate of stock-turn is 12 and the projected sales are £120,000, then the initial stocks will be £10,000 at retail prices. However, this method neglects the fact that sales will vary from month to month and will probably be well below the norm in the first few months of trading, resulting in too much stock being carried for the first few months when sales are low. A refinement is to apply the RST per annum as a ratio of stock to sales for the sales pattern over a shorter term, say two or three months. For example, a shop with expected RST of 12 per annum and sales of £18,000 for the first quarter would require initial stocks of £5,940. Neither method is perfect so you may quite legitimately choose a compromise between the two or some alternative method based on detailed knowledge of the stock requirements of your particular business.

2. Frequency of deliveries: The more often a business can obtain deliveries, the fewer days, weeks or months in advance it has to buy stock. A business that only receives deliveries every two months faces the situation of having stock to sell in March bought/delivered in January. In times of rapid expansion this can cause severe cashflow problems as stocks have to be built up rapidly from relatively low cash inflows.

3. Payment terms: If a business has to pay cash on delivery, then purchases in any one month will have to be paid for in that month. However, if a business can secure, for example, one month's credit, then January's purchases will not show on the cashflow forecast until February, February's until March, and so on. Therefore, the impact of poor delivery frequencies on the cash flow can be lessened by securing trade credit.

Calculation of a purchasing budget is fully discussed in Chapter 13.

Capital expenditure

For your major purchases (fixed assets) you must draw up a detailed schedule of amounts and timings of payments. This is simple to do and you, like most people, will probably find that most of this expenditure will occur in the pre-start up period of the business.

Personal drawings

This has nothing to do with profits but is quite simply the amount you will draw from the business to finance your personal needs. The best way to estimate this is to draw up your own personal cash flow forecast as suggested earlier.

Loan repayments

Like most businesses you will have to borrow money and consequently there will be loan repayments. These will include both capital and interest repayments. As far as the profit and loss account is concerned, the interest will be charged as a cost and the capital repayments will come out of profits, but for the cash flow forecast no distinction need be made. Remember the cash flow forecast is only concerned with cash in and out.

Note: You may not know exactly how much you will need to borrow until you have compiled your first cash flow projection. You can make the necessary adjustments later.

Overdraft interest and bank charges

You will not know the size of the overdraft you will require until you have completed your 'first' cash flow. Let the bank do the calculations for you and then make the necessary adjustments to the cash flow forecast.

Taxation

Depending on the nature and scale of your business, you may pay taxes to the Inland Revenue, National Insurance contributions (for your employees and yourself) and Value Added Tax (VAT). Similar taxes to VAT are found in the USA, such as sales and inventory taxes, where they vary from state to state and county to county. American readers are well advised to contact their local tax collector's office in order to get full information on such taxes in their locality and then carefully examine the effect(s) they may have on cash flow.

Fortunately taxes on profits will not have to be paid until after year one. However, self-employed National Insurance contributions will be paid out on a monthly basis. PAYE and NI deductions from employees will also be on a monthly basis, but payable to the Inland Revenue one month in arrears.

VAT payments (see Chapter 10) will be paid quarterly in arrears on the difference between the VAT elements of sales and purchases invoiced in each quarter.

Note: The Customs and Excise offer several schemes to help retailers with VAT. These are considered in Chapter 10.

A cash flow example

Important note: To make the following example realistic VAT, PAYE, and National Insurance contributions have been included. You should be warned that the regulations appertaining to these 'taxes' may have altered since the time of writing. In particular, regulations governing VAT are complex so you should clarify any doubts you have about it and your business with your local VAT office or accountant. For more information on 'taxation' consult Chapter 10. Also, assumptions made about the type and scale of costings, although feasible, should not be interpreted as being the norm for this type and scale of business.

Steve has recently been made redundant from the local steel works and has decided to open a car accessory shop with his £17,000 redundancy money. The shop is to be called Pitstop and will commence trading in August 19 --. He has carefully researched the market for his business and the costs involved and put together the following information on which he has based his cash flow forecast in Fig. 6.12.

Sales

Figure 6.11 shows the breakdown of Pitstop's sales for the first twelve months.

Pitstop will allow one month's credit to local garages – so cash from August's credit sales will be received in September, cash from September's credit sales in October, and so on.

All cash in from sales will be shown inclusive of VAT.

Pitstop's sales pattern

	Cash sales		Credit sales		Total sales	
	ex. VAT	plus VAT	ex. VAT	plus VAT	ex. VAT	plus VAT
August	4,800	5,520	1,400	1,610	6,200	7,130
September	5,000	5,750	1,600	1,840	6,600	7,590
October	5,300	6,095	1,700	1,955	7,000	8,050
November	5,600	6,440	1,900	2,185	7,500	8,625
December	6,800	7,820	2,400	2,760	9,200	10,580
January	5,100	5,865	1,000	1,150	6,100	7,015
February	5,800	6,670	1,500	1,725	7,300	8,395
March	6,200	7,130	1,800	2,070	8,000	9,200
April	6,600	7,590	2,000	2,300	8,600	9,890
May	6,700	7,705	2,100	2,415	8,800	10,120
June	7,000	8,050	2,400	2,760	9,400	10,810
July	7,100	8,165	2,600	2,990	9,700	11,155
	72,000	82,800	22,400	25,760	94,400	108,560

6

Pitstop's purchasing budget

	Total sales ex. VAT	Purchasing budget @ retail ex. VAT	Purchasing budget @ cost ex. VAT	Purchasing budget @ cost VAT inc.
Start up:		12,800	8,960	10,304
August	6,200	7,000	4,900	5,635
September	6,600	7,500	5,250	6,037
October	7,000	9,200	6,440	7,406
November	7,500	6,100	4,270	4,911
December	9,200	7,300	5,110	5,876
January	6,100	8,000	5,600	6,440
February	7,300	8,600	6,020	6,923
March	8,000	8,800	6,160	7,084
April	8,600	9,400	6,580	7,567
May	8,800	9,700	6,790	7,809
June	9,400	10,000	7,000	8,050
July	9,700	10,500	7,350	8,452
	94,400	114,900	80,430	92,494
Year two:				
August	10,000	?	?	?
September	10,500	?	?	?

Figures rounded to nearest pound

Fig. 6.11 Breakdown of Pitstop's sales and purchasing budget

Purchases

The business expects to operate on a 30 per cent profit margin. Therefore, the cost of stock purchases should be 70 per cent of the selling price.

The business is expected to have annual rate of stock turn of six (two months' stock will be held on average). Therefore, an opening stock of £12,800 (at retail prices, excluding VAT), £8,960 at cost, excluding VAT (i.e. reduced by the 30 per cent gross margin, 70/100 × £12,800), will be required to support the first two months of trading, August and September. Stocks will be repurchased to maintain this ratio of stock to future sales, so that the purchasing budget for July will be based on projected sales for September, August for October, and so on. On this basis the purchasing budget over the course of the year is projected as in Fig. 6.11.

Purchases will be paid for cash on delivery. After month six, one month's credit will be given by suppliers of stock. Therefore, there will be no cash outflows on stock purchases in February.

Overheads

Item	Cost per annum	Payment basis/Comments for cash flow
Shop rental	4,000	Quarterly in advance £1,000
Rates	480	Monthly £40
Telephone	240	Quarterly in arrears £69 (inc. VAT)
Power	1,000	Quarterly in arrears (high in winter)
Insurance	900	Annually in advance
Van lease	1,200	Plus £180 VAT. Monthly in advance £115 (inc. VAT)
Petrol	720	Plus £108 VAT. £69 per month (inc. VAT)
Advertising	3,400	Plus £510 VAT.
		August: £690 (inc. VAT) (initial promotion) December: £690 (inc. VAT) (Xmas promotion) April: £460 (inc. VAT) (Spring promotion)

		Other periods: £230 (inc. VAT) per month
Accountant	1,620	Plus £243 VAT
Solicitor		£805 (inc. VAT) start up £575 (inc. VAT) year end £161 (inc. VAT) remaining quarters
General expenses	1,200	Plus £180 VAT Budgeted at £115 (inc. VAT) per month
Wages	4,080	Two permanent part-time shop workers paid weekly. Monthly £280 net of NI & PAYE
	18,840	

Capital expenditure

Purchase of existing business inclusive of lease, fixtures and fittings and goodwill as assets of the business. Exempt from VAT. Total expenditure: £6,000

Additional capital expenditure:

Item	Cost	Timing	Inc. VAT
Electronic till	£1,000	on start up	£1,150
Display equipment	£2,000	on start up	£2,300
Storage equipment	£1,000	on start up	£1,150
Sub-total:	£4,000	on start up	£4,600
Second till:	£1,000	in December	£1,150
Total	£5,000		£5,750

Therefore, total expenditure inclusive of VAT on fixed assets should be £11,750

VAT

Steve has agreed to submit his VAT return every quarter in arrears. The first return will be due at the beginning of November.

The business will pay VAT (@ 15%) on purchases of stock, certain overhead costs (as noted in above) and fixed assets (as noted above) and charge VAT at the same rate on sales. The estimated VAT payable to, or refundable from, HM Customs and Excise at the end of each quarter is calculated by subtracting the VAT payable on purchases of stock, services and fixed assets (Input tax) from the VAT charged on invoiced sales (Output tax). The total sales forecast (Fig. 6.11) is used to calculate the total of output taxes collected or due (in the case of credit sales). The schedule of monthly stock purchases is used to calculate the quarterly input taxes paid or due to be paid (in the case of purchases acquired on credit after February). Note, however, that even though payment for stocks received in February will not be due until March, the delivery will be invoiced in February.

Calculation of VAT figures

Quarter August to October inclusive

Output – tax payable on sales

Total sales excluding VAT: £19,800, therefore
Total VAT payable on sales (i.e. 15/100 × £19,800):   £2,970

Total A: £2,970

Less

Input – tax refundable

Stock purchases:

Total purchases excluding VAT: £25,550, therefore
Total VAT refundable on stock purchases
(i.e. 15/100 × £25,550):   £3,832

Capital expenditure:

Total expenditure on VAT rated fixed assets: £4,600
Total VAT refundable therefore (15/115 × £4,600):   £600

Overhead expenditure:

Total expenditure (invoiced) on VAT-rated overheads:
          Van lease: 345

Petrol:	207
Advertising:	1,150
Professional fees:	966
Telephone:	69*
General:	345
Total:	3,082

VAT element refundable (15/115 × £3,082):   £402

Total B: £4,834

* Note: Even though the telephone bill will not be payed until November it is included in the VAT calculations for the first quarter because the date of the invoice (the tax point) will fall in October.

Net VAT payable (A–B) = (£1,864). You can see that for the first quarter the Customs and Excise will actually owe Steve quite a sum of money! This is because Pitstop will have paid more VAT than it will have collected (due to the major purchases of fixed assets and opening stock). Steve will receive the money in November.

6

Quarter November to January inclusive

Output tax

Total sales excluding VAT: £22,800
Total VAT payable on sales (i.e. 15/100 × £22,800):   £3,420

Total A: £3,420

Input tax

Stock:

Total purchases excluding VAT: £14,980
Total VAT refundable on purchases (i.e. 15/100 × £14,980):   £2,247

Capital expenditure:

Total expenditure on fixed assets excluding VAT: £1,000
Total VAT refundable: (15/100 × £1,000):   £150

Overhead expenditure:

Total expenditure (invoiced) on VAT rated overheads:

Van lease:	345
Petrol:	207
Advertising:	1,150
Professional fees:	161
Telephone:	69
General:	345
Total:	2,277

VAT element refundable (15/115 × £2,277):   £297

Total: £2,694

Net VAT payable (A–B) = £726

Quarter February to April inclusive

Output tax

Total sales excluding VAT: £23,900
Total VAT payable on sales: Total A: £3,585

Input tax

Stock:

Total purchases excluding VAT: £18,760
Total VAT refundable on purchases: £2,814

Overhead expenditure:

Total expenditure (invoiced) on VAT rated overheads:

Van lease:	345
Petrol:	207
Advertising:	920
Professional fees:	161
Telephone:	69
General:	345
Total:	2,047

VAT element refundable (15/115 × £2,047):   £267

Total B: £3,081

Net VAT payable (A–B) = £504

Quarter May to July inclusive

Output tax

Total sales excluding VAT: £27,900
Total VAT payable on sales: Total A: £4,185

Input tax

Stock:

Total purchases excluding VAT: £21,140
Total VAT refundable on purchases: £3,171

Overhead expenditure:

Total expenditure (invoiced) on VAT rated overheads:
Van lease:	345
Petrol:	207
Advertising:	690
Professional fees:	575
Telephone:	69
General:	345
Total:	2,231

VAT element refundable (15/115 × £2,231):   £291

Total B: £3,462

Net VAT payable (A−B) − £723
(payable in August of second trading year)

Totals for the year

Total output taxes: £14,160
Total input taxes: £14,071

Net VAT payable: £89

Projected profit and loss account

(Net of depreciation and finance charges)

Sales:		94,400
Purchases:	80,430	
Less Planned closing stock:	14,350	
Cost of sales:		66,080
Gross profit (i.e. profits before overhead costs)		28,320
Less Overheads:		18,840
Net profit before taxes:		9,480

Personal drawings

Steve has decided to draw £500 from the business each month to cover his personal needs

Payment of National Insurance and PAYE

Steve will not pay any taxes on the profits of the business until after year one. However, he will have to pay:
* To the Inland Revenue's tax office monthly (in arrears) the National Insurance contributions and tax deducted from the 'wage packets' of his two part-time shop workers plus employers' NI contributions. Steve has estimated these at £60 per month.
* His own Class 2 National Insurance contributions, costing approximately £18 per calendar month.

Pitstop's cash flow forecast

An examination of Pitstop's completed cash flow forecast reveals:
1. For the first seven months, Pitstop will not have enough cash to meet its needs. This is because the initial capital injection of £17,000 is not sufficient to cover both capital expenditure and working capital requirements.
2. The cash deficit is severe for the first three months – an overdraft facility of some £10,000 will be required, until the VAT refund on fixed assets and stock purchases is received in November.
3. From November, monthly cash surpluses steadily reduce the cash deficit until a positive cash flow position is reached in April. A minor cumulative cash deficit of £724 is the result of the grouping of quarterly bills and is overcome in the following month.

4. Predictably, the one month's delay in paying for stock purchases from February gives a boost to Pitstop's cumulative cash flow position (by reducing net working capital requirements) from that date onwards. In fact, it can be easily seen that if Pitstop fails to secure one month's credit by February, or March at the latest, a positive cumulative cash flow position would not be reached by the end of the year. So if Steve could not introduce more capital from other sources, modify expenditure or reduce credit sales and increase cash sales the business would prove an unviable proposition even though it would be making healthy profits.

Where are Pitstop's profits? – the balance sheet

The relationship between Pitstop's expected net profit of £9,480 and its cash in hand at the end of the year of £1,378 might not be readily obvious. You are probably curious about the whereabouts of two items: the original £17,000 capital and the £9,480 net profit. The answer is simply that some of the profits will have been drawn out of the business by Steve and some will have been retained and used, along with all of the original capital, to fund the purchase of fixed assets and net working capital requirements. Let's look at the picture in more detail.

Over the course of the year Steve will have drawn £6,216 out of the business to cover his own personal living expenses and National Insurance contributions, leaving £3,264 profit left in the business. Adding the retained profits to the original capital invested tells us the total amount of capital that will be invested in Pitstop at the end of the year – £20,264. As only £1,378 is left as cash, the rest must be in the assets of the business.

Let's list them to find out if this is true.

First the major assets of the business:

Lease of premises:	£6,000
Fixtures and fittings:	£5,000
	£11,000

Next its current assets:

Cash on hand (from the cash flow):	£1,378
Stock: two weeks' stock on hand to finance August and September sales in year 2. Total from the purchasing budget:	£14,350
Debtors: cash from July's credit sales not received yet:	£2,990
Makes a total of:	£18,718

	Aug	Sept	Oct	Nov	Dec	Jan
Cash in:						
Capital:	17,000					
VAT refunds:				1,864		
Cash Sales:	5,520	5,750	6,095	6,440	7,820	5,865
Credit Sales:		1,610	1,840	1,955	2,185	2,760
	22,520	7,360	7,935	10,259	10,005	8,625
Cash out:						
Opening stock:	10,304					
Stock:	5,635	6,037	7,406	4,911	5,876	6,440
Rent:	1,000			1,000		
Rates:	40	40	40	40	40	40
Telephone:				69		
Gas & Electric:				200		
Insurance:	900					
Van lease:	115	115	115	115	115	115
Petrol:	69	69	69	69	69	69
Advertising:	690	230	230	230	690	230
Acc/solicitor:	805		161			161
General:	115	115	115	115	115	115
Wages:	280	280	280	280	280	280
NI/PAYE:		60	60	60	60	60
Class 2/NI:	18	18	18	18	18	18
Capital exp.:	10,600				1,150	
Overdraft chg:						
VAT payments:						
Personal:	500	500	500	500	500	500
Total cash out:	31,071	7,464	8,994	7,607	8,913	8,028
Monthly Balance:	(8,551)	(104)	(1,059)	2,652	1,092	597
Opening Balance:		(8,551)	(8,655)	(9,714)	(7,062)	(5,970)
Closing Balance: (Net Cash Flow)	(8,551)	(8,655)	(9,714)	(7,062)	(5,970)	(5,373)

Fig. 6.12 Pitstop's cash flow forecast

Feb	Mar	April	May	June	July	Totals:
						17,000
						1,864
6,670	7,130	7,590	7,705	8,050	8,165	82,800
1,150	1,725	2,070	2,300	2,415	2,760	22,770
7,820	8,855	9,660	10,005	10,465	10,925	124,434
						10,304
	6,923	7,084	7,567	7,809	8,050	73,738
1,000			1,000			4,000
40	40	40	40	40	40	480
69			69			207
350			300			850
						900
115	115	115	115	115	115	1,380
69	69	69	69	69	69	828
230	230	460	230	230	230	3,910
		161			575	1,863
115	115	115	115	115	115	1,380
280	280	280	280	280	280	3,360
60	60	60	60	60	60	660
18	18	18	18	18	18	216
						11,750
						0
726			504			1,230
500	500	500	500	500	500	6,000
3,572	8,350	8,902	10,867	9,236	10,052	123,056
4,248	505	758	(862)	1,229	873	1,378
(5,373)	(1,125)	(620)	138	(724)	505	
(1,125)	(620)	138	(724)	505	1,378	

6

However, Pitstop has not had to find all of this money. It has financed some of these current assets from outside sources. It owes money to a number of creditors. We must list and subtract all of these short-term liabilities from its current assets to find out how much Pitstop has had to use to fund its own working capital.

Current liabilities:

The last delivery of stock has been invoiced but no
payment has been made: £8,452

The gas and electric bills should have been
received but payment will be delayed till August: £150

The same with the telephone bill: £69

A total of £60 has been deducted from July's wage
packets but has not yet been paid to the IR: £60

Finally, Pitstop owe the Customs and Excise a
VAT payment for the last quarter of the year: £723

Making total liabilities of: £9,454

Therefore Pitstop's net working capital at the end
of its first year is (Current assets – Current liabilities):   £9,264

If we now add the Fixed assets to the net current assets
will find the total amount of funds that are tied up in the   _____
business at the year end.   Total assets (net) £20,264

Which is, as we predicted, the total net assets have been financed by Steve's original capital and profits retained in the business.

We have just completed a balance sheet of what Steve's business will look like at the end of his first year of trading. If you take away all the detail, it's not that complicated. It is simply a list of where the business has got its money from (liabilities) and what it has done with it (assets) – or, what it owes and what it has. The two lists are separated into long-term assets and liabilities and short-term (current) assets and liabilities. Try balancing the assets and liabilities yourself by completing the blank balance sheet in Fig. 6.13. (For more information on balance sheets and final accounts see Chapter 12.)

Try and answer the following questions about Steve's proposed business (the answers are at the end of the chapter):

Let's look at the worst possible position for Pitstop, given the present sales and costs:

(a) If debtors took two months instead of one month to pay up; and
(b) If Pitstop failed to secure one month's credit from its suppliers of stock.

- How much would this increase net working capital requirements by the end of the first year?
- Would the business be viable? If not, why not?

Note: You can answer the question by simply recalculating Pitstop's net working capital for the year end, but for a fuller picture recalculate the cash flow forecast and draw up a new balance sheet. For owners of desk top computers with some familiarity with spreadsheet programmes, a spreadsheet file enabling calculation of cash flow forecasts is contained in Appendix 6.

6

Summary

You will need to calculate very carefully how much money you need to start and operate the business. The key to the successful management of your resources is in careful scrutiny and planning of your working capital requirements and cycle. A cash flow forecast is essential to any business. Never ever forget that cash is the life blood of any business. Once forecasts have been made and budgets set, actual performance of the business should be closely monitored (see Chapter 12) and any deviations investigated at once.

If your business idea has passed the tests of these last three chapters, you could have a potentially successful business. However, if it hasn't then don't despair – take it through the cycle again and see if it can be successfully modified. If the situation is worse than that then you can only be pleased that you never ventured any money on the enterprise and all that you have spent is time and effort. Try again!

Fixed assets

Total (A): _____

Current assets

Prepaid bills:

Stock:

Debtors:

Cash in hand:

Total (B): _____

Current liabilities

Trade creditors

Stock:

Electricity:

Gas:

Telephone:

Bank overdraft:

VAT provisions:

Tax provisions:

Total (C): _____

Net current assets or net working capital (B–C): _____

Net assets employed in the business: _____

Financed by

Owner's capital introduced:

Profits retained:

Fig. 6.13 Balance sheet format

Checklist

1. What are your business needs?
2. Have you made a fixed asset requirements list?

3. Do you know the amount of capital each will require?
4. Have you considered the alternatives such as buying second-hand, leasing, renting, etc.?
5. Can you delay the purchase of some fixed assets?
6. Are they all really needed?
7. How much stock will you carry on average?
8. How does this compare to other shops of a similar type?
9. Can you obtain more frequent deliveries?
10. Can you reduce your stock-holding by any other methods?
11. What is the length of working capital cycle?
12. Can it be reduced?
13. How much trade credit can you secure?
14. Can you obtain stock on consignment?
15. How many days' credit will you give?
16. How many will you take?
17. Have you the necessary information on sales revenue, credit sales, costs and other outgoings to compile a cash flow forecast?
18. Have you produced a cash flow forecast?
19. Have you looked at the best and worst cash positions?
20. Have you relooked at your:
    • working capital cycle
    • fixed asset schedule
    • market for increasing cash sales
    • overheads
    • timing of costs
    to improve your cash position over time?
21. How much of your profits will have to be retained in the business at the year end to finance future expansion?

6

Answers to the cash flow forecast and balance sheet problem

If Steve failed to secure trade credit and his debtors took longer than expected to pay up, the cash position of the business over the course of the year would never be in the black. In fact, the average overdraft facility required would be in excess of £9,000! The conclusion that must be drawn is that the business will require a larger injection of capital at start up to be viable. Steve would probably have to acquire a long-term loan to finance 'hard core' working capital.

Pitstop's adjusted projected year end balance sheet appears in Fig. 6.15.

	Aug	Sept	Oct	Nov	Dec	Jan
Cash in:						
Capital:	17,000					
VAT refunds:				1,864		
Cash Sales:	5,520	5,750	6,095	6,440	7,820	5,865
Credit Sales:		1,610	1,840	1,955	2,185	
	22,520	5,750	7,705	10,144	9,775	8,050
Cash out:						
Opening stock:	10,304					
Stock:	5,635	6,037	7,406	4,911	5,876	6,440
Rent:	1,000			1,000		
Rates:	40	40	40	40	40	40
Telephone:				69		
Gas & Electric:				200		
Insurance:	900					
Van lease:	115	115	115	115	115	115
Petrol:	69	69	69	69	69	69
Advertising:	690	230	230	230	690	230
Acc/solicitor:	805		161			161
General:	115	115	115	115	115	115
Wages:	280	280	280	280	280	280
NI/PAYE:		60	60	60	60	60
Class 2/NI:	18	18	18	18	18	18
Capital exp.:	10,600				1,150	
Overdraft chg:						
VAT payments:						
Personal:	500	500	500	500	500	500
Total cash out:	31,071	7,464	8,994	7,607	8,913	8,028
Monthly Bal:	(8,551)	(1,714)	(1,289)	2,537	862	22
Open Bal:		(8,551)	(10,265)	(11,554)	(9,017)	(8,155)
Close Bal:	(8,551)	(10,265)	(11,554)	(9,017)	(8,155)	(8,133)
(Cumulative Bal)						

Fig. 6.14   Adjusted cash flow forecast

Feb	Mar	April	May	June	July	Totals:
						17,000
						1,864
6,670	7,130	7,590	7,705	8,050	8,165	82,800
2,760	1,150	1,725	2,070	2,300	2,415	20,010
9,430	8,280	9,315	9,775	10,350	10,580	121,674
						10,304
6,923	7,084	7,567	7,809	8,050	8,452	82,190
1,000			1,000			4,000
40	40	40	40	40	40	480
69			69			207
350			300			850
						900
115	115	115	115	115	115	1,380
69	69	69	69	69	69	828
230	230	460	230	230	230	3,910
		161			575	1,863
115	115	115	115	115	115	1,380
280	280	280	280	280	280	3,360
60	60	60	60	60	60	660
18	18	18	18	18	18	216
						11,750
						0
726			504			1,230
500	500	500	500	500	500	6,000
10,495	8,511	9,385	11,109	9,477	10,454	131,508
(1,065)	(231)	(70)	(1,334)	873	126	(9,834)
(8,133)	(9,198)	(9,429)	(9,499)	(10,833)	(9,960)	
(9,198)	(9,429)	(9,499)	(10,833)	(9,960)	(9,834)	

6

Fixed assets:

	6,000
	5,000
Total (A):	11,000

Current assets:

Prepaid bills:

Stock:	14,350
Debtors:	5,750
Cash in hand:	
Total (B):	20,100

Current liabilities:

Trade creditors

Stock:	
Electricity:	150
Gas:	
Telephone:	69
Bank overdraft:	9,834
VAT provisions:	723
Tax provisions:	60
Total (C):	10,836

Net current assets or net working capital (B-C) :   9,264

Net assets employed in the business: 20,264

Financed by:

Owner's capital introduced:	17,000
Profits retained:	3,264
	20,264

Fig. 6.15   Pitstop's adjusted projected year end balance sheet

7 Raising the money

How much is needed? □ What will the money be required for?
□ Sources and methods of finance □ Presenting your case □
Summary

How much is needed?

The first step, of course, is to establish the capital required to start and operate the business. Chapter 1 encouraged you to assess what personal finance you could raise and Chapter 6 should have enabled you to calculate how much will be needed and perhaps more importantly when it will be needed.

What will the money be required for?

The next step is to itemize what the finance is required for. This will set you on the right path to identifying the appropriate kind of finance to secure. In the course of establishing your fixed and working capital requirements you will, by implication, have identified the purposes for which they are required. The most appropriate method of finance for a particular purpose is indicated in the list below, while the next section deals in more detail with the methods and sources of finance available.

● **Identifying the 'right kind of finance' – a summary**

Purpose	Method
• **Short-term finance** **Debtors, stock, raw materials, and other general working capital requirements**	**Overdrafts** **Creditors**
• **Long-term finance** **Fixed assets, longer term working capital requirements**	**Loans (medium/long)** **Hire purchase** **Grants** **Mortgages** **Equity/venture capital**

Sources and methods of finance

Short-term finance

The overdraft is perhaps the commonest and simplest form of finance available. You and your bank agree a limit to which you can overdraw on your account. You can then use part or all of that overdraft facility as and when you need it. This makes this form of finance very flexible. In addition, although the interest rate for overdrafts is usually a few percentage points above bank base rate, the fact that you only take out the 'loan' when you need it can make it cheap to operate.

Overdrafts are ideal to cover such requirements as temporary cash flow problems. They should not, however, be used to cover the purchase of fixed assets or cover long-term working capital requirements. The reasons for this are that overdrafts have fluctuating interest rates and can be reduced or even called in by the bank at very short notice. This makes long-term financial planning with this method of finance extremely difficult. Moreover, it exposes the business to the real threat of insolvency. Consider the situation below where a business attempts to finance most of its working capital requirements with an overdraft facility:

Current assets:

Stock:	£3,000
Debtors:	£1,000
	£4,000

Current liabilities:

Overdraft:	£4,000

If the bank called in or reduced the overdraft it might possibly force the business into bankruptcy as the debtors and stock could not be so easily or quickly turned into cash to repay the overdraft on demand.

To stand any chance of securing a business overdraft the very least you must do is to produce a fully justified cash flow forecast as described in Chapter 6.

Creditors

Securing trade credit from suppliers is, as previously discussed in Chapter 6, a good way of reducing your net working capital requirements and therefore your overall borrowing. The obvious advantage of this method is that it is interest-free. However, the problem is that some suppliers are reluctant to grant such terms to new businesses. Possibly you will have to trade on a cash-on-delivery basis until you build up a good track record with your suppliers.

Short-term loans

These are obtainable from banks and finance houses and have limited uses. They are less flexible than an overdraft and can work out considerably more expensive when you don't use the full sum borrowed. However, they are usually easily arranged if the amount required is relatively small.

Medium- and long-term finance

Loans

Obtainable from banks and other financial institutions, loans are ideal for the purchase of fixed assets. Banks offer a variety of commercial loans repayable over from one to ten years. Interest rates can be fixed or variable. You must shop around to see what is on offer. For instance, some packages contain repayment 'holidays' where you do not make your first repayment until some months after the loan has been advanced, giving your cash flow a boost in the early period of trading when it is, perhaps, most needed.

For the larger and longer-term capital loan, the lending organization will require personal guarantees and security. Where the loan is a 'major' advance to be used to finance the main assets of the business, the lending institution will look carefully at the 'gearing of the business'. They will want to know how much you are putting into the business. For small businesses, banks will want to see you put at least as much into the business as they are going to do. Therefore, you will find it difficult to raise a loan in this way if you have less than a 50 per cent stake in your own business.

Note: Many small businesses prefer dealing with a bank, as the business relationship is more personal. If the bank is kept informed of the progress of your business, building mutual trust and respect, it is likely to be more sympathetic than other, more impersonal, lenders when problems occur.

Hire purchase

Buying business equipment on hire purchase is just the same as buying household goods on hire purchase. The main advantage of using this method is that it is relatively easy to arrange and secure. The main disadvantages are that interest rates are usually considerably higher than other forms of finance and any default on the loan may be pursued vigourously by the lender!

Mortgages

This type of finance is familiar to most people. Commercial and semi-commercial (when the mortgage is used to purchase a part-residential and part-commercial property) mortgages are advanced for the purchase of specific premises. The maximum loan advanced is usually up to 60 per cent of the valuation of the premises, but sometimes up to 90 per cent of valuation in the case of semi-commercial mortgages. Interest rates can either be fixed or variable and the period of the loan can be in excess of 20 years.

Equity finance

This is, by definition, the most permanent form of finance. This is where an individual or organization takes a share in your business. The main disadvantage is obvious: you can lose overall control of your business. The advantages are that there are no repayments involved and the launch of a business venture that you could not previously finance becomes possible.

Equity finance for new businesses goes under the name of 'venture' capital. As there are many sources and types of venture capital available you should obtain specialist help.

Grants

I am sure everybody would love to start their shop with 'free money'. There are many types of grants available from nearly as many different institutions and organizations, ranging from charities to local and central government bodies. It would take nearly the rest of this book just to go into the sources and types of funds involved. Partly because of the multitude of grants and schemes and their sometimes changing availability and nature, you are best advised to consult one or a number of the organizations listed in Appendix 7: 'Sources of Further Information'.

The availability of grants and criteria for acceptance of applicants are dependent or based on some or all of the following factors:

1. The area in which you intend to set up your business is an important factor. Most governments are keen to rejuvenate rundown localities such as inner-city areas and under-populated rural areas, particularly those that are suffering from a net migration of population.
2. With a general increase in unemployment in the western world, your business is more likely to be eligible for a grant if it is going to create employment.

3. A number of grants and schemes are aimed at specific groups of the population: the disabled, the 'socially disadvantaged', ethnic minorities, the unemployed, etc.

Reducing your need to borrow

At the beginning of Chapter of 6 you were encouraged to assess the financial needs of your business. Use this section to re-examine these needs – can they be reduced, redrafted or reorganized to reduce the amount you need to borrow?

Premises

Rent rather than buy? This can greatly reduce capital outlay but at the same time it diminishes your capability to borrow further funds as little can be offered to the lender as security for the loan.

Equipment, machinery, fixtures and fittings, etc.

Rent, lease or buy second-hand? The disadvantage here is that operating costs can be higher, but will this be offset by not having to pay charges and interest on loans to acquire the item that would have to be otherwise purchased? What are the benefits derived from releasing capital by this method for other purchases? Another factor to be considered is that rental and service agreements often offer service and maintenance. This helps you budget more easily this aspect of operating costs. If you are only going to use an item occasionally, can you hire it for short periods?

7

Stock

- Is your estimate for average stock level excessive?
- Can you adopt a different trading policy that involves a smaller range of goods to be carried without unduly harming sales potential?
- Can you obtain more frequent deliveries?
- Can you obtain stock on credit?
- Can you negotiate terms with suppliers where you only pay for the stock when you sell it (known as obtaining supplies on consignment)?

Debtors

- Can you increase your cash sales?
- Can you reduce the number of days' credit given to your customers?

Costs

- Have you re-examined all of your costs?
- Can any be reduced?
- Can you link wages to sales?
- Can payment of your overheads be spread over a greater period of time?

Presenting your case

The main reason why applications for business loans fail is that they are poorly researched and even more poorly presented. If you have researched and planned your business idea following the suggestions and techniques put forward in this book, you should not make this mistake. The most important thing to remember is that the lender sees the loan in terms of his/her organization making an investment in your business. They will, of course, want to know if their investment will be a profitable one for them. The key question in the forefront of their minds will be: 'Is there evidence of *ability* to *repay* the loan?' With a person who is employed, this is relatively easy to assess by referring to the applicant's job (i.e. how secure it is), their salary and outgoings. With a business, in particular a new business without a prove 'track record', there is little solid evidence to prove the all important ability to repay. This explains why a bank would rather lend £10,000 to an employed person with a relatively secure job to buy a car than lend the same amount to a person wishing to set up a new business. From the lender's point of view, one is relatively risk-free and the other fraught with risk. The lending organization must therefore be convinced of your business's ability to repay. The only way to do this is to prepare and present a *business plan*. This is a concept you are already familiar with from Chapter 2.

The business plan

The lender is likely to want satisfactory answers to the following, or similar, questions before he grants the loan.

What is the business? Does it sound like a viable concern?

Information required is a brief summary of the business idea:

- Basic information: business name, address, legal identity (e.g. sole trader, partnership, limited company) (See Chapter 11.)
- Management of the business – brief and concise, e.g. key personnel, functions, etc.

Nature of your proposed business. What marks it as different from your competitors? Essentially projecting to the potential lender 'what business you are in'. This can be best summed up by restatement of the 'Unique Selling Proposition' you were encouraged to formulate at the end of Chapter 3.

Are you the right type of person to run this type of business?

Information required is a summary of:

* Personal details.
* Relevant work experience, skills and education.

How much am I being asked to invest and what for?

Information required (see Chapter 6):

* Exact amount of money you want.
* Period you want to borrow it for.
* What exactly you are going to use it for – working capital, premises, fixtures and fittings, etc.

Does the business have a sufficient market for its product or service? Will it be able to reach and exploit it?

Information required (see Chapters 3, 4 and 14):

* Summary of customer groups with particular reference to expected revenue they will generate.
* Positive attributes of the site and location chosen.
* Market share expected.
* Estimates of sales for each month in your first year.
* Estimates of sales for second year.
* How you will reach and sell to your customers.
* All projections and statements backed up with evidence of credible market research.

Will the business make a viable profit?

Information required (see Chapter 5):

* Details of costs and sales including timings.
* Projection of when the business will be earning profits.

- Break even analysis, showing the effect on the business of best and worst expectations.
- Expected return on capital employed.

Is the proposed business properly financed? Does it have sufficient capital?

Information required (see Chapters 6 and 12):

- Projected balance sheet for start of business and end of first year's operation. This will show how the capital invested in the business will be used. It will also show the lender your intended equity in the business, that is, how much of the net assets employed in the business you are going to finance from personal funds. Most banks will expect you to have at least a 50 per cent holding in the business.
- Cash flow projection with explanatory notes. This is essential to show the lender your expected borrowing requirements over time. It demonstrates that the business will be able to remain solvent (i.e. be able 'to pay its way'). The cash flow should include repayments of the loan applied for – obviously essential as key evidence to the lending organization that you will be able to repay the loan.
- Details of the working capital required and how it will be financed.
- Demonstration that you have allowed for unforeseen costs and capital requirements.

In addition, you will have to include details of the security and personal guarantees offered in case the business fails.

The actual way you lay out your loan application (business plan) is up to you to decide as long as you make sure you satisfactorily answer the potential lender's key concerns. Many banks now produce their own guides to how you should lay out your business loan application. They are usually in the form of a checklist of questions – the simple advice is, make sure you answer them!

When compiling your business plan adhere to the following guidelines:

1. **Have it typed double spaced with wide margins (this is to allow the lender to make notes as he or she studies it).**
2. **The application should not be over-long. Try and go for a positive and concise presentation of the facts. Use diagrams and graphs where appropriate.**

3. **Adopt a layout that makes sense and is easy to understand. Lay out the application in sections, number the paragraphs and pages so that you can easily refer the reader to relevant information, graphs, and diagrams.**

The complexity of the application will of course depend on the nature and scale of your business. If you find the task of compiling the report is beyond you it is possible to pay for it to be produced. Obviously, you will still have to do the hard work of producing the information on which it is to be based!

Once completed, the application should sent to or left at the lending organization's offices a week before the interview to allow the lender to study it. At the actual interview, quite naturally you will be nervous, but try and project an air of confidence (however, don't 'go over the top'!). Be positive, don't evade questions, be frank (lender's with experience are not easily fooled) and, above all, don't waffle. Dress smartly but conservatively for the occasion and, very importantly, watch your body posture. Many of us have very irritating habits that we are only partly aware of, such as continually tapping on desks, slumping in chairs, leaning too far forward when talking, or looking anywhere but at a person when we are talking to them. Watch out for your bad habits. Remember, you have to sell *yourself* as well as your *business*.

7

Summary

Every shop at some time in its life will require finance from external sources. You will need to know not only how much you need to borrow, but also when. In choosing a finance package it is important to consider the type of finance in relation to the specific use it will be put to.

The key questions any lender will ask are: 'Is there ability to repay?' 'Is there adequate security?' and 'Does the applicant have sufficient equity in the business?' The business plan is the crucial factor in any loan application.

8 Store image, design, layout and merchandising

Exterior design □ Store interior and layout □ Security and store layout □ Summary □ Checklist

In many ways this chapter starts where our discussion and work on location and site selection left off. Just as the site and location must be attractive to customers, so must be the exterior appeal of the shop, its interior design and the way the merchandise is presented for sale on the fixtures.

Exterior design

Imagine a potential customer, a passer-by, walking down the street – his or her first impressions are important. How can you get the customer's attention and then encourage them to come into the shop? Attention must be given to the components of the exterior of the shop:

- The sign and facia.
- The geometry of the shop front.
- The shop entrance.
- The window/window display.

The sign and facia

To be effective, the shop's sign must distinguish your shop from others, capture the customer's attention and quickly identify the broad type of merchandise sold. The key component of the shop facia is, of course, the name.

A lot of time and consideration should be given to the choice of name for the shop. Firstly, it should be consistent with the image you want to convey. For instance, 'Sue's Fashion Store' would not be consistent with an image of designer labels or high fashion. A more appropriate name might be 'Body Designs' or 'Simply Elegance'. In the 1960s the now famous 'Chelsea Girl' chain rose to success partly on its choice of name. At the time, 'Chelsea' was considered to be the fashionable part of London and

Girl' obviously signified the age range. The name has now lost much of its original meaning but this is balanced by the fact that the chain is established and well-known. More subtle, the name 'Next' conveys a sense of the future, signifying to its customers that the store is at the forefront of style and design in clothes. Sometimes putting 'The' in front of a name can convey that the shop is unique, the leader of its type, etc. I am sure that 'The Body Shop' is pleased that it placed 'The' in front of its name, considering how many imitations there have been since its rise to success!

Sometimes shops are named in connection with where the shop is located, such as Blackpool Wine Stores (fictitious name). This has the advantage of identifying where the shop can be found and, in some cases, enhancing its credibility. However, great difficulties are experienced if you want to move to a different location or open up other branches in different areas. Similarly, a name that identifies too closely the type of merchandise you sell can present problems if you expand your merchandise range.

Choosing the name of your shop will undoubtedly take a lot of time. The objective, if possible, is to choose a name that will convey to your customers your 'unique selling proposition' (see Chapter 3) in a clear and unambiguous way. Additional slogans can be added to the facia to highlight your key selling points (e.g. Spar's '8 till late'). Be very careful not to pick names that are pretentious or that can have two interpretations, one of which is offensive or unattractive to your customers. To guard against these and similar problems, make up a short list of possible names, survey a sample of customers, and test their reactions to the choice of names. To do this, the simplest and most effective method is to use some form of projective technique. The idea is to get a spontaneous response to a given situation without it being clouded by conscious thought – hopefully revealing the 'true' feelings of the customer. The two most commonly used projective technqiues are word association and sentence completion. The customer is asked to say the word that immediately comes to mind when he or she hears or sees a particular name or complete a sentence such as:

People who would be attracted by the name 'Body Style' are ...

The choice of lettering and colour scheme combined with the name of the shop facia is very important. They all add up to a symbol or logo by which the shop may be identified. Incorporation of distinctive colours in the facia has paid off well in many cases, e.g. note the success of the red facia and 'green pine tree' symbol in identifying the Spar convenience store.

Geometry of the shop front and the entrance

The choice is basically between a straight front, some form of recessed and angled front, or a completely open frontage. The recessed front has the advantage of allowing the customers to study the window display without obstructing passers by. It also allows you to create more window display space and can provide a more interesting frontage. Its prime disadvantages are that it will erode your internal selling space and at night-time perhaps attract loitering from drunks etc.

Open frontages can be used in enclosed precincts and arcades. This is where the shop has no physical frontage at all. This gives the feeling of complete openness and encourages the customer to come into the store and browse. You should, however, be aware of the increased security risks with such a design.

Display windows

The window area can be used in many ways:

- To show a selection of merchandise offered for sale.
- To feature special promotions.
- To create an overall image.

The key function of the display is to attract the customers' attention and encourage them to enter to shop. The first decision to be made is whether to have an open or closed back display. An open display allows the customer to see right into the shop so that your internal selling area itself becomes part of the overall display. With exceptions, such as jewellers, this is the more common approach being adopted in the high street today.

The basic principles of window display are:

- **Merchandise from different ranges, where there is no connection, should not be displayed together.**
- **There should be balance and line in the display, otherwise it will look chaotic. There are basically two forms of balance: symmetrical and asymmetrical. The way you line up and balance your display will have a different impact. Merchandise lined up in curves or horizontally will generally have a soothing tranquil effect, whereas, the use of diagonal and vertical lines will have a more dramatic impact.**
- **The selection and use of colours and lighting are very important in creating images and feelings. Colours should be chosen with care to communicate the ambience appropriate to your overall image and the selling points of the merchandise. Use of the colour wheel in Fig. 8.1 can be helpful in selecting colours for use with each other. Using the colour wheel is straightforward. For harmonious**

effect choose colours that are next to each other. For more dramatic results choose colours that are opposite to each other. Further, certain colours also have psychological effects. For example, red is strongly associated with heat, passion, love and danger, whereas greens and browns can create a feeling of gloom, and yellows gaiety. The overall impact of colour will vary depending on the combinations used, the overall theme of the display and the merchandise selected.

- Remembering that window displays will act as an advertisement for the shop when it is closed, all displays should be well lit. However, over-bright lighting can 'wash out' the impact of the display. To give a specific example, a display of TV sets would benefit from low background lighting to enhance the appearance of the picture (assuming the sets are switched on). All window displays can be improved by careful positioning of spot lights of different intensities and colours. Concealed lighting can also have interesting effects.
- Don't make the mistake of placing too much merchandise in the window as this can be confusing. A display does not need to contain merchandise at all. However, with certain shops such as jewellers or hobby shops, mass merchandise displays can be very interesting to customers.
- Where merchandise is displayed, it is productive to place it in settings that 'show off' its principal benefits.
- Finally, all displays should be kept clean and changed quite frequently.

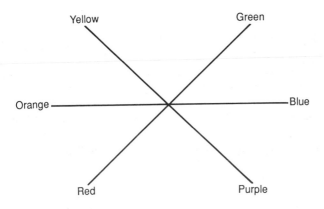

Fig. 8.1 The colour wheel

Store interior and layout

The store atmosphere

The impression created on the outside must carry through into the store itself. In creating an appropriate store atmosphere, consideration must be given to factors similar to those applicable to exterior design, such as colour and lighting. The atmosphere that the customers detect is dependent on what their senses tell them and how that sensory information is interpreted. All the senses, smell, sound, sight and touch must be taken into account.

No customer will want to shop in a store that smells of stale tobacco smoke or mustiness from unclean carpets or damp walls. Sales areas must be kept free of unseemly smells. Air fresheners (not to be over-used!), a frequent cleaning and redecoration programme and good ventilation is the answer. Of course, pleasant smells associated with certain merchandise (e.g. cosmetics, bakery products etc.) should be encouraged.

The use of background music in shops is a widely-debated topic. There are shops where it is definitely desirable (e.g. record shops and teenage fashion 'boutiques') and others where it is definitely not (e.g., high class fashions). In other shopping situations, research has shown that some customers even find music that is designed to soothe the customer irritating, while others do not. This is easily explained by the widely differing tastes in music. Consequently, the decision to pipe music into a store is your decision. Personally, I would not favour its use. Care should also be given to the acoustics of the shop. If a quiet relaxed atmosphere is required then the floor and wall coverings should be selected for their sound absorbing properties.

Particularly in clothes shops, merchandise should be displayed in such a way that it can be touched and felt by the customer. Many clothes sales are made as a result of the fabric 'feeling good'. Also, a shop wishing to project an air of class and exclusivity should use fixtures and fittings that feel good to the touch – such feelings will be associated with the merchandise and thereby help sales.

The sense of sight conveys approximately 80 per cent of all the information we receive about our environment. Stand by the front door of your shop. What will the customer see on entrance? What impression do you want to create? Everything from the colour and condition of the ceiling and walls, to the overall layout of the shop and the lighting used, will create an overall *immediate* visual impression. For example, dark coloured ceilings will psychologically diminish the height of the store.

Layout

Having considered the exterior design, overall atmosphere and image, let's now turn our attention to the way the merchandise will be physically laid out in the shop. With self-service and self-selection selling methods there is almost an infinite variety of possible physical layouts ranging from the grid iron pattern (as favoured by the supermarkets) that seeks to control the flow of customers around the store, to the free-flow designs increasingly found in clothes shops and department stores. Both have the aim of trying to get the customer to see and buy as much of the merchandise as possible. On the whole, the grid iron pattern is more suitable to the volume sales of low value items such as grocery and the free-flow layout is more consistent with that of higher value merchandise.

Merchandise categories, groupings and good layout practice

Having decided on the general shape of the layout, consideration must be given to how merchandise will be grouped and where it should be located in the layout to maximize sales. Merchandise can be categorized in a number of ways.

1. **Demand lines**. These are the lines that are most frequently bought. In most types of business, research has shown that the 80/20 rule applies. That is 80 per cent of the profit is generated from only 20 per cent of the merchandise on sale (more about this in Chapter 13). In researching your business you should seek to identify these lines in some detail. Once identified, they should be spread around the store to encourage the customer to visit all parts of the shop. Importantly some demand lines should be placed close to the entrance of the shop to start customers buying and, therefore, slow down their shopping trip. Such positioning gives other lines more chance of being purchased as the customer begins to browse.

2. **Related, reminder and impulse lines**. These are the lines that are not the main object of the shopping trip. Careful attention to where they are placed in the store will hopefully remind people to buy as an afterthought. Some items are bought on impulse (e.g. confectionery). As such they should be placed where customers have a chance to see them and time to make the decision to buy (e.g. typically, till points).

3. **Promotional lines.** These are the lines that you feature on the basis of price or some other attribute. They should not be placed too close to demand lines as they will detract from each other. Promotional lines should be well spaced and signed to encourage maximum customer flow throughout the store.

You can adopt variations on the two principal ways of grouping merchandise. You can decide to group in generic order. That is place merchandise in terms of some shared characteristic. For example, in a clothing business this may mean placing all coats together, all skirts together, all accessories together, all blouses together, and so on. However, when looked at from the customers' point of view this is not necessarily the best order. For instance, when purchasing a skirt a matching top is often sought, when purchasing beach wear towels, sun tan lotion and sandals are often considered. Similarly, a Father's Day gift display may consist of brief cases, shavers, after shave cologne and pens. This approach to merchandise layout, in making use of related merchandise and basic knowledge of customer buying behaviour, often leads to increased sales.

Once overall positioning is decided upon, equal care must be given to basic common-sense observations such as 'eye level is buy level' – meaning that as a general rule on vertical shelf units, the best sellers should be placed at eye level with the slowest sellers above them and the medium sellers below. Also, you should note that vertical grouping of merchandise is preferable to horizontal grouping as customers tend to survey fixtures in an up-and-down rather than a side-to-side manner.

Customer circulation in the store

As already discussed, care in grouping and locating your merchandise will certainly help maximize customer flow around your shop. However, what the exact pattern of circulation in the store is likely to be, which positions will be possible dead spots and which will be high sales areas is hard to predict. As a rough guide, observations of customer buying behaviour seem to indicate that the ends of island fixtures and the centre of merchandise runs seem to constitute the best selling areas.

Efficient allocation of display space

The basic rule in retailing is that display space should be allocated to merchandise on the basis of its sales performance. For example, if a range of merchandise accounts for 20 per cent of the the sales revenue of the store, it should accordingly be given 20 per cent of the selling space. As discussed in Chapter 5, the proportion of total store sales to be found in each merchandise group can be gleaned from *The Retail Business Monitor*. Once the business is trading, detailed sales data can be obtained (see Chapter 13) to make more informed decisions.

Generally the more sales space you give to a line, the faster it will move. However, some caution should be exercised here. Experience has shown that this works only for demand lines and slow moving lines are little affected by alterations to the sales space allocated to them.

Security and store layout

The risk of theft of merchandise (I prefer not to call it shop lifting for theft is what it is) and cash can be greatly reduced if care is taken in laying out your shop. Particularly avoid blind spots in the layout where the customer cannot be seen because other fixtures obstruct the view of sales staff. Consequently, there are advantages in not having centre sales fixtures above shoulder height. The placement of security cameras and or mirrors strategically around the store should also help to minimize such risk.

High value merchandise should either be placed where it can remain under constant supervision or be secured by electronic loop alarms or similar device. Also, do not place high value items close to the doors from where a thief can make a fast exit. Till points, where possible (for the same reason) should not be placed in very close proximity to the door (till snatches are a frequent and often violent occurrence these days). However, at the same time, the sales counter does not want to be placed in a position where the entrance or exit to the store cannot be seen.

To help deter night break-ins good security lighting should be in operation in all parts of the shop. Finally, you are advised to consult your crime prevention officer by contacting your local police station. Their advice is expert (from years of experience) and free!

8

Summary

The aim of exterior design and display is to first contrast the shop in some favourable way – make it stand out from its neighbours. In doing so the shop name, frontage and display should grab the attention of the targeted customers and instil in them the desire to enter the shop. The customers' expectations from viewing the store from outside should be reinforced as they enter. Attention must be given to developing an overall store atmosphere.

Once in, the customer should be encouraged to start buying straight away. Great care should, therefore, be given to the way you group and locate your merchandise to encourage the customer to visit and buy from as many different locations in the store as possible. To make maximum and efficient use of available selling space, allocation of fixture space should be on the basis of merchandise sales performance. Finally, equal care should be given to security considerations in laying out your store so as to minimize theft by customers.

Checklist

---

1. Have you chosen a name that matches the perceptions of your targeted customers?
2. Is its meaning clear and unambiguous?
3. Does it conform with current regulations governing business names (see Chapter 11)?
4. Have you chosen a colour and/or logo that will be attractive and immediately identifiable by your targeted customer groups?
5. What style and shape of shop frontage is most appropriate?
6. What use of lighting, balance, proportion, colour, and merchandise will you use in your displays?
7. What will be your themes in your first three window displays?
8. What will the customer see on first entering your store?
9. What first impressions will be created?
10. What overall pattern of layout is most appropriate, grid iron or free-flow?
11. What criteria will you use to most effectively group and locate your merchandise?
12. How do you intend to start the customer buying?
13. Which merchandise will be demand lines?
14. Where will you locate them to maximize sales?
15. What steps have you taken to identify possible best selling positions?
16. What potential security hazards are there in your intended layout?
17. How can you minimize the risk of theft by customers?
18. Have you contacted your crime prevention officer?

---

9 Buying the shop

What's for sale? □ Why is it being sold? □ How well has it performed in the past? □ The balance sheet - what is the business worth? □ Buy freehold or leasehold? □ Planning permission □ Summary and checklist

What's for sale?

In most localities an estate agent who deals in commercial properties can be found. This will perhaps be your starting point, to identify what's on the market in your locality and the range of prices for different types of shop. In addition, you will also find that most estate agents have a commercial division. Plus, your local and specialist papers such as 'Daltons Weekly' should be checked for private sales. Finally, you can place advertisements in the business wanted sections of the local and specialist press.

When you visit a commercial estate agents you get information similar to that which you receive when house hunting. This will also include general business information on sales and profits and some estimation of its potential. Much of this, however, can be taken for what it is – sales talk. Don't forget the estate agent is representing the vendor's interests first and your's second. None the less this is useful in compiling a short list of shops to investigate further.

Why is it being sold?

Perhaps your first question on visiting a shop that is for sale is: 'Why is it being sold?' No doubt the vendor will not be short of answers – reasons given ranging from retirement and ill health, through family problems, to moving on to a larger business. The reasons given may not represent the whole truth. This book as whole should have provided you with the type of questions you would ask of both the vendor and yourself to elicit the real reasons. High on your list will be:

1. Are there any developments, present or future, that will diminish the trade of the shop? For instance:

- Parking restrictions are going to be imposed in the vicinity.
- Bus routes have been changed or cut.
- A new main road is going to be built, cutting the catchment area in half.
- A new shopping parade or precinct in a nearby housing estate that makes up a large part of the catchment area for the shop.
- A large store is going to built in the vicinity.
- Reputable retailers are moving away from the shopping area, subtracting from the centre's pulling power.
- A large employer in the area is planning to close down or make large scale redundancies, severely reducing the spending power of the shop's customers.
- A similar shop with a better selling proprosition has opened recently.

2. How many similar outlets are there within the area – is the location over-supplied? It might be the case that the shop is operating in a location where it and the competition have saturated the market.
3. How long has the vendor owned the business? How long did the previous owners stay? The shop may represent a bad buy. It is possible that the business only owes its existence to the fact that losses or poor performance have been financed by frequent changes of ownership. However, it is possible that the opposite might be true, that the business has done well for previous owners who have rapidly moved on to larger operations (possible, but unlikely!).
4. If leasehold, are high rent increases due?

Methods to check on these possible eventualities have already been covered in other parts of the book. Check out all the possibilities. If you are satisfied that the real reasons for sale do not pose a serious threat to your plans you can proceed to examine the business in greater detail.

How well has the business performed in the past?

You must obtain from the vendor copies of the business's final accounts for the previous three years. If the vendor refuses then there is no point in proceeding any further with your interest in the shop! The final accounts are made up of two principal documents, the profit and loss account and the balance sheet. Both were introduced in Chapters 5 and 6, and are dealt with at length in Chapter 12. Briefly, the profit and loss account will give details on sales matched against costs for each year's trading. The balance sheet will give a snapshot picture at the end of each year of what the business owns and what it owes, or to put it another way, what it possesses and where it got the money from to pay for it.

Sales performance

Let's start with the profit and loss accounts. This will give the shop's track record over the last three years. The first item of interest is the sales figure. This will be given exclusive of VAT. The task will be to assess the trend in sales over the past three years. Hopefully, the shop will show some increase in takings. However, you should note that part of the increase in sales will be the result of price increases, i.e. inflation. For instance, a shop showing a 5 per cent increase in sales in the profit and loss accounts over the course of a year when inflation is also running at 5 per cent, would in actual fact be experiencing no increase in real sales at all – it would be standing still. Therefore, the *real* sales trend must be established. This is achieved most easily by revaluing all the sales figures at the prices prevailing in the first year of trading given. The Retail Price Index is used to do this (use of the RPI was introduced in Chapter 4).

You can use the RPI for all items (i.e. general rate of inflation), but for more accurate results, the RPI that measures the price increases for the broad category of merchandise in which the shop's principal sales fall, should be used. Each year's index number represents the price level for that year. Expressing, for example, the 1983 index number as a percentage of the 1986 number will give the percentage by which the 1986 sales figure must be deflated (i.e. to give 1986 sales at 1983 prices). However, care must be taken to match the profit and loss account year end date with an appropriate year in the RPI table. For instance, eleven twelfths of the sales figure shown in an account with a year end date of January 1989 will have taken place in 1988, so that to use the index for 1989 in the deflator would produce misleading results.

Now let's work through an example to show how the process is actually carried out.

If the profit and loss account for a shop you are contemplating buying gives the following sales figures:

Year	£ Sales
1983/4	101,280
1984/5	103,190
1985/6	105,320

(Note: the trading year is from November to November so that the majority of sales fall into the calendar years 1984, 1985 and 1986.)

9

and the RPI for clothing and footwear (source: *Annual Abstract of Statistics*, Table 18.1) gives the following price levels:

Year	RPI
1984	214.6
1985	222.9
1986	229.2

then the sales figures can be revalued at 1983 prices as follows:

Year	Deflator	Sales	Adjusted sales	% Decrease
1984	214.6/214.6 ×	101,280	= 101,280	–
1985	214.6/222.9 ×	103,190	= 99,347	1.9%
1986	214.6/229.2 ×	105,320	= 98,611	0.7%

Overall real decrease in sales from 1984 to 1986: 2.6 per cent

The example clearly shows the benefit of doing these calculations. At first sight the unadjusted sales figures seem to indicate a steady increase in takings. However, when inflation is taken into account the real picture is revealed showing a dismal downward trend.

Further analysis can be done on the sales figures by comparing the shop's real sales trend with the sales trend for the sector of retailing over all. To continue our example, the sales of clothing in the UK between 1983 and 1986 revalued at 1980 prices were (source: *Annual Abstract of Statistics*, Table 14.10):

Year	£ million sales (at 1980 prices)	% increase
1984	11,562	–
1985	12,365	6.9%
1986	13,279	7.4%

Overall real increase in sales from 1984 to 1986: 14.9 per cent.

With this further analysis the shop is shown to be in an even worse state, with it experiencing over a two and half per cent drop in real sales when the market for its category of merchandise has expanded by nearly 15 per cent!

Trends in profits

The next item to be examined is the gross profit figure. The same analysis applied to the sales should be carried out to reveal the real trend in profits. The gross profit margin (i.e., profit/sales × 100) should be calculated and compared to the norm for this type of shop.

A low gross profit margin can be attributed to one or a combination of the following factors:

- Lower than normal prices. This is fine if it results in increased sales volume and profits (see Chapter 5). However, this might also indicate that competition in the area is forcing down prices to an unacceptable level.
- The level of wastage and/or theft of stock is high.
- Higher than normal cost prices as a result of poor turnover preventing advantage of supplier discounts being taken and/or poor selection of suppliers.
- Poor sales/profit mix (see Chapter 5, pages 115–21), i.e. a high proportion of total sales are locked into low profit margin merchandise.

A high gross profit margin can be attributed to one or a combination of the following factors:

- Higher than normal prices. What is the pricing policy/image of the shop? If you were to buy the business, will a reduction in the price level (see Chapter 5) bring in a more than proportionate increase in sales volume, to the extent that it will boost overall gross profit?
- Lower than normal cost prices as a result of a high rate of stock turn, enabling discount to be obtained from suppliers and direct dealings with manufacturers, without the need to buy in any real bulk from the cash and carry. Calculate the rate of stock turn from the accounts (see Chapter 12) and compare with the norm for this type of shop (see Chapter 1).
- Low wastage. If it is a fresh food shop, will you be able to do as well as the present owner in controlling the wastage? How many years of experience does he or she have compared to your skill and experience?

There is always a possibility that the gross profit figure may be inaccurate or misleading. The profit could simply have been inflated to make the business look more attractive for sale. Where there is such a one-off upsurge in profits this becomes, without valid and verifiable reasons, blatantly obvious. The way the end stock is valued can have a dramatic effect on the gross profit. Over-valuation will increase the value of the

	Year 1		Year 2	
Sales:	80,000		100,000	
Opening stock		20,000		25,000
Purchases		70,000		87,500
		90,000		112,500
Closing stock		−25,000		−37,500
C.O.S.	65,000		75,000	
Gross Profit	15,000		25,000	
Margin	19%		25%	
RST (average)	2.8		2.4	
Represented as weeks' stock holding	18.5 weeks' stock		21.6 weeks' stock	

Fig. 9.1 Example of effect of inflated stock values on gross profit

closing stock, reduce the cost of sales and accordingly increase the gross profit. You should, therefore, look for and regard with suspicion any significant variation in the opening and closing stocks as a proportion of the cost of sales over the period. For example, in Fig. 9.1 both the gross profit and the percentage margin have improved dramatically. At first glance this appears to be the result of a 25 per cent increase in sales. But by doing some simple checks in comparing the stock levels over the period of two years, doubt is cast on the authenticity of the profit figure for year two. Given that the difference between the opening and closing stocks represents a general increase in sales over the first year, the year end stock for year one is realistic. However, the closing stock for year two looks quite abnormal. The give away is the poor rate of stock turn for year two. With such an increase in sales, one would expect the rate of stock turn to increase not decrease. By the end of year two the business is carrying over three weeks' worth more stock than it did at the end of year one. A closing stock figure in the region of £30,000 to £32,500 would be more realistic. This would be in rough proportion to the expected future sales increase. Such a stock figure would result in pushing up the cost of sales figure past £80,000 and bringing down the gross profit figure by several thousand pounds. This would then result in a fairly similar margin and rate of stock turn to year one. Of course, this judgement of the figures could be inaccurate – there could be valid reasons for the decline in the RST and vast improvement in the margin. None the less the example (although rather artificial) does illustrate the effect of inflated stock values on gross profit – and demonstrates the kind of 'thinking' that should be done. At the very least the vendor should be questioned as to whether different methods have been applied to value the stocks.

Stock valuation

If you are buying a shop as a going concern, then you will buy the 'stocks at valuation'. To prevent yourself from losing a large amount of money on such a transaction, never accept the vendor's valuation of the stocks, firstly, because the stocks may represent poor selling merchandise that you will have to mark down by a considerable amount to sell when you take over, and secondly, there are a number of ways of valuing stocks and, if left up to the vendor, it is obvious that he or she is going to choose the method which is most advantageous to them. The stock value figure is going to be a subject of negotiation. As such you should be aware of the main methods in use:

1. The stock is valued at retail selling prices and the average profit margin deducted to arrive at the cost price value. The problems are that:

   - You may have to reduce the retail price to sell
   - The potential profit on the stock may not accord to the average profit margin being used.

2. The stock is valued at original cost. A reasonably fair approach which, in a world of rising prices, will probably be advantageous to the buyer.
3. The stock is valued at replacement cost. Obviously this method is more advantageous to the vendor.

Often an independent valuation is required by a specialist firm. But, whatever the case, you *must* be present at the stock taking to check the figures arrived at and to identify any perishable, damaged and generally unsaleable stock.

Overheads

The middle of the profit and loss account is made up of expenditure on overheads (fixed costs). Look for and question any significant variance between the years. Check out the major cost components. Will you incur greater or lesser costs with the plans you have for your business? You should carry out your own profitability analysis using the methods and techniques fully discussed and described in Chapter 5.

Net profit

After deduction of the overheads, the net profit figure is arrived at. The question is will it be sufficient for your needs? Can it be improved and if so, how? Finally, taxation and the owner's drawings are subtracted to show the profit that has been left in the business.

The balance sheet – what is the business worth?

Definitions and descriptions of the components of a balance sheet and the methods to interpret them are given in Chapters 6 and 12, therefore, I will not dwell on such matters here. Rather our discussion will focus on interpreting the net worth of the assets of the business from the information given in the balance sheet and assessing whether the purchase of the business will represent a good investment from a financial point of view.

The net worth of the business is the sum total of all its assets, less its current (short-term) liabilities. This figure is shown as net assets employed or balance sheet value (terms vary). This figure cannot always be taken literally as a fair valuation of the busines for at least two reasons. Firstly, the figure might include an amount for 'goodwill' and, secondly, the valuation of the assets might be inflated.

Goodwill is an intangible asset and its value is always suspect. It is hard to define and cannot be taken literally to mean that there is a guarantee that the custom generated by the vendor and his or her good relationships with suppliers will automatically transfer with the ownership of the business. For this reason alone, value attributed to goodwill on the balance sheet should be automatically deducted from the net worth of the business.

For each of the other assets you should make your own assessment of the value. Also, ask yourself what you will have to replace and at what cost. The greatest care should be taken, as we have already discussed, in valuing the stock.

A fair price

When you have arrived at an assessment of the net worth of the business it should be compared to the asking price. You will undoubtedly find that the asking price is in excess of your valuation of the net assets. This is fair, because after all you are not buying empty premises but a going concern. Now we bring back what many would call the 'goodwill' we discounted in the first place. You must assess the commercial value of the business. The most common way is to judge the likely return on the investment if you go ahead and purchase the shop. This is done by quite simply taking the net profit figure (before taxation and drawings) and expressing it as a percentage of the asking price plus stock at valuation (if the price does not include the stock). The acceptable bottom line in retailing is 20 per cent, with a good investment being in the region of 30 per cent. In other words, the business should recoup its purchase price from net profits within three to five years. The rough and ready guide is that, from a buyer's point of view, the top price payable is five times the current net profit, with a good price being three times or less the current net profit.

In the end the decision of whether to buy and what price to pay is yours. There will be some kind of trade-off between your assessment of the shop's value and the asking price determined partly by one, or a combination, of the following factors:

- How well the business is doing.
- Its net worth.
- The hidden costs of purchase (e.g. redecoration costs and the replacement of unsuitable fixtures and fittings).
- The likely return on the investment.
- The state of the retail property market and prevailing prices.
- Your assessment of the business potential of the shop.
- The likely future value of the freehold property or lease as applicable.

9

In negotiating the price with the vendor, the foregoing should have given you plenty to bargain with. The most important single piece of advice I can give you here is: never forget the objective of the negotiations by letting it become a personal competition between you and the vendor. At all times let rational thinking determine your decision making and don't be pressurized by the well worn vendor tactic of indicating there are rival bidders interested, offering over your ceiling price. Be clear, before you meet with the vendor for negotiations over the sale, what you will not give way on and what is subject to negotiation. It is better if you go into this situation with a point-by-point agenda for discussion. In this way it is more likely you will control the negotiations and that they will be constructive rather than just wandering discussions. Finally, don't make snap decisions. There will always be other shops for sale, but there are no second chances for those who make a bad buy!

Buy freehold or leasehold?

There is no right answer to this one; it is a matter for you to decide in relation to your business's and personal requirements. Here are some factors to consider.

Buying freehold property is a major capital investment. The main disadvantage is obvious: you will have to raise the finance. The repayments of capital and the interest will probably prove to be greater than the out-goings associated with a leasehold purchase. However, you will be buying an asset that will appreciate in value and thus, in future years, it should provide a sound base for raising further finance for expansion. With the purchase of a lease, the opposite is true; as the years go on the lease is used up, and it will depreciate in value. Further, because of the lack of permanence with a lease and the fact that it decreases in value, you will find it more difficult to raise finance for its acquisition. The opposite is true for freehold property: you will find a range of financial institutions prepared to make long-term loans on such an investment.

Generally you will find that there are more constraints and controls attached to the operation of a shop from leasehold than freehold premises. Both will, of course, be subject to planning permission, but the leasehold agreement is more likely to contain clauses imposing repair and maintenance obligations, and restrictions on uses and alterations.

In both cases a reputable solicitor (specializing in such work) should be engaged. In terms of a lease you need to know every detail of the lease agreement before you enter into the contract. Some of the covenants, as indicated above, can be quite restricting and costly.

Planning permission

The golden rule here is to double check that the premises you intend to acquire can in fact be used for all the activities you want to carry out there now and, just as important, in the future. In the first instance, check with your Local Authority Planning Office and later in detail with your solicitor. You should also note that you will need planning permission for any alterations, including new shop fronts and signs. Further, most alterations and extensions will have to conform to building regulations. The main thing to note here is that seeking such permission can be a lengthy and sometimes costly process. You will certainly need legal advice and, more than likely, the services of an architect and surveyor.

You must also check with your local authority whether the existence of any local byelaws will impose any restrictions or controls on your business. A licence, registration or other permission may also be needed.

Summary and Checklist

Acquiring the right premises is perhaps one of the most important decisions you ever make in your business career. Use the following checklist to help you make sure you have got it right.

1. Have you calculated your present and future space requirements?
2. From Chapter 4 have you determined:
   - The right location?
   - The characteristics of a good site?
3. Have you surveyed the full extent of what is for sale?
4. Have you deciphered the real reasons for the sale?
5. Are any of them prohibitive to you?
6. Does the site of the shop match your specifications?
7. What is the real sales trend?
8. How does it compare to what's happening to sales in the trade?
9. Have you made a full assessment of the profits?
10. Have you examined all the overhead costings?
11. How has the stock been valued?
12. What is your assessment of the net worth of the assets?
13. What is the net profit now?
14. Is it enough?
15. What is a conservative estimate of the shop's future potential?
16. What is its commercial value?
17. How does this compare with the asking price?
18. What is the ceiling price that you are not prepared to exceed?
19. What are the points for negotiation?
20. Have you severe restrictions on the amount you can borrow?
21. If so, have you considered a lease instead of freehold?
22. If buying a lease, have you:
    - Obtained legal advice?
    - Checked the present owner has the right to sell the lease?
    - Checked all the details of the lease?
    - Checked about rent reviews? The rent might be acceptable now, but a fundamental aspect of leases are rent reviews – have you discussed this with your solicitor?
    - Checked the attitude of financial institutions to your borrowing requirements for such a lease?
23. Do you need planning permission? Can it be obtained?
24. Have you made the granting of planning permission a condition of the contract of sale?

9

25. If an off-licence, have you made obtaining the licence a condition of the contract of sale?
26. Have you taken into account any future uses your business may put the property to as it expands?
27. If buying freehold are there any covenants in the deeds which will pose a threat to your business?
28. How easily will you be able to find a buyer for the premises if the business fails? (This is rather negative but worthy of consideration.)
29. Have you calculated the full cost of the premises:
    - Legal fees for buying, planning permission, licence applications, etc.
    - Surveying fees
    - Cost of finance
    - Advance rent
    - Rates
    - Alterations and improvements
    - Insurance
    - Costs of conforming with environmental health, and Health and Safety regulations
    - Service connection charges
    - If already in business, costs to disturbance of business (loss of sales, etc.)
31. Finally, and extremely important, have you identified and engaged the services of a solicitor who is expert in this kind of work?

10 Taxation

Income tax □ Corporation tax □ National Insurance
contributions □ Value Added Tax □ Summary

Income tax

The two things you would be well advised to do before starting in business are:

1. Employ the services of a good accountant. This does not mean that you should not keep your own books, but rather dealing with the Inland Revenue is in many cases best left to the professional. At the very least you will need advice from your accountant on the best kind of book keeping system to operate (see Chapter 12), choice of accounting date (the date when you draw up your final accounts) and the tax rules governing what you can offset against tax and what you cannot.
2. Inform your local Inland Revenue offices of the date you intend to commence trading. This, if nothing elese, gets your relationship with the Inland Revenue off to a good start! They will also supply you with a booklet entitled *Starting in Business*, giving you an overview of taxation and the self-employed.

If you start in business as a sole trader or in partnership (see Chapter 11) you will be taxed on your net profits as shown in your profit and loss account. However, it is possible that the Inland Revenue will slightly adjust the net profit figure because of special rules they apply to the calculation of depreciation on certain assets for tax purposes. Your accountant will advise you of the details and make the necessary adjustments if required. As for the rate of tax you are charged and your tax coding (personal allowances) there is no difference between self-employment and employment.

Besides the nature of the allowances you can claim, the main difference between employment and self-employment for tax purposes is the time period of the earnings/profits on which your tax is based, and the payment dates. As you will be aware, as an employed person your tax is calculated on your weekly or monthly earnings. As a self-employed person the rules are different and quite complicated. You should appreciate that when you first start trading no accurate assesment of your earnings can be made until after you have drawn up your first final accounts some twelve months later. The first thing to note is that you will not have to pay any tax until some fourteen to eighteen months or more after starting up.

Although it is beyond the scope of this book to deal with the full complexities of taxation, it would help you to have some understanding of the overall rules that govern how your tax will be calculated and when it will be payed. Let's have a look at those rules and how they are applied.

1. The Inland Revenue operates on 'fiscal' years ending on 5 April each year. For example, the fiscal year 1987/88 runs from 6 April 1987 to 5 April 1988.
2. You may operate on whatever year end date (accounting date) you wish. You will normally draw up accounts for a twelve month period. However, you can draw up and submit accounts for whatever period you like: three months, six months, etc.
3. You will normally receive tax assesments in the autumn of every year. The amount shown on the assessment will normally be payable in two equal instalments on 1 January and 1 July.
4. The general rule is that the tax assessment is based on the profits of the 12 month's profit and loss account ending in the previous fiscal year. In other words, you pay your tax one year in arrears. For example, the tax assessment you receive in Autumn 1988 (fiscal year 1988/89) will relate to your profits as shown in your profit and loss account that ended in the previous fiscal year 1987/88, and be payable in two equal instalments on 1 January and 1 July 1989.

- Now let's see how these rules apply to somebody setting up in business for the first time.

A trader commences business on 16 October 1987. The trader decides to draw up his or her accounts on 15 October 1988 and the same date for future years. To make the example clearer, let's assume that net profits for the first 12 months' trading are £12,000. Also, for simplicity, let's assume that the tax rate is 25 per cent and that the full net profits are classed as taxable income (i.e. ignoring any personal tax allowances). His or her tax assessments for the first three years will be calculated and be payable as follows:

Tax assessment for fiscal year 1987/88

Taxes will be payable as soon as the tax inspector agrees the final accounts for the first year's trading and issues the assessment. The assessment would probably be issued, in, say, December 1987. It will be based on a proportion of the profits earned in the first year's trading - that is from

October 1987 to April 1988 – which will be calculated as 6/12 × £12,000. The total tax payable within 30 days of the assessment will be £1,500 (i.e., 25 per cent of £6,000).

Tax assessment for fiscal year 1988/89

This will be received at the same time as the assessment for 1987/88. As there are no full accounts ending in the previous fiscal year (i.e. 1987/88) on which to base the assessment, the tax inspector will draw up the assessment on your profits agreed for your first 12 months of operation, that is £12,000. The tax payable, £3,000, will be split into two equal instalments and be payable on 1 January and 1 July 1989.

Tax assessment for fiscal year 1989/90

The Inland Revenue can now apply its normal assessment rule and take the profits agreed for the 12 month trading period that ended in the previous fiscal year. If you have followed these manoeuvres so far, you should see that the trading year that ended in the last fiscal year, April '88 to April '89, is, in fact, the first year's trading that ended in October 1988. Therefore, once again, the assessment is based on the first year's trading. This will be payable on 1 January and 1 July 1990.

If you have worked through the above example slowly (try working out your own example) you should now be able to understand why the first three assessments are based on your first 12 months of operation. This is of great benefit to your cash flow if your profits are climbing at a rapid rate each year. It should be obvious that a low taxable profit in the first year's trading is beneficial in minimizing tax payments in the early years. However, your prime considerations should be commercial and planning to minimize or delay tax payments should not distract you from your prime of objective of maximizing profit.

Corporation tax

If you set up as a limited company you will be taxed as an employee and the business taxed as a separate entity under corporation tax. Your wages/salary will be a cost to the business which, like other costs, can be offset against its tax bill. The tax is usually payable nine months after the end of the company's trading year. The amount of tax payable is a percentage of the company's profits. There are lower rates of taxation for small companies who do produce high profits.

National Insurance contributions

There are four classes of National Insurance contributions. Explanatory leaflets on each type are available from any Department of Social Security office.

- Class 1: These are contributions for employed persons.
- Class 2: These are contributions for self-employed persons. You pay these by either stamping a card or by direct debit from your bank account. You can apply for examption from making these contributions if you have good reason to believe your earnings will fall below the 'lower earnings limit' in any given year. However, if you do this, don't forget that your entitlement to some of the benefits this contribution gives you may be effected.
- Class 3: These are voluntary contributions.
- Class 4: These are further contributions that may have to be made by a self-employed person. They are calculated on your profits. If your profits come to more than the lower limit (£4,590 in 1987/88) you will be liable to pay Class 4 contributions on profits above that lower limit figure to the upper limit figure (£15,340 in 1987/88), at a percentage rate of 6.3 per cent (in 1987/88). For example using the upper and lower limits and percentage rate for 1987/88, if your profits are £12,250, then Class 4 contributions would be due on £7,660 at a rate of 6.3%, a total Class 4 contribution of £482.58.

Value added tax

Value added tax is administered by HM Customs and Excise. Many references have already been made to VAT in earlier chapters. Firstly, you should note that an informative and comprehensive pack of free material is available from your local VAT office. (Look up the number in your telephone directory and contact your local office.)

How it works

To the newcomer, VAT can appear a horribly complicated tax, but in essence the principle is quite straightforward – it is the paper work that goes with it that is laborious and sometimes complex. The tax is, in actual fact, a tax on the *value you add* to goods and services, which is payable by the end purchaser.

• Let's take a simple example to demonstrate the process.

Take the case of a retailer buying and selling goods on which VAT is payable at 15 per cent. Let's imagine the retailer buys goods from a wholesaler at a VAT exclusive cost of £100. He or she will actually pay £115 (cost price plus 15 per cent VAT). Now lets assume the trader sells all of those goods at a mark up of 100 per cent (profit margin of 50 per cent), he or she will receive £200 plus 15 per cent VAT on the selling prices, a total of £230. The VAT he/she paid is known as the 'input tax' and is reclaimable – the VAT he/she charged on the sales, known as his/her ' output tax', is payable to the Customs and Excise. The VAT actually due is the *difference* between the output tax of £30 (VAT on sales) and the input tax of £15 (VAT on cost of goods): a total of £15. This is exactly 15 per cent of £100: the value added to the goods!

VAT and profits

In theory the existence of VAT does not affect the profits. Taking the previous example as an illustration, if VAT didn't exist the gross profit would be: £200 (selling price) – £100 (cost price) = £100. With the existence of VAT the same is true, £230 (amount actually received from sales) – £115 (amount actually paid for stock) = £115 (the amount held before payment of VAT) – £15 (VAT payable) = £100 gross profit. You should be able to see that it is *the customer* who actually pays the VAT on the value you added to the stock and it is *you* who has collected the tax on behalf of the Customs and Excise! The existence of VAT, through forcing the consumer to incur extra expenditure, indirectly reduces overall sales and, therefore, profits.

10

Will you need to register?

For the purposes of VAT, merchandise is classified under one of the following headings:

1. Exempt – meaning that they do not come under VAT regulations
2. Zero rated – meaning that, although they do come under VAT regulations, no tax is charged on these items. Most food for human consumption is zero-rated. However, there are exceptions such as ice cream, crisps and confectionery which are standard rated.
3. Standard rated – merchandise on which the standard rate of VAT at 15 per cent is charged.

You must be registered for VAT if you expect your sales of vatable merchandise (the total turnover of standard and zero rated items) to exceed the VAT threshold in any quarter or twelve month period. At the time of writing, a business expecting its sales of vatable items to approach or exceed £22,100 (inclusive of VAT) per annum or £7,500 (inclusive of VAT) per quarter should register for VAT.

It is your responsibility to register for VAT. It is no excuse to say you did not realize your turnover would be 'that large', the Customs and Excise will still demand the VAT due even if you haven't charged it. The important point to note is that registration must be made at the start of the trading period. If you are going to be liable for registration, notification must be made to Customs and Excise within 30 days of opening. In effect, you have one month from the start of trading in which to estimate whether you will exceed the VAT threshold or not in the course of the quarter, or the year.

The VAT return and the importance of the tax point date

As we have seen, the net VAT payable to or refundable from the Customs and Excise is the difference between the output taxes collected and the input taxes paid. The payment is made when the VAT return is submitted. In the case of a refund, payment will be received after the VAT office has processed your return.

The VAT return, which is a relatively straightforward piece of documentation, is completed every quarter. In completing the return, care must be taken to include only purchases and sales made in the quarter that the VAT return relates to. Tax is deemed as being charged when the merchandise is purchased or sold. The date of receipt or sale is known as the *tax point date*. In the case of credit sales, this is not the same time as the money is received. Similarly, where you have credit terms with your suppliers, input tax is deemed as paid when the invoice is issued to you and not when you actually pay. Therefore, you include in your return only the input tax on invoices whose issue dates fall within that period. The same is true for sales.

VAT calculations

Where the price is exclusive of VAT it is simply a matter of adding on 15 per cent. Where the price includes VAT, the VAT content will be 15/115 parts of the price. Conceptually:

$$\text{VAT content} = \frac{15\%}{100\% + 15\%}$$

For example, if £200 of standard rated merchandise is sold, the output tax will be £26.08 (£200 × 15/115).

Note: VAT is always rounded *down* to the nearest penny.

Coping with VAT: retail schemes

In the course of a day's trading you are likely to sell exempt, zero and standard rated items. This presents the problem of separating the VAT collected from the gross takings. Help in finding a solution to this rather perplexing situation is given by the Customs and Excise who offer the choice of nine retail schemes, A to J. Pamphlets on each of these schemes are obtained from your local VAT office.

Scheme A

This is appropriate only if all of your sales are standard-rated. The output tax is simply calculated by multiplying your VAT inclusive turnover by 15/115.

Scheme B

This is appropriate for retailers who sell both standard- and zero-rated merchandise, but where sales of zero-rated items do not exceed 50 per cent of total sales.

The output tax is calculated by subtracting the value of your zero-rated stock purchases at retail price from the gross takings for the VAT period, and multiplying the remainder by 15/115. Adjustments must be made if there are any additional mark downs or mark ups in the prices of zero-rated merchandise.

Scheme C

This is appropriate for retailers who sell both standard- and zero-rated merchandise but whose turnover does not exceed £90,000 pa.

CTNs, off-licences	16.66%
Grocers, butchers, fishmongers, bakers	20.00%
Greengrocers, radio and electrical (excluding rental), cycle shops, chemists, photographic shops and record shops	40.00%
Jewellers	75.00%

Fig. 10.1 Statutory mark ups under Scheme C

The scheme works, not by taking the VAT content of your actual sales, but, by estimating what the retail value of your sales will be by applying a fixed mark up to your purchases. The mark ups to be used are determined by the Customs and Excise (see Fig. 10.1).

For example, if a record shop purchases £10,000 (inclusive of VAT) standard-rated merchandise in a VAT period, the output tax would be calculated as follows:

Estimated sales = £10,000 × 1.4 (i.e. plus 40% statutory markup)
(VAT inc.) of
standard rated
merchandise
            = £14,000

Output tax   = £14,000 × 15/115
            = £1,820

Important note: If the mark up you are using is less than the one laid down, you will pay more tax using this scheme.

Scheme D

This is appropriate for retailers whose turnover exceeds £500,000. Your taxable turnover is calculated by taking the percentage or fraction of your total taxable purchases which is made up of standard-rated merchandise. That fraction is then applied to your quarterly sales of taxable merchandise to determine the sales of standard rated merchandise. The VAT content is then calculated as before. The formula to calculate the output tax in any VAT quarter is as follows:

$$\frac{\text{Value of standard-rated purchases (VAT inc.)}}{\text{Value of standard and zero-rated purchases (VAT inc.)}} \times \frac{\text{Gross takings (standard) and zero}}{} \times \frac{15}{100}$$

Note: Adjustments are made at the end of each year based on actual purchases. The ratio of standard- to zero-rated purchases is then re-estimated for the year to come.

Scheme E

You work out the selling prices of all your merchandise purchased in the period by applying the appropriate mark up. The VAT content of

stimated sales is then calculated in the normal way. As the VAT can be
ue and payable on the merchandise before the items have actually been
old, this scheme is only really suitable for shops that have a high turnover
f stock.

Scheme F

This is straightforward to operate if you have an electronic till capable of
eing programmed to separate standard, zero and exempt sales. The
utput tax is simply calculated by multiplying the till total of standard
ated items by 15/115.

Scheme G

This is very similar to Scheme D, except that 1/8 th is added to the output
ax payable. If your mark up for zero-rated merchandise is higher than
our mark up for standard-rated merchandise you are advised not to use
his scheme.

Scheme H

This scheme is similar to Scheme G except that you express your
urchases at retail rather than cost price in the calculation, and there is no
equirement to add on 1/8 th to the output tax payable.

Schemes J and H

These are very similar to Schemes G and H, except they are based on yearly
ales.

---

t first sight, all of the schemes (with the exception of F) seem quite
onfusing rather than helpful. All, however, with an appropriate
ccounts system (see Chapter 12) are easy enough to operate. To
elect the scheme most suitable to you:

- Gain a greater understanding by obtaining and studying the
  booklets produced by the Customs and Excise.
- Consult with your accountant.
- By all means, consult with the Customs and Excise direct. They
  should be only too pleased to help!

Other important things to note about VAT

1. The Customs and Excise have wide ranging powers of search and entry Any attempt to defraud the Customs and Excise can easily lead to prison sentence!
2. You will need proof of all your inputs and outputs.
3. If you are not sure about any aspect of VAT in relation to your shop contact your local VAT office before you make a complete mess o things. They should be only too pleased to help. It is in their interest for you to get it right at the outset!
4. In some instances it can actually be beneficial for a business to b registered for VAT. VAT paid on some capital items can b recoverable.
5. VAT, like all taxation, has an effect on your cash flow (see Chapter and Appendix 6).

Summary

Getting your tax affairs sorted out before you go into business is important. Selection of a good account is essential to advise you on all matters relating to taxation. However, do not over rely on your accountant to give you all the answers. At the very least, you require a basic understanding of the way taxation will affect your business. This will give the base from which to make the best use of expensive professional help and guidance.

The Inland Revenue and your local VAT office should be contacted to seek further help and advice. If VAT registration is required, then take care to select a Retail Scheme that will both fit your business's requirements and be understandable to you. Lastly, never make tax considerations the focus of your business decisions. There is a lot of 'business pub talk' about taxation and business that is, basically, rubbish. It is better to make a larger profit and pay more tax than pay no tax at all because you haven't made a profit!

11 Trading as ...

Business names □ Trade marks □ Sole trader □ Partnerships □
Limited company □ Co-operatives □ Summary

Business names

If you intend to set up in business as a sole trader using your own name,
or as a partnership using the partners' names, you will have no problems.
However, to project a better image to your market and suppliers, you may
wish to trade under a business name (as discussed in Chapter 8).

You cannot trade under any name you wish. There are certain names
that you cannot use because they may imply that you are something which
you are not. The Department of Trade produces a useful leaflet called
Business Names - Guidance Notes. This leaflet lists some 90 words such
as 'royal' and 'authority' which, unless you have official clearance, you
cannot use.

If you trade under a business name then you must display on your
premises, letterheads, invoices, sales receipts, etc. the following
information:

● Business name.
● Your name (and name of partners if a partnership, or full name of
  company in the case of a limited company).
● Your permanent business address.

Further, if so asked, you must provide the name and address of the owner
in writing immediately! Failure to meet any of these requirements is a
criminal offence which could result in a fine of £400.

When choosing a business name you should also take care that you do
not take unfair advantage of a competitor by choosing a similar name and
'cashing in' on their reputation/goodwill, or you could find yourself in
court!

Trade marks

If your idea is original in some way and you think it could be easily copied by a competitor, you may consider investigating the possibility of registering your business name, inclusive of any distinctive logo, as a trade mark.

A trade or service mark is defined (by the Trade Marks Act 1936 and Trade Marks [Amendment] Act 1984) as any mark, it could be a signature, a name, a distinctive and original colour scheme, a symbol, etc., that is used or intended to be used in relation to the sale of merchandise and/or services. It is of no consequence whether or not the mark gives any indication of the identity of the person holding the trade mark.

* **Application to register a trade mark is made to the Patent Office, State House, 66–71 High Holburn, London WC1 4TP. Advice on trade mark registrations can be obtained from the Trade Mark Protection Society, 50 Lincoln's Field, London WC2A 3PF.**

Obviously, attempts to register trade marks that are identical or sufficiently similar to others to cause confusion will not be successful. Once granted a trade mark will initially remain in force for seven years. It may then be renewed for a fourteen year term and then renewed indefinitely on the same basis.

The registration of the trade mark will give you exclusive rights over its use. However, be warned; it can be a difficult and costly business proving that somebody has infringed your trade mark. As a small business could you afford the legal expenses? One good idea though is to check with the Trade Marks Registry that the logo or name you intend to use is not already registered by somebody who can afford legal action!

Sole trader

Legally, all businesses fall into one of the following main categories:

* Sole trader
* Partnership
* Limited company
* Co-operative

Each has it's own advantages and disadvantages. Which form you should choose depends on weighing up the pros and cons in relation to your business's needs – but there is no 'right' answer. Your accountant and solicitor should be able to advise you and help you come to a decision. What follows is a brief description of each form and a summary of the main advantages and disadvantages.

Setting up as a sole trader is perhaps the simplest way of entering into business. From a legal point of view there is nothing you have to do to set up in business as a sole trader.

Advantages

1. Easy to set up. There are no legal formalities.
2. You have total control of the business.
3. You are taxed as an individual.
4. Accounts do not have to be disclosed to the public.
5. Easy to wind up.
6. Some tax advantages in the short-term.

Disadvantages

1. You are totally responsible and liable for all business losses. If the business goes bankrupt, so do you. Your creditors will be entitled (through the courts) to seize your personal, as well as business, possessions.
2. Does not have the status of, say, a limited company.

Partnerships

If two or more people go into business together without registering as a limited company or co-operative, they are forming a partnership. Again, you can enter into business like this without any legal formalities. However, you would be ill-advised to enter into a partnership without a formal partnership agreement, even more so if you are entering a partnership with a relative or close friend. The main reasons for this are to prevent severe disagreements about how the business should be operated and, should the partnership be wound up or sold, how the proceeds should be distributed. Remember all may seem rosy now but the best of friendships do not always last for ever, particularly when the friendship is exposed to the stresses and strains of running a business. The partnership agreement is there to protect you, your friendship and the business.

Partnership agreements should cover the following as applicable:

- Who is responsible for what?
- How many hours should each partner devote to the business?
- When and for how long can each partner take his/her holidays?

11

- How much can each partner draw out of the business?
- Will cheques to be drawn on the business's bank account require more than one partner's signature?
- How are major decisions to be reached? One vote per partner, or otherwise?
- Will there be any system for settling disputes between partners?
- How are the profits to be divided?
- How long should the partnership last?
- How much notice should be given by each partner if one wants to withdraw?
- How will the proceeds of the business be split up if the partnership is dissolved?
- Will there be a provision for accepting new partners into the business?
- What happens if one partner dies? Will the partnership be automatically dissolved?

The list could be almost endless! There are obviously all kinds of eventualities to be considered. Some partnership agreements, because of the nature of the business, are simple while others are more complex. What should be in your partnership agreement? Sit down with your partner(s) and work out the rough details and then go and see your solicitor for further advice.

Advantages

1. A good way of pooling complementary skills and knowledge
2. A way of starting a busines that requires more capital than you have at your disposal.
3. Can help share the work load and pressures associated with running a small business.
4. Other advantages similar to those of being a sole trader, except you are not in total control.

Disadvantages

1. Each partner is responsible for all business debts even if incurred by another partner.
2. There are some legal costs involved in drawing up a partnership agreement.
3. There is always a risk of personality clashes ruining the business.
4. The death or bankruptcy of any one partner, unless there are arrangements to the contrary, will automatically dissolve the partnership.
5. Can be difficult to expand the business by introducing new partners.

Limited company

The word limited in this context means your liability to repay the business's debts is 'limited' to the amount you have agreed to contribute to the business. Therefore, if the business goes bankrupt your personal possessions cannot be seized to pay the company's debts. This is, as you can imagine, the greatest attraction of forming a business in this way. However, there are a number of disadvantages (see later). A limited company has a legal identity which is separate from its shareholders. Like an individual, the company itself can enter into contracts with other organizations and individuals, sue and be sued and prosecuted, without involving its shareholders in the proceedings. Put simply, once a limited company is formed it exists in its own right and will remain in existence indefinitely, even if it ceases trading, until such time as action is taken to wind it up.

A limited company is formed with a minimum of two shareholders. A director must be appointed from the shareholders and a company secretary appointed (who can be an outside person). With a small business, this is usually the business's accountant or solicitor. Further to this, a limited company prior to registration must produce, and later adhere to, two principal documents, the Memorandum and Articles of Association. These are complex documents but can be simply summarized as follows. The Memorandum sets out the main objectives of the company; these are usually set quite wide to allow the company to sell or manufacture other products and services as it expands. The Memorandum also details the company's share capital. The Articles of Association set out additional rules by which the company will be governed; in many ways it is similar in content, but not style, to some aspects of a partnership agreement. To the lay person both documents can be incomprehensible as they tend to be full of 'legal jargon'. Most use standard phrases and therefore you will find that many Memorandums and Articles of Association are similar. As you can see, specialist advice from a solicitor is needed if you wish to form or 'buy' a limited company.

If you wish to have limited company status, there are two options open to you. You can buy one 'off the shelf' or start one from scratch. Buying one 'off the shelf' means buying an existing company that has no assets and is not trading. These 'off the shelf' companies are offered for sale in the UK by specialist companies known as company registration agents. They keep a stock of companies (that they have properly registered) suitable for a range of businesses. On transfer of the company to its new owners, all that has to be done is for the existing shareholders (nominees of the company registration agent) to resign, allowing the purchasers to become the new

11

shareholders and appoint directors. Because there is less 'legal work' to be done in buying a ready made company, it is the cheapest method. However, the way you intend to establish your business may demand that you start a company from scratch. If this is the case, expensive legal work can bump the costs from hundreds to thousands of pounds!

If you form a limited company, you as one of the directors will have the following responsibilities:

- You will have to attend properly conducted board meetings.
- You will have to disclose private interests and shares in the company.
- You must take reasonable steps to make sure you know what is 'going on' in your company and act in a manner that is honest and diligent.
- Accordingly, if you allow the company to trade whilst knowing it can't meet its debts you may well find yourself personally liable.
- You may not borrow money from the company.
- You cannot exceed the powers granted to you in the Articles of Association.
- You must be elected by the shareholders and, accordingly, you can be removed by them.

Advantages of being a limited company

1. Limited liability.
2. Higher level of status/improved image.
3. Capital may be increased by selling shares.
4. You will be an employee of the company and therefore entitled to Department of Social Security benefits (UK).
5. Management structure of the business is better defined.
6. The business is not affected if shareholders die or become bankrupt.
7. Disposal or acquisition of shares can easily be arranged.

Disadvantages

1. Limited liability status can be, for all intents and purposes, removed with the increasing practice of lending institutions asking for personal guarantees from directors and major shareholders.
2. Can be very costly to set up.
3. The business will have to make public their accounts. This means telling your competitors what your sales, costs, assets, liabilities were last year!
4. You will probably need continuing professional advice to meet your legal obligations as a limited company.

5. As an employee of the company you will have to pay tax as you earn.
6. You can only start trading after your company has been properly formed.

Co-operative

Setting up a co-operative is only suitable for those people wishing to set up in business who have a strong desire to adhere to and practise democratic/collectivist principles. The main characteristics of a co-operative are as follows:

- The business is owned and controlled by those working in it.
- Membership of the co-operative is usually open to all employees, but sometimes subject to special conditions.
- Profits are not shared on the basis of the amount of capital put into the business by an individual, rather, profits are distributed in proportion with the amount of work done by each member.

For further information, help and advice about co-operatives refer to Appendix: Sources of further information and advice .

11

Summary

Most retailers wish to become well known to their customers. It helps if a trading name can be selected and used to promote customer awareness and identification with the shop. If the shop becomes successful, you will want to protect that trading name. Therefore it is a good idea to explore the possibility of registering it as a trade mark. Equally, you should take care not to select a name or some other mark or symbol that is already registered by another business. Even if such a mark is not registered it is possible that the business concerned may take civil action against you under common law for 'passing off' as that business and trading on its goodwill.

Selecting an appropriate legel identity for your business is a matter for serious consideration. Each form has its own advantages and disadvantages. With a partnership, a detailed partnership agreement is a must. This is just as important even when the partners are relatives or close friends. All readers should consider the possible advantages of trading as a limited company. The costs and formalities, as discussed in this chapter, are certainly not prohibitive.

12   Keeping track and avoiding problems

The importance of keeping accounts □ Bookkeeping systems □ DIY systems: Variations on the analysed cash book □ Bookkeeping and VAT □ Electronic tills and bookkeeping □ Recording and keeping track of credit sales and purchases □ Final accounts □ Interpreting final accounts: are big problems on the way? □ Summary □ Appendix

The earlier chapters of this book dealt at length with carrying our research and making plans to ensure that your business gets off to a healthy start. Once up and running, your business will need to be kept on track. The key aim of this chapter is to help you think about and set up business systems to monitor your business's performance and to identify problems early enough for you to take corrective action and avert disaster. The idea is to manage events rather than events managing you!

The importance of keeping accounts

Many new small shops do not review their financial position until the end of their first year of trading when they are forced to produce profit figures for the Inland Revenue. This is far from satisfactory and any business operating in such a way will have survived by luck alone. Each week local and national newspapers are littered with unfortunate bankruptcies where the owner claimed not to know the 'true picture' until it was too late.

A good accounting system, besides meeting the requirements of the taxation authorities, should allow you to easily extract the necessary information to answer such questions as:

- What is my cash position now?
- What profit am I making?
- What are my overheads?
- What are my variable costs?
- How much do I owe?
- How much is owed to me?
- How much net working capital do I have at my disposal?
- What is the value of my fixed and current assets?

From your work with Chapters 5 and 6 you should now realize that the answers to these questions are crucial to cash flow projections and break even calculations – two very important decision-making tools to use when, for instance, you are considering a plan to increase sales by adopting a lower pricing level.

Setting up and keeping an accurate set of accounts is, therefore, the basis for making profitable business decisions and should not be seen as an after-hours chore for the benefit of the taxman!

Bookkeeping systems

The accounting process can be seen in two parts, the first developing and keeping an accurate, full and useful record of the business's financial activities and the second, the interpretation of those records. The first part is what most people refer to as bookkeeping and it is this that we will consider first.

The sole trader or partnership can exercise considerable freedom in the way they keep their books. In selecting which system to use you should consider the following factors:

- Simplicity. If you don't have bookkeeping experience you need to avoid complex systems. Do not waste your time by buying accounting text books. It is unlikely that your shop will need a complex sophisticated system involving double entry principles. If your business is going to be that big then it would be advisable to employ the skills of a suitably qualified accountant, leaving you free to make decisions on the information produced. Your job is to manage the business not learn the finer details of bookkeeping. The accounting system should be simple enough to be understood by yourself and anybody who may take over responsibility for the business while you are away on holiday or ill. In addition the bookkeeping process should not take up too much time, otherwise the danger is that the records will not be kept up-to-date.
- Usefulness. As mentioned above, one of the key reasons for keeping records is to extract useful information on which to base decisions. A system that is over-complex and not easily understood may not produce the information quickly enough to identify problems in time or to exploit profitable opportunities.

There are a number of 'bookkeeping systems' that can be used by the small business. These can be summarized as:

- The double entry method
- Off the shelf systems
- Computer systems
- The DIY system – the analysed cash book

The double entry method

I do not recommend this method for most small businesses because, although the principle is straightforward enough, the practice can be quite complex. It is only really suitable for the larger and more complex business and, even here, old manual systems are being replaced by computerized accounting packages. For those who may want an overview of the method read on, others may prefer to skip this section.

Most of you will have heard of the 'double entry' system but unfortunately much mystery surrounds it. It shouldn't, for the principle is elementary. In any business there are numerous transactions between buyer and seller and obviously each transaction has two sides. Each participant in a transaction both gives something and receives something. Hence, any business transaction can be recorded twice in the accounts of the business.

To take a simple example, if a shop buys in stock to the value of £5,000 and pays for it by cheque then it will give £5,000 from its bank account and receive £5,000 to its stock account. In bookkeeping the giving and receiving have special names. The account that 'gives' is credited and the account that receives is 'debited'. Therefore, in the above example the bank account would be credited £5,000 and the stock account debited £5,000. This will seem wrong to most people – you probably thought that the bank account should be debited by £5,000 as money has been paid out. The source of the confusion is that the statement of account that you see is part of the bank's accounts and not yours. Accordingly it is a mirror or reverse image of your own accounts. The bank has received (debited) a reduction in its liability to you (i.e. money it owes you) by giving (crediting) cash from its 'cash account'. The simple rule is that the debit and credit entries in the accounts of the person or business you deal with will be the opposite to debit and credit entries in your own accounts:

Business A	*Business B*
Buys stock for £5,000	Sells stock for £5,000
Debit stock account (the receiver)	Credit sales account (the giver)

12

Gives £5,000 cheque	Receives £5,000 cheque
Credit bank account (the giver)	Debit bank account (the receiver)

Both businesses make two entries into their accounts to record the one transaction and the advantage of the double entry can be readily seen that when credits and debits are totalled they will equal each other. If they don't, then there must have been a mistake in entry or calculations. As and when the accounts or books are 'balanced' any errors should be detected, ensuring accuracy.

Off the shelf systems

There are many companies producing bookkeeping systems for use by small shops. Such systems are available in 'book' or 'pack' form from most stationers. They range from a few pounds to three to four hundred pounds for the more complex systems. All come with instructions (some easier to understand than others!) and some include pre-printed stationery.

The obvious advantage of using this method is that it is ready made for you to use. However, if your business does not 'fit the system' you can have problems. Because of this, most small businesses adopt a modification of an off the shelf system, create their own, or use a flexible computer-based system.

If you consider this method as a possibility, shop around and look at each system in some detail before coming to a decision. Your accountant should be able indicate a choice of suitable systems for your business.

Computer-based accounting packages

If you are considering buying computer hardware for some other aspect of your business then it would be well worth considering the purchase of an accounting software package. If you are already familiar with other business software, you will find them relatively easy to operate. There are a number of 'cheap' accounting software packages available for the desk top micro. At the time of writing these start from as little as £50. The majority have the advantage of being 'user definable', a jargon term meaning that they can be easily adapted to suit the requirements of a particular business.

Alternatively, you can create your own accounting package using a spreadsheet based on a variation of the do-it-yourself system described in the next section. You will find the spreadsheet formulas for use on Super-Calc Spreadsheet versions two to four in Appendix 6.

If you have no experience of computers, you would be well advised to think carefully before deciding to purchase one. Although a complete business computing package, including hardware (monitor, disc drives and printer) and software (programs), can be acquired for less than a thousand pounds (the Amstrad range of business micro's being amongst the most popular in the UK), there are a number of factors to be taken into account.

1. A computer can save you an enormous amount of time and money if you and your staff know how to adapt it and use it in your type of business. However, there are many examples of small business people who bought expensive computers and found they could not afford the time or money to train themselves and their staff in the necessary skills, or found that the systems did not live up to the salesperson's promises, with the result that the expensive purchase never left its packaging! Therefore, you would be well advised to gain some appreciation of what is involved before coming to a decision. One cheap and effective way is to attend a short business computing course at your local college before you start in business.
2. Don't make the mistake of taking 'a sledge hammer to crack a nut'. Computers are only a really cost-effective investment when you have large amounts of information to process. Can your accounts be done more quickly, easily and cheaply with a calculator costing a few pounds and a note book?

DIY systems: variations on the analysed cash book

The analysed cash book is a simple but effective system for recording all cash coming into and out of a business. As such, it can be easily modified to suit the requirements of most businesses.

All you need to create your own analysed cash book is a large hard-bound book. You can buy books ready made for the job. You will find that each page is ruled and divided into columns ready for you to enter the receipt and payment headings applicable to your business. You use the left hand columns to record receipts and the right hand ones to record payments. An example of an analysed cash book appears in Fig. 12.1.

You can divide the receipts and payments sides of your cashbook into as many sections as you want. On the receipts (or cash in) if you sell some merchandise on credit you will wish to distinguish between money coming in from cash sales and money coming from customers settling all or part of their account. You will also need a column to record money coming from other sources, such as the occasional sale of fixed assets and capital injections into the business from loans or your personal bank account. The

RECEIPTS

Date	Details	Ref	Acc no.	Bank	Cash	Cash sales	Credit sales	Other	
Oct	Bal b/f			50.00	80.00				
1	Till	C6			110.45	110.45			
1	J Smith		45	40.00			40.00		
2	Till				114.98	114.98			
3	Cash From Bank			(98.00)	98.00				
5	Capital (Loan)			200.00				200.00	
6	Cash to Bank			90.00	(90.00)				
				282.00	313.43	225.43	40.00	200.00	

PAYMENTS

Date	Details	Chq. no.	Inv. no.	Bank	Cash	Stock	Misc.	Overheads	Drawings
Oct									
1	Brands Ltd	21	540	97.80		97.80			
1	Rent				60.00			60.00	
1	Stationery		45		5.46		5.46		
3	Advert	22	34	80.34			80.34		
4	Legal fees				75.90			75.90	
5	Brands Ltd		987		82.34	82.34			
6	Petrol	23		10.00			10.00		
6	Self				50.00				50.00
				188.14	273.70	180.14	95.80	135.90	50.00

Calculations check

Receipts:

From cash sales:	225.43	Stock:	180.14
From credit sales:	40.00	Misc:	95.80
From other:	200.00	Overheads:	135.90
	———	Drawings:	50.00
	465.43		———
Open bal. cash:	80.00		461.84
Open bal. bank:	50.00	Total:	461.84 (Bank & cash cols.)
	———		
	595.43		
Total bank & cash cols.	595.43		
	———		

Balances

	Bank	Cash
	282.00	313.43
	188.14	273.70
	———	———
	93.86	39.73

Note: Both the cash and bank balances should be checked against the actual amounts in the cash box and bank account and any shortages recorded.

Fig. 12.1 Analysed cash book

purpose of the column headed up 'Acc no.' is to identify the customer account that should be debited (reduction of customer's debt) when cash is collected from credit sales. The purpose of the column headed up 'Ref no.' (you may choose some other title) is to identify where the documentation such as invoices, till rolls, details of sales, etc. are to be found in your filing system (more on that subject later).

The rule applying to cheques received in payment is to count them as cash until they are transferred to the bank. When bankings are made, subtract the amount from the cash column and add the amount to the bank column. In Fig. 12.1 you can see how I transferred £98 to the bank on the 3 October and then transferred £90 back to the business's 'cash box' on the 6 October.

On the payments side you should have sections for items that involve frequent payments. For items where infrequent/occasional payment is made you would be advised to have at least one column for grouping all overheads (fixed costs) together and one for all variable or direct costs. This will make it easier when you wish to extract information to use such decision-making tools as break even analysis. Where payment is made by cheque you should record the cheque number. The column headed up 'Invoice number' is for recording your supplier's invoice number. This will help you to identify if, when and by what method a payment was made in the event of any enquiries. You may wish to add a further column headed up 'Reference no.' or 'File no.' to identify where a copy of the paid invoice or bill is to be found in your filing system.

Periodically you should total your cash book – weekly or monthly as is appropriate for your business. The purpose of this is partly to check your cash and bank balances and partly to verify the accuracy of your entries and calculations. First check your calculations as shown in Fig. 12.1. Then verify your cash and bank balances as follows.

- **Cash balance. Count your cash in hand at the end of the period. It should equal the difference between your net receipts and payments. If it doesn't, re-check your cash, entries in the cash book and calculations. The balance to carry forward to the next period is the *actual* cash balance.**
- **Bank balance. To verify the cash book bank balance with an actual bank statement do the following:**

  1. **To the last balance on the statement, add all monies paid in but not yet shown on the statement.**
  2. **Subtract all cheques drawn but not yet presented to the bank (i.e. shown on the statement).**

The result should match the balance shown in your cash book.

If the standard format of the cash book doesn't suit you, then try experimenting with variations on the theme. At the minimum, your system will have to have checks for accuracy built into it, be able to produce cash and bank balances and classify both receipts and expenditure according to the needs of your type of business.

Bookkeeping and VAT

(VAT is discussed in detail in Chapter 10.)

If you are going to be registered for VAT then you will need to modify the example in Fig. 12.1. The cash and bank columns are left unaltered, receipts and payments being entered inclusive of VAT. A VAT column is added to both the receipts and payments side to record VAT collected on sales and VAT paid on purchases. The amount, exclusive of VAT, is then entered in its appropriate column to show the true value of sales and cost of payments to the business.

Calculation of VAT payable to the Customs and Excise at the end of the period is a simple matter of subtracting total VAT paid from total VAT collected. However, if you buy or sell on credit then you must:

1. Add the VAT elements of invoices received but not paid and credit sales made but cash not received in the VAT period.
2. Discount the VAT paid and charged on payments made and cash received at the beginning of the period that relate to invoices and credit sales with tax points (dates of issue) in the previous VAT period. You will have already paid the VAT on those!

If you wish to separate total sales into VAT-rated and exempt products and services, you will have to add further columns to the receipt side of your cash book.

An example of a simple layout for a cash book to record VAT inputs (VAT on sales) and outputs (VAT on payments) is shown in Fig. 12.2 – again, it can be added to as desired.

An alternative layout

A simpler, but equally effective, layout is shown in Fig. 12.3. Analysis of receipts and purchases is still present but the cash bank columns for receipts and expenditure are combined. Receipts are shown as plus entries and expenditure as minus entries (in brackets). This layout has the advantage of immediately producing cash and bank balances without

Receipts

Date	Ref	Details	Bank	Cash	Sales Analysis			VAT
					Exempt	Zero	Standard	
Oct		Bal. b/f	100	100				
1	C4	Till		300	300	-	-	-
1	C5	Till		115	-	-	100	15
2	C6	J Smith	230			-	200	30
2	C7	Till		100	-	100	-	-
			330	615	300	100	300	45

Payments

Date	Ref	Details	Bank	Cash	Stock	Misc.	Over-heads	Draw-ings	VAT
Oct									
1	23	Brands Ltd	-	460	400	-	-	-	60
2	24	Cash & Carry	-	115	100	-	-	-	15
3	25	Brands Ltd	-	50	50	-	-	-	-
				625	550	-	-	-	75

Fig. 12.2 Simple layout for cash book to record VAT inputs and outputs: Example 1

recourse to the additional arithmetical checks associated with the previous layout shown. A spreadsheet version of this format is given (on spreadsheet file) in Appendix 6.

Electronic tills and bookkeeping

Modern electronic tills, ECRs (Electronic Cash Registers), can be bought for as little as £500. The purchase of one is highly recommended. Nearly all such tills have the following capabilities:

1. A price look up (PLU) facility. This allows you keep a record of the sales of individual items. Its principal use is in stock control and ordering which we will consider in some detail in the next chapter.
2. The ability to record the sale of merchandise in different groups and provide totals of each group on request. So that for instance sales may be recorded by:

Entry details			Balances			Receipts			Payments			
Date	Details	Reference or Chq. no	Cash	Bank	Total	Till Sales	Credit Sales	Other	Stock	O/heads	Other	Total
	Balances from acc¹ c/f:		80.00	50.00	130.00							.00
1/10	From till		110.45		110.45	110.45						.00
1/10	From J Smith			40.00	40.00		40.00					.00
1/10	Cash to Bank		(90.00)	90.00	.00							.00
1/10	To Brands cash/c			(97.80)	(97.80)				97.80			97.80
1/10	Rental payment		(60.00)		(60.00)					60.00		60.00
1/10	Stationery		(5.46)		(5.46)					5.46		5.46
2/10	From till		114.98		114.98	114.98						.00
3/10	Cash from bank		98.00	(98.00)	.00							.00
3/10	To Gazette (advert)			(80.34)	(80.34)					80.34		80.34
4/10	Legal fees		(75.90)		(75.90)					75.90		75.90
5/10	To Brands cash/c		(82.34)		(82.34)				82.34			82.34
5/10	Capital (loan)			200.00	200.00			200.00				.00
6/10	Petrol			(10.00)	(10.00)					10.00		10.00
6/10	Drawings for self		(50.00)		(50.00)						50.00	50.00
			39.73	93.86	133.59	225.43	40.00	200.00	180.14	231.70	50.00	461.84

Fig. 12.3   Simple layout for cash book to record VAT inputs and outputs: Example 2

- Individual line.
- Department (i.e. merchandise group).
- VAT classification.

3. Also an ECR can give:

- The sales taken in individual hours of the day.
- The number of customers served in a sales period.
- The total amount of money paid into customer credit accounts.
- The cash takings.
- The total amounts collected from the till for transferral to the safe or to the bank account.
- The total cash that should be in the till.
- The total of all sales transactions paid for by cheque.
- The total of all sales transactions paid for by credit card.

Clearly, the information that a modern ECR can record and summarize is of immense value to any retailer. The information can be used for everything from maintaining till security and minimizing the possibility of theft by the till operator, through providing valuable customer information, to efficient stock control. However, some ECRs on the market have limited functions and you would be well advised to check with the dealer that the model you are considering buying has at least the above mentioned capabilities. Other considerations when making the purchase are the reputation of the make and dealership in terms of reliability and the back up service. For instance, does the dealer offer free installation and initial training? Also importantly, does the dealer offer an immediate replacement (at the very least, same-day service is required) in the event of the ECR breaking down?

The use of ECRs in stock control, as already mentioned, will be considered in the next chapter. Here we will be concerned with matching systems to the ECR to maintain security at the till point and ease the process of bookkeeping.

It is possible for any sales assistant to be tempted to steal from the cash register. The best way of preventing this from happening is to have a good system for checking and controlling cash register transactions.

The basic strength of any such system is to be able to know, at any time, how much should be in the till. It is then a relatively simple task of counting the till contents (minus the float) and comparing the total with what should be in the till to determine whether the till is short or over. An ECR enables you to do this quite easily.

The total takings reading of an ECR can be reset to zero by taking what is known as a 'Z' read. The 'Z' read will give you details of the takings including the total monies taken (including cheques and credit vouchers) and the total cash remaining in the till since it was last reset. If you reset the till by taking a Z read at the beginning and end of each till operator's shift, then the 'Z' read will give details of all the transactions that occurred during that shift. Cashing up the till is then simply achieved by matching the cash in till read to the till contents (minus float).

An alternative to resetting the till every time you want to cash up is to take an 'X' reading at the beginning and end of each shift. The 'X' reading gives the same information as the 'Z' reading but does not reset the till. Subtraction of the opening reading from the closing reading will give the takings for each shift. To illustrate, if the total sales reading at the start of the shift is £1,000 and the total sales reading at the end of the shift is £1,500, then the money taken (inclusive of cheques and vouchers) should be £5,000. However, to simply obtain the cash in till figure there is no need to do this, unless a detailed sales breakdown for the shift or period of trading is required. The cash in till read on both 'X' and 'Z' readings will always be true. The only adjustment that needs to be made to this figure between shifts is to allow for cumulative till overages and shortages. A simple example of a system to monitor each sales assistant's till balances is given below:

	Cash in till read	Contents	Till	Operator
Williams	100.00	99.90	(0.10)	(0.10)
Brown	140.80	140.50	(0.30)	(0.20)
Smith	178.50	178.60	0.10	0.40

Assuming that the till was zeroed at the beginning of Williams' shift, the ten pence till shortage must be attributable to Williams. Brown manages to increase the till shortage from ten to thirty pence. Brown is therefore twenty pence short of her shift. Smith inherits a thirty pence till shortage, but by the end of the shift manages to turn it into a ten pence overage. Smith is, therefore, a total of forty pence over on her shift.

At first sight the problem of operating such a simple system is that there is no allowance for removal of money from the till. This can easily be rectified by adding a cash collection column to the till control sheet. The simple cashing up process at the end of each shift is as before, for the cash in till read will still be accurate because the ECR will automatically deduct monies paid out of the till from the running cash-taken total.

Such a simple system is attractive and would suffice for a shop not registered for VAT, or operating VAT retail schemes based on purchases rather than sales. The cash collections are simply transferred to the analysed cash book under the receipts from till column, and that is the end of that! But if you wanted to operate VAT Scheme F (see Chapter 11), which requires sales receipts to be classified as exempt, zero and standard rate, such a procedure fails to give the required information. That is, with most ECRs, the paid out read (cash collection) does not give the necessary breakdown of sales. The problem is not a large one and there are a number of alternative solutions.

To give just one possible method, details of the cash collections made from the till(s) can be held on a daily till control sheet prior to being analysed at the end of each day's trading (with the benefit of full 'X' readings). The full day's trading analysed for VAT content can then be transferred to the analysed cash book each evening.

The details of your till reconciliation procedures are up to you. The system you end up with should be designed to:

● Suit your business and VAT scheme.
● Have cross checks built into it to prevent mistakes.
● Ensure that only one sales assistant is responsible for the till in a given period.
● Be capable of reconciling the till readings with the till contents and cash collections for each till operator.

The format of your till control system will largely depend on whether you decide to zero the till:

● At the end of each shift
● Daily
● Weekly
● Monthly
● Quarterly

12

Each has its own advantages and disadvantages. Obviously zeroing the till at the end of each shift makes the cashing up process for each sales assistant an easy task. However, you will then have to add up all the reads taken to obtain daily or weekly takings. Some businesses prefer to zero the tills on a weekly basis. This has the advantage of allowing you, at any time of the week, to obtain a sales total in just a few seconds by taking an 'X' read. Also, all the main adjustments to the accounts are done on a weekly instead of daily basis. You could, of course, elect only to zero your till(s) at the end of each VAT period, therefore making the calculation of VAT output tax collected relatively easy. The decision should be taken with care. What ever you decide upon make sure the design:

- Suits your business and VAT scheme.
- Has cross checks built into it to detect clerical errors quickly.
- Ensures that all sales assistants' till balances can be accurately monitored.

Once the system is designed, put it through a dry run. Does it work as well as you anticipated? Are there any ways in which it can be fiddled? Above all, maintain till key security. When you purchase your ECR you will be given at least three types of key:

- An operator key, which will allow only normal customer transactions to be registered.
- An 'X' key which will allow X reads and till mistakes to be rectified.
- A 'Z' key which will allow 'Z' reads to be taken and till mistakes to be rectified.

It is obvious that sales assistants should never be allowed access to the 'Z' key and use of the 'X' key should be tightly controlled. There are two main ways the till can be directly fiddled. The first is by the operator zeroing the till part way through a shift and pocketing the takings up to that point. Even if the 'Z' key is kept secure, it is possible an operator may have obtained a duplicate or master key from elsewhere. This is easy enough to detect because all 'Z' readings are automatically numbered by the till. Secondly, and more common, the till operator can defraud you by erasing takings from the till by using the till in the void mode. To prevent this happening you should insist that all mistakes that have to be corrected with the void key are carried out by yourself or, at the very least, checked by another (preferably) senior sales assistant. Each void should be recorded on a 'void sheet'. The void sheet should be totalled and matched against the read of total voids given on the X reading. Any discrepancy might indicate improper use of the void capability on the ECR.

- If you are going to employ staff, a sensible and detailed list of rules and regulations will help maintain both till security and staff management relations. There is nothing guaranteed to sour staff relations more than a till that has had a number of staff on it without any proper till balances being taken, being down £5 at the end of the day. In such a situation *everybody* feels under suspicion.

Recording and keeping track of credit sales and purchases

For a shop trading solely on a cash or cheque basis, the analysed cash book will meet most of its bookkeeping needs. However, if you are making credit sales and purchases you will be well advised to keep additional records. The purpose being to:

- Monitor the amount outstanding on individual accounts.
- Check statements of your account with suppliers.
- Enable you to identify slow payers and send out reminders.
- Rapidly calculate, at any one time, the amount owed to you by debtors and the amount owed by you to creditors.

One simple way to provide these additional records is to buy two files or suitable boxes and a pack of plain stiff white cards of a suitable size. Create one file for creditors (people who you buy on credit from) and one for debtors (people who buy on credit from you). Using the sheets of white card open an 'account' for each debtor and creditor (as shown in Fig. 12.4).

As you make credit sales or purchases enter the necessary details into each account. When cash or cheques are received or sent, enter the details first in your cash book and then transfer the details into each account.

Weekly checks of your debtors followed by speedy reminders by phone or letter as required should reduce the problem of slow payers. To keep running totals of debts outstanding and total credit sales you may wish to keep a separate summary. In any case you should check on a regular basis the average number of days your debtors are taking to pay. This is the relatively simple matter of using the calculation below.

$$\text{Average days' credit taken} = \frac{\text{Total debtors' accounts}}{\text{Total credit sales for the period}} \times \text{Number of days in the period}$$

Example:

Period: October, 31 days

$$\text{Average days' credit taken} = \frac{£2,780}{£2,500} \times 31$$

$$= 35 \text{ days}$$

You should note the trend in the average collection period. If it is steadily worsening then you should investigate quickly and take necessary action, otherwise very serious cash flow problems could be on their way!

Example of a debtor account card

Date opened: 1/10
Name: J Smith
Tel: 14356

Account No: 45
Address: 12 John Street, Langton FY5 5AD
Credit limiit: £100.00
Terms: 30 days

Date	Details	Received	Returns	Paid Cash	Paid Chq.	Bal	Comments
1/10	Open/bal	–	–	–	–		
1/10	Goods	£25.56	–	–	–	25.56	
3/10	Payment	–	–	10.00	–	15.56	
1/11	Letter	–	–	–	–	15.56	Reminder sent
6/11	Payment	£15.56	–	–	–		

Example of a creditor account card

Date opened: 1/10
Name: Melody Ltd
Tel: 23734

Account No: 5
Address: 12 Cocker Street, Langton FY5 9AD
Credit limit: £500.00
Terms: 30 days

Date	Details	Received	Returns	Paid Cash	Paid Chq.	Bal	Comments
1/10	Open/bal	–	–	–	–		
1/10	Goods	£515.00	–	–	–	515.00	
3/10	Goods ret	–	15.00	–	–	500.00	Credit note Rec.
1/11	Payment		–	500.00	–	–	
6/11	Goods	£400.00	–	–	–	400.00	

Note: Both account cards can be modified to provide extra detail. For example, the creditor's card above would benefit from having columns to record the invoice/delivery note number and a file reference number.

Fig. 12.4 Examples of debtor and creditor account cards

You should also compare the number of days' credit taken by your debtors with your actual credit terms. If you offer 30-day payment terms and your customers are taking 50 days on average to pay, then obviously your credit control needs to be tightened up. Remember, major cash flow problems are not caused by the occurrence of bad debts (those which are never paid) but by the growth of slow payers.

Similarly, you should periodically check the average number of days' credit you take from your suppliers – see below.

$$\text{Average days' credit taken} = \frac{\text{Total creditors' accounts}}{\text{Total credit purchases for the period}} \times \frac{\text{Number of days in the period}}{}$$

Your aim is simple (but not so easy to achieve): to reduce the days taken to collect debts while increasing the days' credit taken from suppliers. The more successful you are in this direction, the lower your net working capital requirements will be (see Chapter 6).

Final accounts

To answer such questions as:

- What is my net profit?
- What is my gross profit?
- What costs have I incurred?
- What is the value of the assets my business possesses?
- What is my net working capital?
- What are my total current liabilities (short term debts)?
- What is the total value of my current assets? etc.

You will have to prepare a set of final accounts which, after interpretation, will provide quite a comprehensive picture of your business. They consist of two summaries of the business's financial performance and position:

- The profit and loss account: details the business's actual sales, costs and profits over a certain period of time.
- The balance sheet: details what the business has (assets) and what it owes (liabilities) at one particular moment in time.

Let's look at each in turn.

The profit and loss account

This gives a summary of the business's sales and costs over a period of time, showing the gross and net profit (or loss) that has been achieved. Figure 12.5 shows an example of a profit and loss account for a small retailing business.

How to compile your profit and loss account

1. Sales for the period is the total of all cash and credit sales (excluding VAT). To obtain this, add together:

	£	£
Sales		120,000
Cost of Sales		
Opening stock:	17,000	
Purchases:	82,000	
Available to sell in the period:	99,000	
Less Closing stock (goods left unsold):	21,000	
Cost of goods sold:		78,000
Gross Profit		42,000
Overheads		
Rent:	5,000	
Electricity:	2,000	
Maintenance:	1,000	
Transport:	2,000	
General selling expenses:	2,500	
General:	1,500	
Depreciation:	3,000	
Loan interest:	5,000	
Total overheads:		22,000
Net profit before tax:		20,000

Fig. 12.5   Profit and loss account: 1/11/88 to 31/10/89

- The total of all credit sales invoiced in the period (less the ex VAT value of any goods returned) and
- All cash sales for the period.

2. Opening and closing stocks are obtained from actual physical stock counts at the beginning and end of the period. The stock should be valued at cost price. (There are various valuation methods available – consult your accountant.)
3. All purchases invoiced in the period are totalled, excluding VAT. Merchandise returned is subtracted from the total before entering them in the profit and loss account.
4. The cost of goods sold is calculated by working out what was available to sell at cost price (opening stock plus purchases in the period) minus what you are left with at the end of the period (closing stock). The value of your closing stock is not a cost because it has not been used in the period. Rather it is something you have and is therefore an asset (see Chapter 5).

5. Overheads are again totalled for the period from your cash book/ bookkeeping system and entered in the profit and loss account exclusive of VAT. However, where you have paid out for overheads in advance of their use, for example, three months' rent in advance, just before you closed your accounts for the period, you should not include them in the profit and loss account. This is a 'pre-payment' for an overhead you have not yet used and is, therefore, an asset (something that you have) and not a cost. When you open up a new cash book for the next accounting period the amount estimated as pre-payment in the last accounting period should be entered in as an opening balance in the appropriate column, otherwise you will fail to record the payment as a cost in the next accounting period (the one in which it will be incurred). Alternatively you could keep a separate record of pre-payments.

Where you have used an overhead but not yet been billed, for example you could have used two months' electricity (as it is paid quarterly you will not receive a bill for at least another month), you should estimate the amount used in the period and add it to the costs for the P/L account. When you open a new cash book for the next period the amount estimated should be shown as an opening negative balance in the 'electricity' column, otherwise you will end up double-counting the cost in the next accounting period when you actually receive the electricity bill for the full quarter. Alternatively, you could keep a separate record of the 'accruals' (costs incurred but not yet invoiced/billed).

The thing to remember is that the profit and loss account sets out to try and match sales and costs for a certain time period regardless of whether money has been received and paid out. The sales figure at the top of the account refers to the value of products and services that have been *received* by customers and the costs detailed should refer to the value of materials, stocks and services *used* in the period.

12

Compiling the balance sheet

The balance sheet is a list of items that you own (called assets) and the types/sources of finance you used to fund those assets (called liabilities). Or to put it more simply, a list of where you got the money from and a list of what you did with it. Your total liabilities will always equal your total assets because what you own must have been paid for at some stage. The two lists will, of course, be constantly changing as the business acquires or disposes of its assets, acquires loans, depreciates its assets, retains more profit in the business or draws on its capital, and so on. Therefore, a balance sheet is like a snapshot – it only relates to one single moment in time. Let's take a snapshot of an imaginary business's financial position at its start up.

The owner starts a business on 1 October 1988 with £10,000 of his or her own money and a £7,000 loan. Of this £7,000 is used to acquire premises, £2,000 to acquire stock and £1,000 as payment in advance for the rental of equipment. He or she acquires a further £3,000 of stock on credit from a supplier. To obtain a clearer picture let's make two lists, one for assets and one for liabilities:

Assets

Premises:	£7,000	
Cash:	£7,000	(i.e. started with £17,000, spent £10,000)
Stock:	£5,000	(i.e. bought £2,000 and acquired a further £3,000 on credit, none sold so stock level will be £5,000)
Pre-payments:	£1,000	(i.e. rental in advance)
	£20,000	

Liabilities

Creditors:	£3,000	(i.e. stock bought on credit)
Loan:	£7,000	
Capital:	£10,000	
	£20,000	

It should come as no great surprise that the two lists balance. However, in their present form they are not as informative as they could be. Let's transfer them to a properly laid out balance sheet (Fig. 12.6).

In Fig. 12.6, showing the re-drawn balance sheet, we have, by separating the assets and liabilities into sections, gained a more accurate picture of the business. A further look at the balance sheet may reveal to you the reasoning that has been applied in dividing up and listing the assets and liabilities. Look at it again and you will notice that both the assets and liabilities have been ranked in order of their permanence (i.e. starting with those that are most difficult to turn into cash). Therefore, assets start with those that are 'fixed' and move on to those that are 'current'. Within each section, individual items are also listed in order of their permanence, e.g., stock is listed before cash. Let's look at each section in more detail.

Assets

Fixed assets. We have already discussed at some length the characteristics of fixed assets in Chapter 6. They are items with a 'measurable money value' that the business has not bought for resale and are expected to be kept for a long period of time (usually more than a year). Typical examples are premises, equipment, cars, vans, etc. However, do not make the mistake of classifying items that have been acquired on some form of rental or leasing agreement: such 'assets' do not belong to you – they are assets of the leasing or rental company.

As discussed in Chapter 6, the value of fixed assets can change. If there has been a provision in the profit and loss account for depreciation then this figure must be deducted from the previous value of the fixed assets (a process known as 'writing down'). As the money equivalent of the depreciation figure has not actually left the business (it hasn't been paid out to anybody!), the amount by which the fixed assets have been written down will still be present in one or a range of the other assets of the business. In other words, the balance between assets and liabilities will not be affected.

Fixed assets:		
Premises:		7,000
Current assets:		
Stock:	5,000	
Pre-payments:	1,000	
Cash-in-hand:	7,000	
		13,000
Current liabilities:		
Creditors:	3,000	
Net working capital:		10,000
(current assets – current liabilities)		
Net assets employed:		17,000
Financed by:		
Bank loan:		7,000
Owner's capital introduced:		10,000
		17,000

Fig. 12.6   Balance sheet at 1 October 1988

Current assets. These are assets that have a short life; typical items listed under this heading are as follows:

- Stock holdings for resale (figure is obtained by an actual stock take).
- Prepayments: these are bills for services in advance of their use. As they have not been used, they are not costs but assets.
- Debtors: people who owe you money. For example, sales on credit that you have not collected the money on. Calculated by adding together all the outstanding balances on your debtor account cards.
- Cash-in-hand is the sum of your cash and bank balances at the time the balance sheet is compiled.

Liabilities

These are split into long-term liabilities (listed under 'financed by') and short-term liabilities (listed under 'current liabilities').

Current liabilities. These are loans of money that can be called in at short notice by the lender. Typical items listed under this heading are:

- Accruals: provision for services used but not yet invoiced for.
- Creditors: the value of outstanding invoices and bills to be paid. Calculated by adding together all the outstanding balances on your creditor accounts.
- Overdrafts, outstanding balances on credit cards and the balance of outstanding loans.

Net working capital. This is the difference between total current assets and total current liabilities. The importance and nature of working capital has already been fully discussed in Chapter 6. The figure represents the total amount of money the business is presently having to invest 'out of it's own pocket' in its day-to-day operations. The other part of gross working capital (i.e. total current assets) is funded by current liabilities.

Net assets employed. This gives the total value of all the assets employed in the business, after allowing for current liabilities.

Financed by. This section shows where the money came from to finance the acquisition of the total net assets of the business. There are a number of sources of finance:

1. Owner's equity (i.e. the amount the owner has invested in the business from his/her personal funds) is made up of:

- Owner's capital introduced. This shows the money put into the business by the owner. If the business is a limited company this will read 'share capital'.
- 'Paper profits'. The owner's capital investment (equity) can be increased by a 'paper profit' resulting from the revaluation of fixed assets. For example, if premises increase in value from £30,000 to £35,000, then the owner's holding in the business will increase by £5,000. A reduction in the owner's equity will occur where there is a revaluation of fixed assets downwards. However, depreciation of fixed assets accounted for in the profit and los account will not affect the owner's equity. As noted above, the actual total sum of depreciation will not have physically left the business and accordingly will be absorbed in the financing of other assets of the business.

2. Profits retained. It is not the case that profits are always withdrawn from the business; often they are left to provide the necessary capital to allow it to grow. This figure is calculated simply by taking the net profit figure and subtracting your personal drawings from the business (as recorded in your cash book). The residual element is the profit that has been retained in the business (unless there are further drawings on profit to make repayments (net of interest) on long-term loans). Where the owner has withdrawn more than the net profit, he or she will have withdrawn part of the capital they introduced into the business. This is usually termed 'drawings on capital' or some like term. Similarly, where the business make a loss the owner's capital will be reduced.

3. Long-term loans. These include such items as bank loans and hire purchase agreements. The figures shown here are the actual balances outstanding net of interest (the interest being a cost and therefore accounted for in the profit and loss account).

12

To check that you have understood what has been discussed so far about the profit and loss account and the balance sheet, try and answer the following questions. The answers appear in the appendix at the end of the chapter.

Today is 31 October 1988. John, a friend of yours, has come round to see you for some help. He thought he would have a go at producing his own first set of final accounts. He has got as far as producing the following information. The trouble is that it is all jumbled up and he doesn't know what to do next. Can you produce a profit and loss account and balance sheet for John?

1. **Started business on 1 November 1987.**
2. **Capital introduced at the start of the business: £16,000.**
3. **Sales for the period: £60,000.**

4. **Purchases of stock for the period: £40,000.**
5. **Closing stock figure: £5,000.**
6. **Debtors: £1,000.**
7. **Creditors: £3,000.**
8. **Cash-in-hand: £1,000.**
9. **Drawings: £12,000.**
10. **Overheads: £10,000.**
11. **Depreciation of fixtures and fittings: £1,000.**
12. **Shop premises: £10,000.**
13. **Initial cost of fixtures and fittings: £5,000.**

Use the profit and loss account and balance sheet blanks in Fig. 12.7.

Profit and loss account: period:

	£	£
Sales:		
Cost of sales:		
Purchases:		
Closing stock:	_____	
Cost of sales:		_____
Gross profit:		
Overheads:		
Depreciation:	_____	
		_____
Net profit before taxes:		
Drawings:		_____
		_____

Balance sheet at _____

	£	£	£
Fixed assets:			
Current assets:			
Current liabilities:			
Creditors:		_____	
Net working capital:			_____
Net assets employed:			_____

Financed by:
Bank loan:
Owner's capital introduced: _____

Fig. 12.7   Profit and loss account and balance sheet blanks

- **If you have the necessary information, compile a balance sheet of how your business will look at start up. To gain further practice and understanding, try to compile a forecast of how your business will look and perform at various stages in its first year. Start with a projected profit and loss account, move on to produce a cash flow forecast and then, finally, draw up a projected balance sheet. Use the worked example at the end of Chapter 6 as a guide.**

Interpreting final accounts: are big problems on the way?

There are a number of techniques you can use to interpret final accounts. Their use serves two purposes: to monitor and control your business and to assess the performance of a business that you may be considering buying (see Chapter 9). What follows is an overview of the main techniques of interpretation.

Gross profit percentage margin

$$\frac{\text{Gross profit}}{\text{Sales}} \times 100$$

Easily calculated, and can be compared to averages for the type of business concerned and also to previous years.

Net profit as a percentage of sales

$$\frac{\text{Net profit}}{\text{Sales}} \times 100$$

Percentage return on capital employed

$$\frac{\text{Net profit}}{\text{Net assets}} \times 100$$

A useful calculation. It should be compared with the pre-tax interest your money could earn if invested in another venture. Useful for assessing investment opportunities.

Percentage analysis of costs

$$\frac{\text{Item cost}}{\text{Total costs}} \times 100$$

Calculate each major cost item in the profit and loss account as a percentage of total costs. Watch for any major variation between periods. Find out the reason.

Net working capital as a percentage of sales

$$\frac{\text{Net working capital}}{\text{Sales}} \times 100$$

This will give an estimate of the amount of working capital to fund a higher level of sales. For example:

$$\frac{\text{£4,000}}{\text{£20,000}} \times 100 = 20\%$$

Therefore, a rough estimate of the net working capital to finance a higher level of sales, say £24,000, can be obtained by calculating 20% of £24,000, indicating that an increase in net working capital would be required from £4,000 to £4,800.

Liquidity ratios

The current ratio

$$\frac{\text{Current assets}}{\text{Current liabilities}}$$

This should be greater than 1. If it is below 1, it means that the business will not be able to meet its current liabilities if they are called in.

The acid test or 'quick ratio'

$$\frac{\text{Current assets} - (\text{Stocks and work in progress})}{\text{Current liabilities}}$$

As this ratio excludes assets that are not quickly convertible into cash, it provides a more accurate picture of whether the business can meet its day-to-day commitments. If this figure is below 1 or falling, it strongly indicates that there are serious cash flow problems and that the business may be insolvent.

The number of times working capital has circulated in the business in a given period

This is good indicator of the efficiency of the business. The result of the calculation below can be compared to previous years and to other similar businesses. The faster the circulation of working capital, probably the more efficiently the business uses its resources. An increase in the circulation of working capital can be brought about by a reduction in net working capital requirements, an increase in sales with a lower than proportionate increase in net working capital, or both.

$$\text{Number of times NWC has circulated} = \frac{\text{Sales for period}}{\text{Net working capital}}$$

Rate of stock turn

The importance of this figure has been fully discussed in Chapter 6. It is a measure of how often average stocks have been turned over (sold) in a given period. The figures should be compared over time and with performance standards for your business.

Note: If you are reviewing final accounts with the view to deciding whether to buy a business, carefully checkout any suspicious deviations in rates of stock turn. Manipulation of closing stocks upwards can produce an artificially high profit figure.

Days' credit given and credit taken

These should be monitored regularly. The techniques have already been covered in this chapter.

To gain some practice in the use of these interpretation techniques, apply them to John's final accounts you compiled in the previous section. To give you something to compare the results with, assume that the type of business John is involved in gives an average gross margin of 45 per cent and a rate of stock turn of 14. Also assume that John sells all of his goods on 30-day credit terms. You will find my answer in the Appendix at the end of this chapter.

Summary

It is inviting disaster to start trading without good systems to give quick and accurate information about the financial health of your business. You will need such information to identify and act on problems before they become unmanageable and to react quickly to changing market conditions. The secret of producing such information is a simple but effective bookkeeping system that is regularly updated and analysed. The purchase of a modern electronic cash register is strongly advised. Your profit and cash position should be monitored at regular intervals and compared to your previous projections. Close monitoring of debtors (if appropriate) is required to avert cash flow problems.

To ensure smooth performance of your business, try and plan for all eventualities and have systems to identify and act on routine problems.

Appendix

Answers: The financial picture for John

Profit and loss account: period:

	£	£
Sales:		60,000
Cost of sales:		
Purchases:	40,000	
Closing stock:	5,000	
Cost of sales:		35,000
Gross profit:		25,000
Overheads:	10,000	
Depreciation:	1,000	
		11,000
Net profit before taxes:		14,000
Drawings:		12,000
Retained profits:		2,000

Balance sheet.   Date:

Fixed assets:

	£	£	£
	Cost	Depreciation	Net
Premises:	10,000	–	10,000
Fixtures & Fittings:	5,000	1,000	4,000

Current assets:

Stock:	5,000	
Debtors:	1,000	
Cash-in-hand:	1,000	

Current liabilities:		7,000
Creditors:		3,000
Net working capital:		4,000
Net assets employed:		18,000

Financed by:

Owner's capital introduced:	16,000	
Retained profits:	2,000	
		18,000

12

Analysis

Gross margin = 42%
Net margin = 23%
Return on capital employed = 78%

Current ratio: 2.3
Acid test: 0.66
Rate of stock turn: 7

John is making a good rate of return on the capital invested – his next best alternative might be a building society account at a rate of return of ten per cent. Just looking at his percentage margin it looks like he is doing very well, the average for his trade being 45 per cent. However, when you take into account his rate of stock turn which is half what his competition is doing things don't look too good. A number of things could be happening here:

- He is carrying too much stock, which might be the result of poor buying or carrying the wrong stock or too wide a range.
- He is charging too much for his goods, attempting to make too much unit gross profit, at the expense of sales.

If we now turn our attention to the balance sheet, we can see an even worse picture unfolding:

Current ratio: 2.3 is acceptable, but ...
The acid test reveals a ratio of less than 1 : 0.66, which means that the business could be approaching insolvency! There must be serious cash flow problems on the way, or already there. John certainly needs to produce a cash flow forecast and take some remedial action quickly. He should perhaps be trying to retain more profit in the business or, since he has good equity in the business, taking a medium-term loan to finance 'hard core' working capital. In the longer term, if he changes his trading policy and increases his rate of stock turn, he should bring down his working capital requirements.

Let's now turn our attention to number of days' credit taken and given:

Days taken = 31 from creditors
Days given = 18 to debtors

There are no problems here, he pays his bills on time and gets the money in from credit sales well – and before time.

- Although this is very much an artificial example and, in many ways unrealistic, it does show the benefit of using these ratios.

13   Buying, stock control and ordering systems

Stock assortment policy: model stock plans □ Selecting suppliers □ Working out a purchasing budget □ Buying in bulk □ Monitoring sales and ordering systems □ Stocking for profit □ Checking for and controlling stock losses □ Summary

Stock assortment policy: model stock plans

Your shop is not going to be successful unless the right merchandise is bought in and offered for sale. As with all major decisions, deciding what to stock should be largely determined by what you know about your targeted customers. Chapter 3 should have helped you to gather the necessary information on this count. In the case of buying an existing shop, further information will be gleaned from the existing proprietor. Once trading has started, sales information (if collected and studied in detail) will provide an excellent basis for further decision-making in this area.

In addition to the information obtained from the vendor, newcomers to a particular retail trade will gain an insight into the broad ranges of merchandise to be carried by reference to the *Retail Business Monitor*. This type of information has already be used to make detailed break even calculations based on sales and profit margins (see Chapter 5). The *Monitor* gives the principal merchandise groups and their percentages of total retail sales for many different types of retail operation.

After decisions have been made relating to broad merchandise groups, you will be in the position to consider the more detailed question of how many and which merchandise lines to stock in each group. Again much valuable information can be obtained from the vendor and studying trade publications. However, because even a small convenience store can carry literally thousands of different lines, to prevent instant confusion, the best way forward is to decide what your guiding principles will be in relation to stock assortment.

Firstly, are you going to go for depth or width in assortment? A wide ranging stock assortment describes a ranging policy that includes a large variety of products, but not necessarily a deep selection of colours, sizes, brands, etc. for each type of product offered for sale. For instance, a small grocery store stocking the full range of canned vegetables from peas to asparagus, but only offering one or two brands and sizes in each category would have a wide stock assortment but have little depth. Where a deep-ranging policy is operated, a large and comprehensive choice of brands colours, sizes, etc. is offered. Deep-ranging is typically found in specialist shops where, by definition, the number of products and groups of products offered for sale are limited. To give some examples: Sock Shop is an extreme case of deep-ranging policy; a delicatessen is likely to have comprehensive depth in cooked meats, whereas a convenience store is only likely to carry a few pre-packed, demand lines in this merchandise group.

In practice, you will have to strive for a balance between width and depth in your assortment policy. The two limiting factors to the variety you can offer are, quite simply, the finite sales space available and the size of your purchasing budget. Care must be taken to develop a balance that will match customer expectations and be in keeping with the desired image you wish to project (i.e. your 'unique selling proposition' developed in Chapter 3).

Once broad guiding principles have been established, the task is to determine the principal demand lines within each group. Research has shown that roughly 80 per cent of the sales of any retail outlet will come from only 20 per cent of the lines carried! Obviously, these lines need identifying. These will form the back-bone of your stock range and, as such, the basis of your model stock plan. You can start building in the detail of your stock plan by asking to what degree other products are related in the customer's mind to the demand lines stocked. Continue to do this until a suitable balance of width and depth in stock assortment is achieved.

Where there is no previous sales information to work on, the task of deciding on a model stock plan is difficult. If you find yourself in this position because either you are opening a shop from scratch or the previous owner never kept detailed order-sales information (by no means uncommon!), then you will have to rely on market research (Chapter 3) or suggested model stock plans provided by your suppliers. One of the many advantages of dealing direct with manufacturers or belonging to a voluntary group such as Spar, is that through their detailed knowledge of the market they can identify the demand lines within their ranges and build a stock plan around these fast movers for you. The main problem with this approach though, is that the information on which the merchandise planning is based is derived from regional and national sales information. Unfortunately the market you serve may be far from typical. Sometime ago, in developing the confectionery stocking plan in a small shop, I took the sales representative's advice on stock assortment. In the main it worked well, but the sales of one of their national leading brands was dismal – to say the least. It took me three months to clear six outers (boxes) of this merchandise that the representative assured me would 'move off the shelves' in the space of two weeks! This should serve as a warning: never let sales representatives make all the decision and do not be over-tempted by special offers.

Once trading, detailed analysis of sales will allow you to steadily refine your model stock plan to maximize sales and profit. We will consider how to do this later on in the chapter.

Selecting suppliers

The choice confronting most retailers is whether to deal with one or a combination of the following:

- Cash and carry warehouse and the more traditional wholesalers.
- Voluntary group wholesalers (see Chapter 1).
- Direct with manufacturers.

In the 1950s, pressure from the emerging supermarkets and other multiple chains in all areas of retailing forced change on the traditional wholesaler or 'middleman'. Some, as already discussed, formed into voluntary groups such as Spar, Londis, VG, etc. and others radically changed their selling approach and became what are now loosely referred to as cash and carrys.

The location and types of cash and carrys in your area can be found by refrence to the *Yellow Pages* and commercial directories. To trade with a cash and carry all you will need is some proof (e.g. business cheque book, letterheads, etc.) that you are in business, or intending to start a business. The cash and carry is similar to a supermarket in the way it operates. The warehouse is usually laid out in aisles, you select the stock you require and take it to the payment point.

With food cash and carrys, for example, the merchandise is sold in quantities ranging from 12 to 48 per box (more commonly referred to as 'outers'). The main advantage of dealing with a cash and carry is that there is no minimum order requirement; you can buy as few or as many outers as you wish on each visit. The main disadvantages are:

- You will usually pay a higher cost price than if dealing direct with the manufacturer.
- Valuable time is taken up travelling to and from the cash and carry.
- You incur the transport costs.
- You will not necessarily get the same level of advice and service provided by manufacturers and voluntary group wholesalers.

13

If you are going to use cash and carrys, shop around for the best prices: their price competitiveness varies enormously. For example, I dealt direct with the manufactuerers for my soft drinks supplies, but when one of the deliveries was late, I was forced to visit my local cash and carry to buy in stocks of Coca-Cola. On examining their prices, I found that I could have bought the stock cheaper at my local supermarket! The opposite can be true: in my area I found it more profitable to buy crisps from the cash and carry than direct from the manufacturer.

Dealing direct with manufacturers is often better than buying in from cash and carrys, the main draw-back being that you will have to buy in reasonable bulk. The minimum order is usually set around 20 to 30 outers. Some manufactuers also stipulate that you must place an order every month or six weeks to keep open your account with them. One of the principal advantages of opening an account with a manufacturer is that you will usually have 30 days from the invoice date to pay. As such, though, you will be required to provide references (e.g. a reference from your bank is ideal) to confirm that you will be able to meet payments. The other advantages of dealing direct are:

- Often excellent advice can be obtained on stock planning and merchandise layout.
- Often free display fixtures and advertising material can be obtained.
- No time is wasted by having to pick up the order yourself.
- Transport costs are usually paid by the manufacturer.
- Most importantly, the cost prices are usually more competitive than those found in cash and carrys.

In selecting suppliers, you should consider the following factors/ questions:

- How frequently do they deliver?
- What are their cost prices?
- What is the minimum order that can be placed?
- What discounts are offered?
- What transport and time costs will be involved?
- What is the depth and width of their range?
- What is the quality of their range?
- How reliable are they at delivering on time?
- Do they often suffer from out-of-stock situations?
- What are the payment terms?
- Does the merchandise offered meet your standards of quality? On this point it is worth noting that the success of Marks & Spencer, perhaps

the most envied multiple on the high street, has been built on careful selection of suppliers on the basis of quality.
● What additional services do they offer?

Working out a purchasing budget

In planning ahead it is important to know how much you will have to allocate for the purchase of stock on a monthly or weekly basis. There are two ways to arrive at a merchandise budget. The first, and least complicated, is the one used in the cash flow example in Chapter 6. This is where the budget is derived from the rate of stock turn and the sales forecast. For example, given a rate of stock turn of 12 per annum, a store would have to carry one month's stock in hand. The stock will turn over (i.e. be sold) every month. The stock bought in one month will have to support the following month's sales. Therefore, the merchandise budget for November would be calculated to support December's sales, as illustrated in Fig. 13.1.

	Nov	Dec	Jan	Feb	Mar
Sales Forecast:	10,000	15,000	12,000	10,000	8,000
Merchandise Budget					
@ Retail price:	15,000	12,000	10,000	8,000	?
@ Cost price:	11,250	9,000	7,500	6,000	?
(less a 25% margin)					

This example assumes an RST of 12 and a gross margin of 25%.

Fig. 13.1 Calculating a merchandise budget

As can be clearly seen from the example in Fig. 13.1, this method is easy to operate. The only problem is that it assumes that you will wish to manage your stock levels so that the stock holding to sales ratio (i.e. RST) remains exactly constant throughout the course of the year. This is slightly unreal and if taken to the extreme is tantamount to saying that an RST is some sort of commandment – that shalt not be broken! In reality, you will wish to build stock holdings past the norm in preparation for peak sales periods and pare them down below norm in sales' troughs. A more accurate (and possibly realistic) method of compiling a stock purchasing budget is to take into account what you have in stock to start off with (opening stock) and what you want to end up with (closing stock). The calculation, known as 'open to buy', is simply:

Planned sales at retail for the coming period
(i.e. what you want to buy in to sell in the coming period)

Plus

Planned closing stock at retail at the end of the period.
(i.e. what you want to end up with)

Minus

Opening stock at retail at the beginning of the period
(i.e. what you have alredy got)

Minus

Planned profit margin

Equals

Open to buy at cost

The open to buy method is illustrated in the example given in Fig. 13.2. As before, the basis for the calculation is the sales forecast. The desired planned closing stocks are derived partly from the expected rate of stock turn and the sales pattern. As already pointed out, the RST is an average ratio of stock holding to sales throughout the year. The example assumes that it is prudent to build stocks past the average at certain times in the year to meet demand in peak sales periods.

Buying in bulk

It is often the case that buying in bulk will enable you to buy at lower cost prices. By taking this option you will certainly increase your gross profits. There is, however, a catch – the cost of holding increased stock levels. The cost of holding stock is made up of a number of components. More stock will mean converting at least some valuable selling space to storage space and, because you will hold the stock for longer, there is always the risk of it going out of fashion, being damaged or spoiled. However, more than any of these, the main cost of holding stock is the capital cost. Remember, money tied up in stocks in *dead money* – not earning any interest. Look at it this way: an increase in average stock holding from £10,000 to £20,000 over the course of a year at, say, a prevailing rate of interest on a normal

	Nov	Dec	Jan	Feb	Mar
Sales forecast:	10,000	15,000	12,000	10,000	8,000
Plus Closing stock:	30,000	20,000	16,000	14,000	12,000
	40,000	35,000	28,000	24,000	20,000
Minus Opening stock:	20,000	30,000	20,000	16,000	14,000
Open to buy @ retail:	20,000	5,000	8,000	8,000	6,000
Less Margin:	5,000	1,250	2,000	2,000	1,500
Open to buy @ cost:	15,000	3,750	6,000	6,000	4,500

● This example assumes a gross margin of 25%. Planned stocks are loosely based on an average rate of stock turn throughout the year of 12 (i.e. two months). Adjustments to planned stocks have been made on the basis of anticipating demand. Stocks are highest in the November/December period to minimize out of stock positions in the Christmas period.

Fig. 13.2   Calculating a merchandise budget: the 'open to buy' method

investment account (at 10 per cent return per annum) is adding, at the very least, an extra £1,000 to your stock holding costs for the year. This might actually wipe out any gains experienced from being able to buy in at lower prices! Clearly, careful consideration needs to be given when confronted with the decision of whether or not to opt for a quantity discount.

Monitoring sales and ordering systems

Electronic tills and sales information

The basis of any good ordering system is a system of detailed sales records. Fortunately, the advent of the modern electronic till has made the recording of sales information automatic. Most modern electronic tills have a price look up facility (PLU). This allows you to allocate a PLU number to each item of merchandise (limited by the number of PLUs available on your till). You program the till with the price and department of that item (this is very simple to do and a straightforward manual comes with most tills). When the plu number is entered into the till both the price and the fact that one more of that item has been sold is automatically registered by the till. Consequently a 'till reading' can be taken at any time to give the total unit and total money sales of each item of merchandise allocated with a plu number. This information can then be easily manipulated to identify fast and slow sellers – invaluable information for refining stock plans, merchandise layout and rationalizing your stock range (i.e. deleting slow-sellers and bringing in new and more profitable lines).

Re-order levels and re-order quantities

Sales information obtained in this way can be used to build an ordering system based on re-order levels and re-order quantities. The system works by establishing a safety level under which stock levels must not fall. This minimum or re-order stock level is determined by:

- The minimum amount of stock required to maintain sufficient sales fixture merchandise levels for display; plus
- The amount of stock required to meet sales between the order being placed and the order being received (known as the lead time).

The final component of the system is the re-order quantity. This is a pre-determined fixed quantity that is re-ordered when stock levels fall to the re-order level.

The main problem with this system is that stock levels need to be monitored closely. There are two options here. You can engage in the rather tedious and impractical task of frequently counting stock, or use PLU sales information to estimate stock levels. If PLU sales information is used, a computer spreadsheet can be used to calculate book stocks on demand. The term book stock means the stock you *should* have (in reality there will be discrepancies with actual stocks as even in the best-run shops there will be theft!). The method to arrive at book stocks is quite straightforward. It is simply a matter of adding opening stock and purchases together (the total amount you could have sold) and subtracting PLU sales to give the amount you should have in stock. To illustrate, if at your last stock take you had 100 cans of lemonade in stock and have since purchased an additional 400 cans and sold 300 cans (according to the PLU read), then you should have 200 cans left (i.e. 500 – 300). This simple process can be laid out on paper or on a computer spread sheet (a full computer spreadsheet to do this job is reproduced in Appendix 6).

Periodically, re-order levels and quantities will have to be reviewed and adjusted to take into account sales trends.

The main manual chore in this process is the actual transference of the PLU sales information to the system. It is of course possible to have the till linked directly to the computer but you should be warned that such a system is, at present, a rather costly investment for the small retailer. Be wary of sales representatives trying to sell you cheap imitations of full blown EPOS (Electronic Point of Sale) systems.

Stock and order cards

An alternative to this system is to use the traditional stock and order card as illustrated in Fig. 13.3. The system works on roughly the same principle as before. The previous stock is added to last order and the present stock level deducted to arrive at the sales for the period (i.e. opening stock + deliveries – closing stock = sales). The new order is placed to cover sales for the next period but takes into account the existing stock level and the desired stock level at the end of the next period. It helps, as shown in the example, to have an ideal closing stock to work to. This should be calculated for each item in the same way as the re-order level is estimated in the previously described system.

In the example the time lapse between orders is one month and the lead time is one week (the planned closing stock is thus calculated to cover a minimum of one week's sales). In the month, the sales for cola are 6 outers (i.e. 1 + 8 – 3). the order for the second month is placed allowing for present stock levels and assuming that sales in the second month will be fairly similar. The actual order is calculated, aiming to reach the planned stock level by the time of the next order. The order of 5 outers is arrived at by adding the planned closing stock to the expected sales and subtracting the opening stock (i.e. 2 + 6 – 3). This all sounds fairly complicated but, with practice, it becomes second nature. After gaining competence a large

Supplier: Halls Limited, Cash Road, Forton, FY9 8QT
Telephone: 123-5678
Lead time: 1 week

13

Stock number	Item	Planned stock	S	O	S	O	S	O	S	O	S	O
123	Cola	2	1	8	3	5						
124	Lemonade	1	2	4	4	0						
125	Cherry	1	1	3	1	3						

Fig. 13.3 Stock and order card

order consisting of hundreds of different items can be successfully completed in a few hours.

If you are going to use a system like this then you may find it advisable to keep a stock and order card for each supplier. Further, it will help you to administer your accounts better if you also keep your account information (see Chapter 12) related to that supplier in the same file.

The stock sheet also serves another purpose when used with an actual stock take, that of identifying stock shortages in great detail.

Stocking for profit

Monitoring deliveries

In Chapter 5, we considered at length the subject of profitability. From that work you should have decided on an overall target profit margin for your shop. This margin will be achieved, not by selling everything at the same margin, but rather by a mix of different sales levels and margins on your stock assortment. The planned operating margin, once in business, needs constantly checking. Any significant deviation could indicate that trouble is on the way. As you will by now appreciate, any fall in your profit margin will mean you will have to sell more to achieve your targeted net profit.

A quick and efficient way to run an almost constant check on your operating margin is to calculate the gross profit on each delivery. This is simply a matter of calculating the retail value of the delivery (i.e. the sales that would be made if all the delivery is sold) and subtracting the total cost of the delivery to arrive at the gross profit. The percentage profit margin can then be simply calculated (i.e. Gross profit/Retail value × 100). However, if you are registered for VAT, care must be taken to calculate the margin from total revenue and total cost figures exclusive of VAT. Remember, your break even calculations, used in profit, price and sales planning, are all based on VAT exclusive figures (see Chapter 10, 'Value Added Tax').

An example of such a delivery profitability analysis is illustrated in Fig. 13.4. With the aid of a computer spreadsheet the task is quick and simple and, in addition, the margin of each line can be calculated (see Appendix 6). As each delivery is analysed the totals should be transferred to a summary sheet, as in Fig. 13.5, to allow you to:

- Check the current profit position on deliveries.
- Isolate suppliers who consistently produce low gross profit margins.

DATE: 15/10/1989   Order reference: 12

Supplier: Turner's Cash & Carry

PLU	ITEM	Retail Price inc. VAT	Qty. per outer	Outer price ex. VAT	VAT rate	Outers Ordered	Cost ex. VAT	Retail ex. VAT	Margin
1	Cola	0.24	24	4.32	15.0%	5	21.6	25.04	13.7%
2	Diet	0.23	24	3.84	15.0%	2	7.68	9.60	20.0%
3	Lemonade	0.19	24	3.56	15.0%	1	3.56	3.97	10.2%
4	Fiz	0.15	60	4.80	15.0%	3	14.4	23.48	38.7%
5	Citrus	0.25	24	4.80	15.0%	5	24	26.09	8.0%
6	Tropical	0.25	24	4.80	15.0%	3	14.4	15.65	8.0%
7	Orange	0.22	24	3.36	15.0%	2	6.72	9.18	26.8%
8	Tangy	0.18	24	3.36	15.0%	1	3.36	3.76	10.6%
					TOTALS	22	95.72	116.77	

Gross Profit on order: 21.05
Percentage margin on order: 18.0%

Fig. 13.4   Delivery profitability analysis

Any major deviation from the planned profit margin should be investigated immediately. Possible reasons might be one or a combination of the following:

- You are selling and, therefore, ordering more merchandise with a low profit margin and less merchandise with a high profit margin, unbalancing your planned sales mix. Monitor sales in detail to isolate the problem. Changes in merchandise layout, pricing and promotion may need to be made.

DATE	SUPPLIER	RETAIL	COST	GROSS PROFIT	MARGIN
10/10	Turners	123.89	99.89	24.00	19.4%
12/10	Browns	234.89	198.78	36.11	15.4%
23/10	Turners	156.89	120.78	36.11	23.0%
28/10	Markdowns	234.89	198.70	36.19	15.4%
	Sub-total	750.56	618.15	132.41	17.6%
1/11	Williams	123.56	101.78	21.78	17.6%
5/11	Discount	178.90	162.80	16.10	9.0%
6/11	Price cut	300.00	250.89	49.11	16.4%
	Sub-total	1353.02	1133.62	219.40	16.2%

13

Fig. 13.5   Checking gross profit trend on deliveries

- One or a number of suppliers have increased their cost prices on key demand lines. You will have to review your selling prices, look for new suppliers or investigate the possibility of finding substitute merchandise that earns a better profit margin.

Monitoring profitability from sales records

If you adopt the PLU/Spreadsheet ordering system described earlier, it is a simple matter of incorporating cost and retail prices into the system to determine profit generated by each line. For those interested in this approach I have included a spreadsheet file in an appendix that will calculate:

- The total gross profit earned to date for each section of the store and the shop as a whole.
- The percentage margin for each line.

Checking for and controlling stock losses

Periodically, I suggest at least every three months, you need to carry out a full stock take to determine the scale of stock losses and work out your actual gross profit. This will involve you in producing a profit and loss account, as described in detail in Chapter 12. Inevitably, there will be a difference between your estimated profit margin (arrived at by the methods described in the previous section) and your actual profit margin. Some of this loss (referred to as stock shrinkage) will be known to you if you have kept detailed records of losses as a result of:

- Breakages and spoilt merchandise.
- Price reductions (mark downs) on intended selling prices.

The reasons for some of the shrinkage, however, will be unknown to you. The size of this loss must be identified. It should be a matter of great concern to you for, until the reasons for the 'unknown shrinkage' are identified and acted upon, this aspect of your stock loss is out of your control.

There are two principal methods to identify stock loss and check and compare actual profit margin after stock take with your estimated profit margin. The first, known as unit stock control, involves establishing a system that will monitor the movement of individual items of stock. The second method is based on valuing stocks and purchases at retail selling prices.

Unit stock control

Unit stock control is a simple method that involves recording the sale of each individual item and subtracting it from stocks. The result is that at any time book stocks can be calculated and compared to actual stocks. Any discrepancy between book and actual stocks, unaccounted for by breakages etc., will tell you the number of items of that stock line that have been stolen (assuming that there are no clerical errors in recording sales, purchases, breakages or in counting stock).

The cost of sales in the profit and loss account will have been increased by the total value of these losses at cost price. Therefore, to determine the percentage margin you would have achieved without these losses is simply a matter of adding back the losses to the gross profit and recalculating the percentage profit margin.

The strength of this system is that it allows you to identify unknown losses by line. It is easy to operate in shops that have a low physical turn-over of high value items. Sales tickets (or similar) are collected as merchandise is sold and, at the end of each day, recorded onto the 'stock sheet'. However, in shops where they physical turnover of merchandise is high the system becomes unworkable without an electronic till with a PLU facility. For those with such tills and a business micro, a spreadsheet based system of unit stock control is reproduced in Appendix 6.

A system of stock control based on retail selling price

With this method stocks and purchases are valued at retail price. The logic applied is that the opening stock, plus the purchases, minus the closing stock, will give the retail value of the stock that has moved off the shelves in the period. If there are no stock losses at all, then the retail value of the stock that has gone will equal the sales for the period. For a full and accurate check, known losses (value of price changes, markdowns, etc.) must be added back to the sales figure and price increases, that have inflated the sales value of existing stock, must be subtracted from the sales figure (see Fig. 13.6).

Once all losses have been calculated, it is important to calculate the effect they have had on your profit margin for the period of trading. If the sales, cost of sales and gross profit for the example given in Fig. 13.6 are as follows:

Sales:	20,000
Cost of sales:	15,000
Gross profit:	5,000

13

	£	£
Sales for the period:	20,000	
Value of mark downs, known stock wastage and cash losses @ retail:	200+	
Value of price increases @ retail:	100–	
Adjusted sales for the period:		20,100
Opening stock @ retail:	5,000	
Purchases @ retail:	19,000+	
	24,000	
Closing stock @ retail:	3,000–	
Value of stock movement @ retail:		21,000–
Shortage or overage for the period:		(900)

Fig. 13.6   Calculating retail value of unknown shrinkage using the selling price method

then the actual profit margin will be 25 per cent. The effect of the losses, £900 (unknown) and £100 (known) can be assessed by adding back shrinkage to produce an adjusted sales and profit figure to give a fairly accurate estimation of the margin that would have been realized if no losses had occurred:

Sales (adjusted)	21,000
Cost of sales:	15,000
Gross profit:	6,000
Profit margin:	28.57%

Care must be taken not to misinterpret these figures. It does not mean that you would have sold an extra £1,000 of merchandise or earned an extra £1,000 of gross profit, but that you would have earned a gross profit equalling 28.57 per cent rather than 25 per cent of actual sales. With a 28.57% profit margin, your gross profit figure would have been £5,714 (i.e. £20,000 × 0.2857). A £1,000 loss of stock at retail prices has resulted in a loss of £5,714 gross profit. The £5,714 represents that stock loss at cost prices (i.e. the retail loss minus the adjusted profit margin).

For a quick check take your actual sales figure and adjust it to take into account known shrinkage and an allowance for theft (in theory any level of theft is unacceptable, however because of its inevitability in reality most large retailers build an allowance of between one and two per cent into their calculations). From this subtract the estimated profit margin (from delivery analysis) to arrive at an estimated cost of sales (including adjustments). Taking the estimated cost of sales away from the actual sales will give an estimation of the current gross profit and gross profit margin. Figure 13.7 illustrates the process. I suggest that you should carry out such checks on a weekly basis in the early life of your shop. The main use of this check is to monitor the effect of mark downs, customer discounts, breakages and spoilage on your profit margin. Of course, any major deterioration in your profit margin should be acted upon without delay.

The estimated realized gross profit figure can easily be verified by taking a full stock check. For instance, in the example given in Fig. 13.7, if a full stock take and compilation of an actual profit and loss account revealed actual gross profits of £6,500 additional losses at cost would be £500. If all known shrinkage records and the stock count had been recorded accurately this additional loss can only be attributable to increased shrinkage by theft.

Recorded sales:		31,000
Recorded sales @ retail:	31,000	
Recorded shrinkage @ retail:	400	
Theft provision @ 2% of sales:	600+	
	32,000	
Less estimated profit margin (25%):	8,000–	
Estimated cost of sales (including adjustments for known shrinkage):		24,000–
Gross profit estimated before stock take:		7,000
Estimated realized gross profit margin: 22.58%		

Fig. 13.7 Quick G.P. check to assess effect of recorded shrinkage on G.P.

13

Summary

Your merchandise plan is part of your overall selling proposition. Accordingly, it should take into account your objectives in the other areas of your marketing mix (i.e. place, price, service and promotion). The merchandise planning process starts with consideration of the requirements of your customers, identifying key lines to carry and building detail by adding related lines to the limits of your purchasing budget.

Detailed estimates of sales are required to develop and refine the merchandise plan. For the retailer who is just starting out the lack of past sales information makes building a model stock plan and calculating a purchasing budget a difficult project. However, indications of likely demand for merchandise can be derived from a combination of first hand market research, seeking advice from suppliers, consulting trade publications, and talking to people in the trade. Once in business, detailed sales information should be recorded and made use of. The purchase and use of a modern electronic till with an extensive PLU facility will make the task of collecting sales data relatively painless. Purchase & use of a business micro & suitable software will allow more detailed & quicker manipulation & interpretation of stock & sales information.

Once the merchandise plan has been refined an efficient system of ordering must be devised to ensure that both out of stock positions are minimized and, equally important, over-ordering does not occur. If you are going to operate a shop with a high physical turnover of low value items then investigation of an integrated computerized system of stock control, to include an ordering system and stock check facility, might be advised. However, remember that training will be required to make use of such a system. For those with knowledge of computer spreadsheets, Appendix 6 gives some ideas and examples of how spreadsheet files may be devised to aid stock control and ordering.

As stock losses, if undetected and unknown, can grow at an alarming rate, it is essential to have a system which can quickly identify the scale of losses. A system that can pinpoint losses down to individual lines is preferable (unit stock control). If this is not possible than one of the other methods to carry out stock checks described in this chapter should be used frequently.

Finally, monitoring profit margins on delivery and detailed recording of wastage will help you to monitor your gross profit performance. This should be a must for all because it helps you to identify and act on problems before they become too big to manage.

14 Forecasting, maintaining and expanding sales

Sales targets

Much has already been said in Chapters 3 and 4 about forecasting sales prior to opening. Such detailed research, coupled with your break even analysis and cash flow forecast, will furnish you with fairly detailed sales tagets for the first six to twelve months in business. How realistic these forecasts will be depends partly on the accuracy of the information you have unearthed and partly on the care you have taken in interpreting it. However, at the end of the day, whether such forecasts will become reality depends very much on whether you are able to put into practice the plan you have devised. The research reveals the potential – you have to exploit it.

In setting sales targets cognizance has to be taken of what is achievable. Investigation of what is likely to happen in the future is often the starting point. Sales forecasting, even when you have been in business for sometime with the benefit of past experience and detailed sales records, is still a notoriously difficult business. It is an exercise that can be tackled by use of both quantitative methods (isolation of trends from past sales data) and more 'subjective' or 'qualitative' methods which take into account changes in the business's immediate environment (e.g. the activity of competitors, etc.) and the larger business environment (e.g. interest rate increases affecting credit purchases).

Science and technology tend to be seen as the holders of truth in our society. The effect is that there is a natural inclination to believe and have confidence in any sales forecast which is based on some mathemtical/statistical technique. However, there is a positive danger in making an assessment of the potential for future sales increases purely on the basis of what has happened to sales figures in the past. If an upward trend in sales is detected from studying past sales records it is important to ask what the contributory factors were that gave rise to the situation.

14

- To illustrate the point, there is the classical example of a well-known soft drinks manufacturer who, on the basis of the marked upward sales trend over the previous two years (I might add very sophisticated statistical techniques were used to confirm the trend 'mathematically' committed literally millions to the building of a new bottling plant to meet the anticipated continuing boom in sales. The sales the following summer were disastrous; nobody (almost unbelievably) had taken into account that previous sales were mainly the result of two glorious exceptionally hot, summers!

Clearly, detailed account must be taken of the environment in which past sales took place, and how factors affecting sales may change in the future (see Chapter 2).

Identification of a sales trend can be made in many ways. On a crude level past sales can be plotted on a graph (as in Fig. 14.1) and a line of best fit drawn. Extension of this line into the future will give some indication of what future sales will be if the upward trend continues. The closer the various sales levels are to the line the more accurate your line of best fit will be. This method assumes that there will be a straight line (linear progression in the trend. Obviously, if the past sales levels are widely scattered then this method cannot be used as no linear (straight line) trend

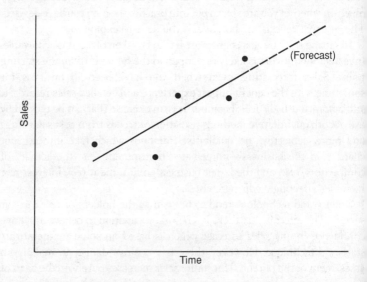

Fig. 14.1 Crude estimates of future sales by line of best fit

is apparent. Use of hand and eye to establish the line of best fit is notoriously inaccurate. A much better predication can be obtained if the slope of the trend line is calculated mathematically. Unfortunately it is outside the scope of this book to go into the lengthy explanation that the calculation of the linear trend line requires (interested readers should consult a business statistical methods textbook on the subject of linear regression analysis).

An alternative aid to forecasting which is easy to use is to identify sales trends by applying moving totals to the past sales figures. By simply looking at past weekly or monthly sales totals that vary due to seasonal fluctuations in customer demand, it will be very difficult to isolate any trend. The objective of applying a moving total to the figures is to clearly show the trend by suppressing the seasonal variation in the sales data.

To calculate a moving total, first you have to select a period of time over which the moving total will pan, say three months. Then it is simply a matter of adding the most recent month's sales to the total, and subtracting the value of sales for the first month. Each month the moving total is moved on, using the same procedure. The greater the period of time the moving total spans, the smoother the trend line will become. It is for this reason that the 'Moving Annual Total' (spanning a period of 12 months) is the most popular.

In the first instance it is likely that sales targets will be set in broad terms, as a single figure to be achieved say over a six or twelve month period. This sales figure needs to be broken down into at least monthly targets but, as no shop expects a constant level of sales throughout the year, there is little point in dividing it by 12 to get a monthly target. Here it is useful to refer to the trading pattern experienced in previous years and apply it to the targeted sales for the coming year. The method used is to calculate a monthly sales index from the previous year's trading (for increased accuracy two years can be used). This is done by dividing the monthly sales by the average sales for the period. The index is then used to break down the sales target for the year into monthly targets. As with all quantitative techniques, consideration should be given to other factors.

The 'targets' derived from the calculations should be just the starting point. For instance, you may wish to attempt, through increased sales promotion activity, to focus on selected months or weeks to increase sales activity in a normally slack period of the year. Good judgement must be applied to all sales information collected.

14

As a guide it is suggested that you should record and periodically analyse the following sales information:

1. Weekly sales:
   - Total.
   - Per section of the shop.

2. Average sale per customer. This is calculated by taking the total sales for the week (as per till reading) and dividing by the number of customers (as per till reading). This is valuable information – it is obviously desirable to earn more sales from hard-won existing customers. Increasing the value of your average sale should be a prime sales objective. Attention to merchandise layout and stock assortment are the main actions that can be taken.
3. Weekly checks should be made on the sales of your best sellers and a full sales check should be carried out monthly.
4. A customer request and complaints book should be kept and reviewed periodically.
5. Sales by day and time (easy if you have an electronic till) should be recorded and reviewed to identify busy and slack periods across the trading week, and identify the peak trading times within each day.
6. Finally, as discussed in Chapter 2, periodically take stock of the environment in which you operate. At the very least, checking in detail what the competition is doing should be a frequent activity.

Developing a sales promotion plan

In nearly every chapter of the book we have discussed the importance of finding out as much as you can about your customers, to plan in detail what is hoped will be a successful selling proposition. To enable that plan to be fully effective, your customers need to be reached, made aware of your existence and your sales proposition, and *sold to*. Many would–be retailers open their shops to find that obtaining a viable market share is a much tougher proposition than they expected.

Effective selling is derived from all of the aspects of the marketing mix discussed in Chapter 3: the merchandise, price, place and service that is to be offered. The final aspect of the marketing mix, promotion, will now be considered.

The first objective of any business start up promotion plan is to tell potential customers of your existence. The second is to get them to visit you. The third is to get them to buy. The fourth is to get them to come back.

This section will therefore deal with the method and means of doing this. Your overall objective is to turn the people who make up your potential target markets into loyal customers.

Developing a sales promotion plan

There are a number of key aspects to developing a sales promotion plan:

1. What do you want to happen (specifically)?
2. What message will make it happen (what message will be sent, how can it be made persuasive)?
3. What media will be used to communicate the message?
4. What will it cost?
5. What profits will it generate?
6. How can you find out if the sales promotion worked?

If you have done a good job in answering the questions posed in Chapter 3 and the book in general you should be in a fairly good position to summarize the information by answering the following two broad questions:

1. What image will your shop attempt to project? This should be built on and from the package of benefits you are offering to your customers (your unique selling proposition).
2. By what means can potential customers be attracted away from the competition? By this stage you should have carried out a detailed analysis of the competition, as suggested in Chapters 3 and 4.

This summary will provide you with the message you wish to send to your potential customers.

14

What do you want to happen?

What do you want your potential customers to do?

Deciding on the message you wish to send to your customers is not as easy as it first appears. First, you must decide what you want them to do and, second, what will have to be in the message to persuade them to do what you want.

What you want them to do is really your set of specific objective(s) for the sales promotion. To help you promote your business start up, in response to the message you send, do you want your customers to:

- note you exist, and become aware of your trading policy?
- visit your shop?
- make requests for further information?
- buy more on each visit?
- buy a particular type of merchandise?
- other?

How are you going to make it happen?

Next, how are you going to persuade your potential customers to respond in a positive manner to the message? As we have stressed throughout, customers will only buy from you if they perceive there are genuine benefits to be derived from shopping at your store. Therefore, your best chance of getting potential custom to do what you want is to point out the benefits of becoming one of your customers. To do this you need to stress more than just the benefits of the actual merchandise being offered for sale. The total selling proposition must be stressed.

This persuasive message, once identified, should become the basis for building an image, something you become known for, such as:

- friendly personal service
- speed and reliability of delivery
- excellent after-sales service and backup

This should be presented well at all times. Good advertisements/sales promotions should follow what has now become commonly known as the 'AIDA' formula. For an advertisement to have a chance of success it must attract a customers' **A**ttention, gain their **I**nterest which, in turn through the message being communicated, generates **D**esire to take the **A**ction of going out and buying the product.

Attention. Most prospective customers scan over poor advertisements without paying attention. You need to stop this browsing with something that will focus their mind. Clever use of graphics, colours, or bold headlines can sometimes achieve this.

Interest. The next step is to gain their attention long enough to transmit the central message. Concentrate on trying to relate to what your research has identified as your customers' most important needs. Try to do it in a simple but interesting way. Don't make the mistake of making the advertisement confusing and boring by trying to communicate too much – keep to the most powerful messages.

Desire. If you have managed to capture their attention long enough and the message is powerful enough then the potential customer should feel the need to purchase the product.

Action. Finally the advertisement should include some aspect that will encourage the customer to come to you and make the purchase. Many advertisements seek to do this by using such phrases as: limited offer, while stocks last, free trial, and so on. Others offer money-off coupons, or make suggestions such as 'come down next week on our late opening night' (including simple directions of how to get there), or encourage the potential customer to give them a telephone call straight after seeing or hearing the advertisement. In fact any ploy can and should be used (as long as it is legal and honest) to instil action in the customer.

Themes and promotional activities

Promotional activities, such as price-based promotions, competitions, etc., are often at the centre of promotional campaigns. They should, of course, be selected to achieve your set promotional objectives. To serve as a guide or as a menu from which to select and possibly to inspire you to think up more original activities, what follows is a brief discussion of some of the possibilities.

Often good use can be made of manufacturers' sales promotions. They spend literally millions on national advertising and you can benefit by timing your in-store merchandise features to coincide with their promotional activity. Ask your suppliers what free in-store promotional material they can provide you with. Many provide posters and free special display fixtures.

Manufacturers' merchandise activities are many and varied. They are familiar to most of us. Whilst they can and should (in most cases) be supported, they also can be copied and made use of in your own promotional activity. Here is a brief listing:

- Money off packs.
- Buy one, get one free.
- Compitition, including bingo games, raffles, give-aways, etc.
- Money-off coupons on subsequent purchases or a related line.
- Multi-packs.
- Free gifts.
- Free samples.

With certain shop types the holding of special events should be investigated. For example, many fashion shops hold successful mini

14

'fashion shows' on their premises. Depending on the promotional objective, these might be held in the evening and be by special invitation only, aiming to build customer loyalty and repeat sales, or, be in the day time and open to all. Similarly, a specialist food shop may hold something like 'a recipe ideas day', where instructions and tips are given on using their merchandise in new and novel ways. Is there anything you could do along these lines?

You may find it appropriate to build promotions around the calender. A clothes shop would promote spring, summer, autumn and winter fashions. Other shops may build themes around:

- Christmas
- New Year and party time
- Planning of summer holidays
- St Valentine's day
- St David's day
- St Patrick's day
- Spring cleaning
- Preparing the car for the summer or winter
- April the first
- Easter
- Gardening activities
- Soft drinks, ices, sun tan lotion, etc. in the summer
- Father's day
- Mother's day
- Back to school
- Guy Fawkes' Night

There are many ideas here, but the list is not exhaustive. Can you think of any more?

The media

There are means of communicating the message to your market segments. The choice of media is as crucial as the message itself. Each medium of communication, from personal recommendation to television, has specific advantages and limitations. Let's briefly consider some of the communication media available to a small business. As a rough rule of thumb, the more personal the advertising medium is, the more persuasive it is likely to be.

Personal recommendation

Personal introduction by present customers to potential customers is prhaps the most persuasive means to attract new custom. Obviously, it is not one that can be used in the start up period but because of its power and nil cost it should be fostered with care as the business grows.

Direct 'personalized' calling

This direct contact by telephone or letter, although of limited use to retailers, has the advantage of being able to target your communication precisely. It may have the effect of making a potential customer feel important and therefore more likely to respond in a positive manner. Others, however, may feel it an affront to their privacy. What would be the reaction of your target markets? Also, if the telephone is used, you have the opportunity to gain direct responses to your 'message'. Your approach, of course, must be carefully constructed and practised before use.

Local newspapers

A mention or feature in the local newspaper can sometimes be secured by new small businesses free of charge as a 'human interest' story. This is always worth investigating.

Yellow Pages

This should be an obvious medium to use, particularly for specialist small businesses. Many consumers use this as a starting point for finding goods and services If you decide to pay for entry it is probably worth while to go for a distinctive box advertisement. Consumers are more likely to investigate the obvious rather than wade through the small print. Also, it is sensible, if you can justify it, to secure an entry under 'A' so that it is read first instead of last!

14

Local newspaper advertising

This is very useful to a new business, to build up awareness that it exists. The charge per advertisement can be quite high, but when compared to the potential number of readers it might reach, the cost per customer can be low. However, the problem with newspapers, and the same is true of radio and TV, is that only a small percentage of the readership may be from the target market you are aiming at. If a large part of the local population is your target market, then this is certainly a good method to use. Remember to place advertisements where your potential customers will see them – the TV page, for instance, could be a good place to advertise VCR tapes.

Local radio stations

These offer widespread coverage for a reasonable cost per thousand listeners. However, for visible effect, the advertisement would have to be repeated regularly over a period, considerably pushing up costs. If this medium is used, careful attention must be given to placing the advertisement at times when your target market is most likely to be listening.

Television advertising

This is perhaps the most expensive form of communication. However, short-duration 'spot' commercials are becoming reasonably priced. In the UK, Channel 4 provides considerable help for the first-time user.

Billboard posters

A relatively cheap form of communication, usually you will have to pay a fee for the poster itself and then three months' rent of the billboard itself. If you decide to use this method, then the location of the billboard must be chosen with care. Perhaps there is a large billboard near to where you plan to open your business, outside an office block where a large proportion of your target market work, or on the bus route they use. Check out the site carefully: is it visible from more than just one direction, is there anything that will distract from whatever message it is attempting to send and will people have ample opportunity/time to see it? The disadvantages of using posters are:

- research has been unable to gauge their effect (the general consensus is that they are not very persuasive);
- people tend to regard them as part of the background, consequently the poster itself would have to be very creative to catch a person's attention.

Leaflets

These have the advantage over posters that they can be targeted at specific groups of potential customers. They are relatively cheap to produce and circulate but are often ignored by the receivers – what did *you* do with the last lot of leaflets that were put through your letter box? However, if you distribute leaflets to small areas at a time, it is relatively easy to monitor the results.

These are but a few of the main methods of communication; here are some others for your consideration:

- Diaries
- Taxis
- Exhibitions
- Local charity magazines
- Exterior of your business vehicle
- Newsagents' windows
- Beer mats
- Milk bottles
- Litter bins
- Carrier bags
- Interiors and exteriors of buses
- Calendars
- Sports team sponsorship
- Packaging

What others can you think of? The choice is certainly vast. Any single medium used on its own will be unlikely to be sufficient. Which do you select? To help you come to a decision, use the following checklist.

1. **Is it consistent with the image of your shop?**
2. **Will it be seen or heard in sufficient numbers by your target group?**
3. **What opportunities will each target group have of seeing or hearing the advertisement?**
4. **How many times will the target group see or hear the advertisement?**
5. **What is the cost of reaching each inividual customer?**
6. **How persuasive do you consider the medium to be?**
7. **Can it be targeted accurately on the group you wish to use?**
8. **Is it complementary to other media you plan to use?**

14

Measuring the success of a sales promotion

You should monitor the outcomes of your advertising and other sales promotion activities for two reasons:

1. To compare the sales the campaign has generated against the costs involved to see whether it has been a profitable activity.

2. To see whether the sales promotion has achieved its stated objectives, so that you can learn from experience, build on good practice, and make sure you don't make the same mistake twice.

There are a number of ways of doing this but as a general guide you should plan and monitor your sales promotions campaigns as suggested below.

Sales promotion plan

Objectives:

Duration (dates):

Theme or message:

Main activity:

Media to be used:

Cost:

In-store promotional support:
(*or* **personal contact support**)

Implications for business organization (e.g. capital and stock requirements):

Method to monitor and check results:

Measuring the success

Promotion:

Duration:

Theme/objective:

Media used:

Comments

Total cost of campaign:
Estimated number exposed to campaign:

Of which estimated target market audience:
Sales objective:
Actual sales increase: _____
Variance (objective – results):

Increase in gross profits after cost of campaign (i.e. Actual sales increase × unit gross profit – total cost of campaign) = £

Customer contact skills

How many times have you walked out of shop and made an oath you would never go there again, or made an enquiry by telephone and been put off visiting a business by the abrupt and sometimes rude manner of the person who you spoke to? Every day businesses are loosing thousands of potential customers in this way and perhaps are not even aware of it. The very least any customer expects (and has a right to expect) is polite and friendly service. With some thought behind the way you deal with customers on a personal level, you can:

- Project a good image, that they in their turn will pass onto their friends.
- Encourage them to come back and make repeat purchases.
- Minimize customer complaints.
- Get them to visit the business.
- Get them to buy.

Here is a simple broad sequence of steps to follow to help you improve your skills at personal selling and service:

1. Keep up standards of dress and hygiene that are appropriate to your business.
2. Have a simple procedure for answering the telephone, for example, 'Good day, Discount Stores, Ann speaking. Can I help you?' This makes a better impression than such responses as '5678' or, 'hello, who is it?' or, 'Discount'. This sounds like common sense, but how many times have you made a telephone enquiry to be greeted in such a poor way?
3. Make sure you and your staff know the benefits your merchandise and services can offer your customers.
4. Choose the right time to approach customers. They usually send non-verbal signals indicating when it is the right time to approach. For instance, people quickly looking through merchandise, checking the labels and looking at their watches, are indicating that they have

14

probably already made up their mind to buy but do not have much time and are perhaps trying to find the right colour or size. You can then simply walk up to them and make a simple opening such as 'Good day, what size are you looking for'.

5. The opening statement is just as important as the timing of the approach. It should be designed to engage the customer in further conversation so that you can identify what they need. Therefore, you should never use the classic 'Can I help you' phrase because the customer can always say no!

6. Identify the customer's needs, then from your knowledge of the products you can select appropriate merchandise or services to show/offer to the customer. Point out the features but base the sale on how the merchandise or service will satisfy the customer's needs. That is what you would do in your advertising – sell the benefits.

7. When showing or demonstrating the merchandise, always handle it with care – this enhances its value in the customer's eyes.

8. Do not make the choice too large as this will confuse the customer. Help the customer narrow down the choice to two or three items. Differentiate between the items but keep pointing out the benefits in all cases. Finally, *hint* that one of the alternatives is better – customers always perceive that they are making the final decision.

9. If the customer hesitates or objects, try to identify the reason and overcome the objection. However, never pressurize as this will lead to bad feeling. Even if a sale is not made then, if the customer is left with a good impression of the business he or she may come back and buy another day!

10. When the sale has been made, you may consider making an additional related sale. However, it should not be attempted if it is obvious and crude … how many times have shoe shop sales assistants tried to sell shoe polish?

11. Finally, treat all complaints courteously and seriously – the often used motto is well worth remembering: 'If you like what we do, tell your friends … If you don't, tell us'.

Summary

Forecasting sales and setting sales targets is an emotive subject. It is fraught with difficulties and dangers. Never forecast sales and set sales targets solely on the basis of assessment of what has happened in the past. Statistical analysis of past sales should always be examined in the context of the wider retail environment in which you operate.

Once sales targets are set, you must address yourself to the question of how they are going to be achieved.

It is crucial that you accurately understand as much as you can about your markets. The most important things to know are the needs that govern your customers' buying behaviour. To sell the product or service you need to act on that knowledge and tell your customers, in the most persuasive (but honest) way you can, that you have what they need!

The way to maximize sales is to plan your sales promotions carefully and monitor the results.

Remember the golden rule: point out the features of your shop and its merchandise but sell the benefits.

Do not try to expand sales too rapidly, otherwise you may end up being unable to 'deliver the goods'.

Sales promotion and selling is an activity that goes on every minute of the day – it is not a spasmodic activity.

Remember that where you have personal contact with customers, properly trained sales staff will be your most valuable sales asset.

The first point of personal contact with a customer, whether it be face-to-face, on the telephone or by letter, makes a lasting impression.

14

15 Keeping on the right side of the law

Sale of goods and services □ Trades Descriptions Acts 1968 and 1972 □ Consumer Credit Act 1974 □ Resale Prices Act 1976 □ Food Hygiene Regulations □ Weights and Measures Act 1985 □ The Shops Act and Sunday trading □ Your premises and the law □ The Theft Act 1968 □ Employment protection legislation □ Trading Standards Office □ Your right to refuse to sell □ Summary

Retailers are subject to a whole host of legislation. This chapter's intention is to give an overview of the main areas. As such it should not be taken as an authoritive or comprehensive guide. Further, information in this field alters rapidly and may well have changed by the time of your reading. You are, therefore, advised to check that all the information given still applies by contacting the authorities mentioned in each section. Up-to-date information can be obtained by consulting a reference such as Croner's *Reference Book for the Self Employed and Smaller Business* (very informative and up-to-date, but quite expensive – can usually be found in the reference section of larger libraries).

Sale of goods and services

The Sale of Goods Act 1979 and The Sale of Goods and Services Act 1984 cover the sale of all merchandise and services to consumers. The most important aspects of this legislation are as follows:

1. The merchandise or service must be of merchantable quality. This quite simply means that they must be fit for sale. It also covers goods bought in a sale. However, if any faults or defects are clearly and specifically brought to the customer's attention at the time of purchase, the customer has no right to reject the merchandise at a later date.
2. The merchandise or service must be fit for the purpose for which it is bought. For example, a lawn mower must be able to cut grass, a rain coat must keep out the rain, but fashion shoes are not fit for country walks! Care must be taken in this area, however, if a customer states the

...y wish to put the merchandise to. For example, if a customer comes into your shop looking for glue to mend their glasses and says so, and you sell the merchandise on that understanding, then if that glue fails to do the job (even if there is a disclaimer on the packaging stating that it is unsuitable for such a task) they will have every right to demand their money back. Further, if the glue damages the optical lenses, you may be liable to pay for the damage.

3. The merchandise must correspond to its description. This includes any description you may make, that is on the packaging, in an advertisement, and so on.

If you breach these implied terms of the contract between you and the customer, the customer has every right to a full refund. Further, as has already been pointed out, you may also be liable for any losses that have been incurred by the customer as a consequence of using the faulty merchandise. The result can be very expensive if the merchandise resulted in the death of the user! Therefore, taking out public liability insurance to cover legal liability for death, injury of illness to a member of the public caused by defects in your merchandise, premises, or services or by the negligence of you and/or your exployees, is essential.

The other important things to note about this legislation are:

1. The customer need only provide proof of purchase; you cannot demand that a customer must produce their receipt to gain a refund for faulty merchandise.

2. As the customer has the right to a full refund where the terms of the contract have been broken by the shop, the displaying of signs similar to:

> 'No refunds given'

or

> 'Sale goods cannot be exchanged or money refunded'

is *illegal*. To do so is to commit a *criminal* offence.

Trades Descriptions Acts 1968 and 1972

These acts cover any descriptions made about merchandise. Any statement made verbally by a sales assistant, in advertising material, on shelf edges, on the packaging or labels, must be accurate and true. The implications of this legislation mean that you must take especial care in the wording of promotional material. For example, the use of a slogan like

Your premises and the law

Offices, Shops and Railway Premises Act 1963

If you become an employer you must register your shop with the local authority. This legislation lays down certain minimum standards relating to temperature, ventilation, lighting, toilet and washing facilities, eating facilities, etc. Importantly, fire precautions must be taken (fire drills, proper means of escape, etc.), including the provision of suitable, properly maintained, fire-fighting equipment.

Under the Fire Precautions Act 1971 a shop that employs more than 20 people or has more than ten employees on the premises at any one time, must apply for a fire certificate.

Health and Safety at Work Act 1974

This is a comprehensive piece of legislation that aims to protect all employees and members of the general public on business premises. It is applicable to all businesses. Employers are obliged by law to take all reasonable steps to ensure the health and safety of all people (employees and members of the general public) on their premises. Further, employers are obliged to tell their employees of their policy towards health and safety (where more than five people are employed this must be in writing).

Any accidents which cause more than three days off work (the day of the accident is not included) have to be reported to the local authority or to the Health and Safety Executive. A detailed report will be required. You should, as a matter of course, keep a detailed record of all accidents, minor or major – obtaining where possible witnesses to the event.

You are advised to consult your local Health and Safety Executive Officer for further information, guidance and advice.

The Theft Act 1968

15

A person is guilty of theft if he or she obtains the property of another person with the intention of permanently depriving that person of it. You will note from the wording that the act of theft occurs if it can be proven that there is an intention to permanently deprive the owner of their property. In practice it is prudent, before making an arrest, to be sure that they have actually stolen the goods: that is, left the premises without paying for the merchandise. Reasonable force may be used to make the arrest.

I strongly advise you to get advice on such matters from your local crime prevention officer before opening up for business.

Employment protection legislation

Employment legislation is wide-reaching, comprehensive and, at times, complicated. Unfortunately, full discussion of this area is out of the scope of this book. There are a range of pamphlets on the legislation available from HMSO bookshops. If you are going to employ people I strongly suggest you purchase *Hiring and Firing* by Karen Lanz, another title in this series.

Trading Standards Office

The Trading Standards department (attached to your local authority) is responsible not only for enforcing the majority of consumer legislation but also for giving advice to traders. Make use of their service by contacting them and gaining further information and advice on any aspect of current legislation.

Your right to refuse to sell

You are not obliged to sell anything to anybody, unless you are refusing on the grounds of race or sex (an offence under the Race Relations Act or Sex Discrimination Act). This is because in the eyes of the law when a retailer places merchandise on display he or she is not offering it for sale, but inviting customers to make an offer (an *invitation to treat*). Thereby, because a contract needs both an offer and acceptance to become valid, there is no obligation for you to sell. This is fortunate in cases where an item has been subject to a major pricing error that could result in a sizable loss. Often customers who find such an error believe it to be their right to force the retailer to sell at the marked price. As the price marked and the fact that the merchandise is on display does not constitute an offer, the retailer has no obligation to sell. Of course, in such a case the customer may have a case under the Trades Descriptions Act. In cases where the error is small, to maintain customer goodwill, I would point out the mistake but still sell the item at the marked price.

Summary

It is important for you to check in detail the law as it applies to your specific type of shop. Your aim should not be to understand the letter of the law, but to become aware of its implications for your day-to-day trading. It should be remembered that the agencies that exist to enforce the law are also there to give help and advice, so make use of them.

Prosecution leads not only to a fine and, in some cases, imprisonment, but also to loss of reputation with your customers due to the ensuing bad press.

The author welcomes comments on this book and can be contacted through Pitman Publishing, 128 Long Acre, London, WC2E 9AN.

15

% Profit Margin before price decrease

% Price Decrease	10	11	12	13	14	15	16	17	18	19	20	21	22	23	24	25	26	27	28	29
1	11	10	9	8	8	7	7	6	6	6	5	5	5	5	4	4	4	4	4	4
2	25	22	20	18	17	15	14	13	13	12	11	11	10	10	9	9	8	8	8	7
3	43	38	33	30	27	25	23	21	20	19	18	17	16	15	14	14	13	13	12	12
4	67	57	50	44	40	36	33	31	29	27	25	24	22	21	20	19	18	17	17	16
5	100	83	71	63	56	50	45	42	38	36	33	31	29	28	26	25	24	23	22	21
6	150	120	100	86	75	67	60	55	50	46	43	40	38	35	33	32	30	29	27	26
7	233	175	140	117	100	88	78	70	64	58	54	50	47	44	41	39	37	35	33	32
8	400	267	200	160	133	114	100	89	80	73	67	62	57	53	50	47	44	42	40	38
9	900	450	300	225	180	150	129	113	100	90	82	75	69	64	60	56	53	50	47	45
10		1,000	500	333	250	200	167	143	125	111	100	91	83	77	71	67	63	59	56	53
11			1,100	550	367	275	220	183	157	138	122	110	100	92	85	79	73	69	65	61
12				1,200	600	400	300	240	200	171	150	133	120	109	100	92	86	80	75	71
13					1,300	650	433	325	260	217	186	163	144	130	118	108	100	93	87	81
14						1,400	700	467	350	280	233	200	175	156	140	127	117	108	100	93
15							1,500	750	500	375	300	250	214	188	167	150	136	125	115	107
16								1,600	800	533	400	320	267	229	200	178	160	145	133	123
17									1,700	850	567	425	340	283	243	213	189	170	155	142
18										1,800	900	600	450	360	300	257	225	200	180	164
19											1,900	950	633	475	380	317	271	238	211	190
20												2,000	1,000	667	500	400	333	286	250	222

% Price Decrease	30	31	32	33	34	35	36	37	38	39	40	41	42	43	44	45	46	47	48	49
1	3	3	3	3	3	3	3	3	3	3	3	3	2	2	2	2	2	2	2	2
2	7	7	7	6	6	6	6	6	6	5	5	5	5	5	5	5	5	4	4	4
3	11	11	10	10	10	9	9	9	9	8	8	8	8	8	7	7	7	7	7	7
4	15	15	14	14	13	13	13	12	12	11	11	11	11	10	10	10	10	9	9	9
5	20	19	19	18	17	17	16	16	15	15	14	14	14	13	13	13	12	12	12	11
6	25	24	23	22	21	21	20	19	19	18	18	17	17	16	16	15	15	15	14	14
7	30	29	28	27	26	25	24	23	23	22	21	21	20	19	19	18	18	18	17	17
8	36	35	33	32	31	30	29	28	27	26	25	24	24	23	22	22	21	21	20	20
9	43	41	39	38	36	35	33	32	31	30	29	28	27	26	26	25	24	24	23	23
10	50	48	45	43	42	40	38	37	36	34	33	32	31	30	29	29	28	27	26	26
11	58	55	52	50	48	46	44	42	41	39	38	37	35	34	33	32	31	31	30	29
12	67	63	60	57	55	52	50	48	46	44	43	41	40	39	38	36	35	34	33	32
13	76	72	68	65	62	59	57	54	52	50	48	46	45	43	42	41	39	38	37	36
14	88	82	78	74	70	67	64	61	58	56	54	52	50	48	47	45	44	42	41	40
15	100	94	88	83	79	75	71	68	65	63	60	58	56	54	52	50	48	47	45	44
16	114	107	100	94	89	84	80	76	73	70	67	64	62	59	57	55	53	52	50	48
17	131	121	113	106	100	94	89	85	81	77	74	71	68	65	63	61	59	57	55	53
18	150	138	129	120	113	106	100	95	90	86	82	78	75	72	69	67	64	62	60	58
19	173	158	146	136	127	119	112	106	100	95	90	86	83	79	76	73	70	68	66	63
20	200	182	167	154	143	133	125	118	111	105	100	95	91	87	83	80	77	74	71	69

Appendix 2

The percentage sales volume decrease that can be supported by a price increase

% Profit Margin before price increase

% Price Increase	10	11	12	13	14	15	16	17	18	19	20	21	22	23	24	25	26	27	28	29
1	9	8	8	7	7	6	6	6	5	5	5	5	4	4	4	4	4	4	3	3
2	17	15	14	13	13	12	11	11	10	10	9	9	8	8	8	7	7	7	7	6
3	23	21	20	19	18	17	16	15	14	14	13	13	12	12	11	11	10	10	10	9
4	29	27	25	24	22	21	20	19	18	17	17	16	15	15	14	14	13	13	13	12
5	33	31	29	28	26	25	24	23	22	21	20	19	19	18	17	17	16	16	15	15
6	38	35	33	32	30	29	27	26	25	24	23	22	21	21	20	19	19	18	18	17
7	41	39	37	35	33	32	30	29	28	27	26	25	24	23	23	22	21	21	20	19
8	44	42	40	38	36	35	33	32	31	30	29	28	27	26	25	24	24	23	22	22
9	47	45	43	41	39	38	36	35	33	32	31	30	29	28	27	26	26	25	24	24
10	50	48	45	43	42	40	38	37	36	34	33	32	31	30	29	29	28	27	26	26
11	52	50	48	46	44	42	41	39	38	37	35	34	33	32	31	30	30	29	28	28
12	55	52	50	48	46	44	43	41	40	39	38	36	35	34	33	32	32	31	30	29
13	57	54	52	50	48	46	45	43	42	41	39	38	37	36	35	34	33	33	32	31
14	58	56	54	52	50	48	47	45	44	42	41	40	39	38	37	36	35	34	33	33
15	60	58	56	54	52	50	48	47	45	44	43	42	41	39	38	38	37	36	35	34
16	62	59	57	55	53	52	50	48	47	46	44	43	42	41	40	39	38	37	36	36
17	63	61	59	57	55	53	52	50	49	47	46	45	44	43	41	40	40	39	38	37
18	64	62	60	58	56	55	53	51	50	49	47	46	45	44	43	41	41	40	39	38
19	66	63	61	59	58	56	54	53	51	50	49	48	46	45	44	43	42	41	40	40
20	67	65	63	61	59	57	56	54	53	51	50	49	48	47	45	44	43	43	42	41

% Price Increase	30	31	32	33	34	35	36	37	38	39	40	41	42	43	44	45	46	47	48	49
1	3	3	3	3	3	3	3	3	3	3	2	2	2	2	2	2	2	2	2	2
2	6	6	6	6	6	5	5	5	5	5	5	5	5	4	4	4	4	4	4	4
3	9	9	9	8	8	8	8	8	7	7	7	7	7	7	6	6	6	6	6	6
4	12	11	11	11	11	10	10	10	10	9	9	9	9	9	8	8	8	8	8	8
5	14	14	14	13	13	13	12	12	12	11	11	11	11	10	10	10	10	10	9	9
6	17	16	15	15	15	15	14	14	14	13	13	13	13	12	12	12	12	11	11	11
7	19	18	18	18	17	17	16	16	16	15	15	15	14	14	14	13	13	13	13	13
8	21	21	20	20	19	19	18	18	17	17	17	16	16	16	15	15	15	15	14	14
9	23	23	22	21	21	20	20	20	19	19	18	18	18	17	17	17	16	16	16	16
10	25	24	24	23	23	22	22	21	21	20	20	20	19	19	19	18	18	18	17	17
11	27	26	26	25	24	24	23	23	22	22	22	21	21	20	20	20	19	19	19	18
12	29	28	27	27	26	26	25	24	24	24	23	23	22	22	21	21	21	20	20	20
13	30	30	29	28	28	27	27	26	25	25	25	24	24	23	23	22	22	22	21	21
14	32	31	30	30	29	29	28	27	27	26	26	25	25	25	24	24	23	23	23	23
15	33	33	32	31	31	30	29	29	28	28	27	27	26	26	25	25	25	24	24	24
16	35	34	33	33	32	31	31	30	30	29	29	28	28	27	27	26	26	25	25	25
17	36	35	35	34	34	33	32	31	31	30	30	29	29	28	28	27	27	27	26	26
18	38	37	36	35	35	34	33	33	32	32	31	31	30	30	29	28	28	28	27	27

% Profit Margin before price decrease

% Price Decrease	10	11	12	13	14	15	16	17	18	19	20	21	22	23	24	25	26	27	28	29
1	10	9	8	7	7	6	6	5	5	5	4	4	4	4	3	3	3	3	3	3
2	23	20	18	16	14	13	12	11	10	10	9	8	8	7	7	7	6	6	6	5
3	39	33	29	26	23	21	19	18	16	15	14	13	12	12	11	10	10	9	9	8
4	60	51	44	39	34	31	28	26	23	22	20	19	17	16	15	14	13	13	12	11
5	90	74	63	54	48	43	38	35	32	29	27	25	23	21	20	19	18	17	16	15
6	135	107	88	75	65	57	50	45	41	37	34	32	29	27	25	24	22	21	20	19
7	210	156	123	102	85	74	65	58	52	47	43	40	36	34	31	29	27	26	24	23
8	360	237	176	139	115	97	84	74	66	59	53	49	45	41	38	35	33	31	29	27
9	810	401	264	196	155	128	108	93	82	73	65	59	54	50	46	42	39	37	34	32
10		890	440	290	215	170	140	119	103	90	80	72	65	59	54	50	46	43	40	37
11			968	479	315	234	185	152	129	111	98	87	78	71	64	59	54	50	47	43
12				1,044	516	340	252	199	164	139	120	105	94	84	76	69	63	58	54	50
13					1,118	552	364	270	213	176	149	128	113	100	90	81	74	68	62	58
14						1,190	588	387	287	227	187	158	137	120	106	95	86	79	72	66
15							1,260	623	410	304	240	198	167	144	127	113	101	91	83	76
16								1,328	656	432	320	253	208	176	152	133	118	106	96	87
17									1,394	689	453	336	255	218	185	159	140	124	111	101
18										1,458	720	474	351	277	228	193	167	146	130	116
19											1,520	750	494	366	289	238	201	173	152	135
20												1,580	780	513	380	300	247	209	180	158

% Price Decrease	30	31	32	33	34	35	36	37	38	39	40	41	42	43	44	45	46	47	48	49
1	2	2	2	2	2	2	2	2	2	2	2	1	1	1	1	1	1	1	1	1
2	5	5	5	4	4	4	4	4	3	3	3	3	3	3	3	3	2	2	2	2
3	8	7	7	7	6	6	6	6	5	5	5	5	4	4	4	4	4	4	3	3
4	11	10	10	9	9	8	8	8	7	7	7	6	6	6	6	5	5	5	5	5
5	14	13	13	12	11	11	10	10	9	9	9	8	8	8	7	7	7	6	6	6
6	18	17	16	15	14	13	13	12	12	11	11	10	10	9	9	8	8	8	7	7
7	21	20	19	18	17	16	15	15	14	13	13	12	12	11	11	10	10	9	9	9
8	25	24	23	21	20	19	18	17	17	16	15	14	14	13	12	12	11	11	10	10
9	30	28	27	25	24	23	21	20	19	18	17	17	15	15	14	14	13	13	12	11
10	35	33	31	29	28	26	25	23	22	21	20	19	18	17	16	16	15	14	14	13
11	41	38	36	34	32	30	28	27	25	24	23	22	21	20	19	18	17	16	15	15
12	47	44	41	38	36	34	32	30	29	27	26	24	23	22	21	20	19	18	17	17
13	54	50	47	44	41	39	36	34	32	31	29	27	26	25	23	22	21	20	19	18
14	61	57	53	49	46	43	41	38	36	34	32	31	29	28	26	25	24	22	21	20
15	70	65	60	56	52	49	46	43	40	38	36	34	32	31	29	28	26	25	24	23
16	80	74	68	63	59	55	51	48	45	42	40	38	36	34	32	30	29	27	26	25
17	92	84	77	71	66	61	57	54	50	47	44	42	39	37	35	33	32	30	29	27
18	105	96	87	80	74	69	64	60	56	52	49	46	44	41	39	37	35	33	31	30
19	121	109	99	91	84	77	72	67	62	58	54	51	48	45	43	40	38	36	34	32
20	140	125	113	103	94	87	80	74	69	64	60	56	53	50	47	44	42	39	37	35

Appx

Appendix 4

The percentage decrease in sales revenue that can be supported by a price increase

% Profit Margin before price decrease

% Price Increase	10	11	12	13	14	15	16	17	18	19	20	21	22	23	24	25	26	27	28	29
1	8	7	7	6	6	5	5	5	4	4	4	4	3	3	3	3	3	3	2	2
2	15	14	13	12	11	10	9	9	8	8	7	7	6	6	6	6	5	5	5	5
3	21	19	18	16	15	14	13	12	12	11	10	10	10	9	8	8	8	7	7	7
4	26	24	22	21	19	18	17	16	15	14	13	13	12	11	11	10	10	9	9	9
5	30	28	26	24	23	21	20	19	18	17	16	15	14	14	13	13	12	11	11	10
6	34	31	29	27	26	24	23	22	20	19	18	18	17	16	15	15	14	13	13	12
7	37	35	32	30	29	27	26	24	23	22	21	20	19	18	17	16	16	15	14	14
8	40	37	35	33	31	30	28	27	25	24	23	22	21	20	19	18	17	17	16	15
9	43	40	38	36	34	32	30	29	27	26	25	24	23	22	21	20	19	18	18	17
10	45	42	40	38	36	34	32	31	29	28	27	25	24	23	22	21	21	20	19	18
11	47	45	42	40	38	36	34	33	31	30	28	27	26	25	24	23	22	21	20	20
12	49	46	44	42	40	38	36	34	33	31	30	29	28	26	25	24	23	22	22	21
13	51	48	46	43	41	39	38	36	34	33	32	30	29	28	27	26	25	24	23	22
14	53	50	47	45	43	41	39	37	36	34	33	32	30	29	28	27	26	25	24	23
15	54	51	49	47	44	43	41	39	37	36	34	33	32	30	29	28	27	26	25	24
16	55	53	50	48	46	44	42	40	39	37	36	34	33	32	30	29	28	27	26	25
17	57	54	52	49	47	45	44	42	40	38	37	35	34	33	32	30	29	28	27	26
18	58	55	53	51	48	46	44	43	41	39	38	36	35	34	33	31	30	29	28	27
19	59	56	54	52	50	48	46	44	42	41	39	38	36	35	34	32	31	30	29	28
20	60	57	55	53	51	49	47	45	43	42	40	39	37	36	35	33	32	31	30	29

% Price Increase	30	31	32	33	34	35	36	37	38	39	40	41	42	43	44	45	46	47	48	49
1	2	2	2	2	2	2	2	2	2	2	1	1	1	1	1	1	1	1	1	1
2	4	4	4	4	4	4	3	3	3	3	3	3	3	3	2	2	2	2	2	2
3	6	6	6	6	5	5	5	5	5	4	4	4	4	4	4	3	3	3	3	3
4	8	8	8	7	7	7	6	6	6	6	5	5	5	5	5	4	4	4	4	4
5	10	10	9	9	8	8	8	8	7	7	7	6	6	6	6	6	5	5	5	5
6	12	11	11	10	10	10	9	9	8	8	8	8	7	7	7	6	6	6	6	6
7	13	13	12	12	11	11	10	10	10	9	9	9	8	8	8	7	7	7	7	6
8	15	14	14	13	13	12	12	11	11	10	10	10	9	9	9	8	8	8	7	7
9	16	16	15	14	14	13	13	12	12	11	11	11	10	10	10	9	9	9	8	8
10	17	17	16	16	15	14	14	13	13	12	12	12	11	11	11	10	10	9	9	9
11	19	18	17	17	16	16	15	14	14	13	13	13	12	12	11	11	10	10	10	9
12	20	19	19	18	17	17	16	15	15	14	14	14	13	12	12	12	11	11	11	10
13	21	20	20	19	18	18	17	16	16	15	15	14	14	13	13	12	12	12	11	11
14	22	21	21	20	19	19	18	17	17	16	16	15	15	14	14	13	13	12	12	11
15	23	23	22	21	20	20	19	18	18	17	16	16	15	15	14	14	13	13	12	12
16	24	23	23	22	21	21	20	19	18	18	17	17	16	15	15	14	14	13	13	13
17	25	24	23	23	22	21	21	20	19	18	18	17	17	16	16	15	14	14	14	13
18	26	25	24	24	23	22	21	21	20	19	19	18	17	17	16	15	15	15	14	14
19	27	26	25	24	24	23	22	21	21	20	19	19	18	17	17	16	16	15	15	14

Appendix 5

Methods of providing for depreciation

There are a number of ways of providing for depreciation of assets. Here we will briefly consider three of the most popular:

- Straight line method
- The production hour method
- Reducing balance method

All of the following methods allocate the same total amount for depreciation, i.e. the full cost of the purchase, less resale value (if any). It is the timing of the costs that differentiates each method.

The straight line method seeks to spread the cost of the asset evenly over its working life. As it is simple to work out it is commonly used, but only really suitable for assets whose resale value declines with time and not usage. The calculation for determining annual depreciation is:

$$\frac{\text{Original cost (or revaluation)} - \text{Resale value}}{\text{Working life (years)}}$$

- For example if a cold store display cabinet is bought for £4,000 with a planned life with the business of four years and an estimated resale value of £2,000, then the annual rate of depreciation will be £500.

The production hour method is more suitable for assets such as machinery, whose resale value may be largely determined by how many hours (or miles, etc.) they have been worked. The calculation again is simple:

$$\text{Depreciation per hour} = \frac{\text{Original cost (or revaluation)} - \text{Resale value}}{\text{Working life in units of usage (e.g. hours, miles, etc.)}}$$

- Example: if an electronic till is bought for £20,000 with a planned working life of 80,000 hours then the hourly depreciation would be £0.25. If the till is operated for 160 hours in one month then the monthly depreciation cost will be £40.00.

The reducing balance method. Both of the above methods fail to take into account the commonly known fact that many assets can lose a higher proportion of their second-hand value in their early life. You will have no doubt recognized this in the many domestic purchases you have made: cars, TVs, washing machines, etc. The reducing balance method seeks to take this into account by attributing larger depreciation costs in the earlier years. This is done by decreasing the value of the asset by a fixed percentage each year. The result is to allocate costs on a 'diminishing sliding scale' as time goes by. However, using this method the value of an asset is never reduced to zero! The formula for calculating the percentage rate to be used is:

$$\text{Annual percentage rate of depreciation} = 1 - n\sqrt{\frac{\text{Residual Value}}{\text{Cost}}} \times 100$$

Note: n is the useful life of the asset.

This calculation looks difficult but is relatively simple with a modern calculator that has logarithm capability. You don't have to understand why the calculation works, but only how to operate it. The procedure to follow on most calculators is clearly laid out in Fig. A5.1. If you have such a calculator, try to apply the reducing balance method on the information in our cold store cabinet example – you will find the solution and the comparison of the methods in Fig. A5.2.

The reducing balancing method may be more complicated to calculate but for many assets it will more accurately reflect reality. It evens out the asset's operating costs over time by counterbalancing the decline in

1) Enter the residual value	2) Press divide
3) Enter the original cost of revaluation	4) Press the equals key
5) Press the log key	6) Press divide
7) Enter the useful life of asset	8) Press the equals key
9) Press inv (invert) and then the log key (to obtain the anti log)	10) Press multiply
11) Enter 100 and press equals	12) Finally subtract the answer from 100

Fig. A5.1   Using a calculator to obtain annual % rate of depreciation (reducing balance)

Annual percentage
rate of depreciation $= 1 - 4 \sqrt{\dfrac{£2,000}{£4,000}} \times 100$

$= 15.9\%$

| | **Reducing balance method** | | | **Straight line method** | | |
| | Depreciation: | | | Depreciation: | | |
Yr end	Net value	Annual	Cumulative	Net value	Annual	Cumulative
Start	4,000	–	–	4,000	–	–
1	3,364	636	636	3,500	500	500
2	2,829	535	1,171	3,000	500	1,000
3	2,379	450	1,621	2,500	500	1,500
4	2,000	379	2,000	2,000	500	2,000

Fig. A5.2 The reducing balance and straight line methods compared

depreciation over the period by the increasing maintenance costs as the asset becomes worn with usage.

In selecting the method to use you must give careful consideration to the type of asset and how it will lose value. In the end you may wish to ignore the above methods and calculate the depreciation of your assets on sound estimates of their resale value after each year's trading periods. Whichever method you choose, you should be aware that the Inland Revenue lay down varying rates of depreciation (capital allowances) for different types of assets. Therefore, before they calculate your tax bill they will alter your depreciation figure.

Now, using a table similar to that in Fig. A5.3, estimate your fixed asset costs. The total cost of your fixed assets for your first year will be the total of column B and the total of column A will represent the part of the capital you will have to find to put into your business.

Appx

Item	A Total Cost £s	Life in yrs	B Depreciation First yr £s	Comments
Capital Required		First yr's cost:		

Fig. A5.3 Charting the cost of your fixed assets

Appendix 6

Spreadsheet applications for small business planning and administration

The intention of this section is not to give a complete guide on how to build and use spreadsheet files: there is simply not enough space! Rather, what is given here are ideas for those with some basic familiarity with spreadsheets, to apply and develop them further to aid in the planning and administration of their businesses.

For those who are unfamiliar with spreadsheets, most come with helpful tutorial manuals. There should also be short adult education courses on the subject available in your area (lasting about 10 weeks). Further, there are now many books on the market for first time users of spreadsheets.

Spreadsheet packages, amongst the more popular are SuperCalc and Lotus, are perhaps the most easily learnt and versatile of all business software programs. A spreadsheet consists of a large 'electronic piece of paper' divided vertically into columns (identified by letters) and horizontally into rows (identified by numbers). Each square, known as a 'cell', is referred to by its column letter and row number (e.g. A1, B67, D6, and so on). Into each cell can be entered numbers or text and – most important of all – formulas. The formulas are easy to write, for instance to add up the contents of cells A1 and A2 and place the answer in cell A3, the formula A1+A2 would be entered in cell A3. The formulas make use of the 4 basic rules of arithmetic:

× multiply
/ divide
+ plus
– minus

Constants can also be included in the formula, for example A1 × (A2/100), would divide the contents of A2 by 100 and multiply the result by the contents of A1. Note, brackets are placed around the calculation you wish to perform first.

The hard part of using a spreadsheet is the chore of designing and entering the formula. However, once constructed they are very easy to use. Once the formulas are in place, data can be changed at will and recalculation is automatic (or at operator request). For example, any figures in the cash flow forecast can be changed and the effect on the overall cash flow can be assessed in seconds – a chore using calculator, pen and paper that would take the best part of 30 minutes. Further, as long as the spreadsheet is constructed properly 100 per cent accuracy is guaranteed on all calculations!

More sophisticated packages offer more advanced mathematical functions, such as square root and a range of financial mathematical functions. However, all the spreadsheet applications in this appendix use only the 4 basic rules of arithmetic and can therefore be created using the most basic spreadsheet packages.

For those with skills and experience and more advanced spreadsheets the basic file duplicated in this appendix can be developed to provide more sophisticated planning and administration aids. For instance, the stock control sheet could be adapted to perform automatic re-ordering if 'If, then' statements are used to identify merchandise that needs re-ordering and a data management system (database), such as found in SuperCalc 3, is used to extract the items and re-order quantities to an order form (prepared in another part of the spreadsheet).

Both the experienced and inexperienced user should find the basic ideas given here are capable of further development.

Multi-product break even

This application is based on the formula given in Chapter 5:

$$\text{BEP} = \frac{\text{Fixed costs}}{(\% \text{ Sales} \times \% \text{ Profit margin}) + (\% \text{ Sales} \times \% \text{ Profit margin})}$$

Study of the cell formulas should clearly show how this break even formula has been transferred to the spreadsheet. You should also be able to see that the application can easily be extended to include as many different merchandise groups as you wish. Detailing the overheads helps if you wish to assess the effect of the change of one overhead cost on the BEPs. Calculation of the BEPP is simply a matter of adding your net profit objective to the overheads.

Cash flow forecast

This is a straightforward application of the standard cash flow forecast format given in Chapter 6.

Stock control sheet

As already discussed, this application is capable of further development depending on your skills and software. The simple logic used is that book stock (what you should have) equates with opening stock plus deliveries minus PLU sales.

Delivery analysis and summary

This is not a sophisticated application; however, it is a time-saver. You could create a file for each major supplier, then all that needs to be done on each delivery is to enter the number of outers of each line received.

Cash book

This again is a simple application. Many would prefer to do this on paper! In this case the main advantage of using a computer to do the job is that accuracy in calculation is ensured.

You could adapt this cash book file to include automatic calculation of VAT inputs and outputs. Further, you could extend it to produce an automatic update of profit and loss. In fact with ingenuity you could link most of the applications given.

The SuperCalc trade and product names, and the following SuperCalc spreadsheets are reproduced by courtesy of Computer Associates Limited, Computer Associates House, 183–7 Bath Road, Slough, Berks. SL1 4AA.

Examples of spreadsheets

Break even analysis

```
    :        A     ::    B   ::   C   ::    D   ::    E   ::    F   ::  G
 1:BREAK EVEN ANALYSIS
 2:_____
 3:
 4:                    OVERHEADS
 5:            Rent:     1,000
 6:           Rates:     2,000
 7:       Telephone:       500
 8:     Electricity:     1,200
 9:       Insurance:       800
10:     Advertising:       900
11:     Accountant:        879
12:       Solicitor:       567
13:        Interest:       100
14:    Depreciation:       210
15:       Transport:     1,000
16:           Misc.:       844
17:                   ----------
18:                      10,000
19:                   ----------
20:
21:MERCHANDISE        PERCENT   PROFIT              BEP      GROSS
22:GROUP              OF TOTAL  MARGIN              SALES    PROFIT
23:                   SALES
24:
25:        Newspapers     22%     27%    .0594   11,905    3,214
26:          Tobbacco     38%      8%    .0304   20,563    1,645
27:     Confectionery     20%     25%    .05     10,823    2,706
28:       Soft drinks      5%     30%    .015     2,706      812
29:           General     15%     20%    .03      8,117    1,623
30:                                               0         0        0
31:                   ----------         -----------------------------
32:                      100%             54,113  54,113   10,000
33:                   ----------         -----------------------------
```

```
    :    A     ::  B  ::  C  ::     D      ::    E   ::   F  ::   G  :
 1:BREAK EVEN ANALYSIS
 2:_____
 3:
 4:             OVERHEADS
 5:     Rent: 1000
 6:    Rates: 2000
 7: Telephone: 500
 8: Electricity: 1200
 9: Insurance: 800
10: Advertising: 900
11: Accountant: 879
12:  Solicitor: 567
13:   Interest: 100
14: Depreciation: 210
15:  Transport: 1000
16:      Misc.: 844
17:           ----------
18:        SUM(B5:B16)
19:           ----------
20:
21:MERCHANDISE   PERCENT  PROFIT           BEP       GROSS
22:GROUP         OF TOTAL MARGIN           SALES     PROFIT
23:              SALES
24:
25:    Newspapers .22    .27    B25*C25   D32*B25   C25*E25
26:      Tobbacco .38    .08    B26*C26   D32*B26   C26*E26
27: Confectionery .2    .25    B27*C27   D32*B27   C27*E27
28:   Soft drinks .05    .3    B28*C28   D32*B28   C28*E28
29:       General .15    .2    B29*C29   D32*B29   C29*E29
30:                            B30*C30   D32*B30   C30*E30
31:           ----------       ------------------------------------
32:        SUM(B25:B30)    B18/SUM(D25:D30) SUM(E25:E30) SUM(F25:F30)
33:           ----------       ------------------------------------
```

	A	B :: AUG	C :: SEPT	D :: OCT	E :: NOV	F :: DEC	G :: JAN	H :: FEB	I :: MAR	J :: APRIL	K :: MAY	L :: JUNE	M :: JULY	N :: TOTALS
1:	:	:	:	:	:	:	:	:	:	:	:	:	:	:
2:	CASH :N:													
3:														
4:	Capital:													SUM(B4:M4)
5:	VAT refunds:													SUM(B5:M5)
6:	Cash Sales:													SUM(B6:M6)
7:	Credit Sales:													SUM(B7:M7)
8:														
9:		SUM(B4:B7)	SUM(C4:C7)	SUM(D4:D7)	SUM(E4:E7)	SUM(F4:F7)	SUM(G4:G7)	SUM(H4:H7)	SUM(I4:I7)	SUM(J4:J7)	SUM(K4:K7)	SUM(L4:L7)	SUM(M4:M7)	SUM(N4:N7)
10:														
11:	CASH OUT:													
12:														
13:	Opening stock:													SUM(B13:M13)
14:	Stock:													SUM(B14:M14)
15:	Rent:													SUM(B15:M15)
16:	Rates:													SUM(B16:M16)
17:	Telephone:													SUM(B17:M17)
18:	Gas & Electric:													SUM(B18:M18)
19:	Insurance:													SUM(B19:M19)
20:	Van lease:													SUM(B20:M20)
21:	Petrol:													SUM(B21:M21)
22:	Advertising:													SUM(B22:M22)
23:	Acc/solicitor:													SUM(B23:M23)
24:	General:													SUM(B24:M24)
25:	Wages:													SUM(B25:M25)
26:	NI/PAYE:													SUM(B26:M26)
27:	Class 2/NI:													SUM(B27:M27)
28:	Capital exp.:													SUM(B28:M28)
29:	Overdraft chg:													SUM(B29:M29)
30:	VAT payments:													SUM(B30:M30)
31:	Personal:													SUM(B31:M31)
32:														
33:	Total cash out:SUM B13:B31)		SUM(C13:C31)	SUM(D13:D31)	SUM(E13:E31)	SUM(F13:F31)	SUM(G13:G31)	SUM(H13:H31)	SUM(I13:I31)	SUM(J13:J31)	SUM(K13:K31)	SUM(L13:L31)	SUM(M13:M31)	SUM(N13:N31)
34:														
35:	Monthly Balance:	B9-B33	C9-C33	D9-D33	E9-E33	F9-F33	G9-G33	H9-H33	I9-I33	J9-J33	K9-K33	L9-L33	M9-M33	N9-N33
36:														
37:	Opening Balance:		B39	C39	D39	E39	F39	G39	H39	I39	J39	K39	L39	
38:														
39:	Closing Balance:	B35+B37	C35+C37	D35+D37	E35+E37	F35+F37	G35+G37	H35+H37	I35+I37	J35+J37	K35+K37	L35+L37	M35+M37	
40:	(Net Cash Flow)													
41:														

Cash flow forecast

Stock control sheet

```
 : A:: B :: C::    D   ::    E   ::  F  ::   6   ::  H   ::   I   :: J:: K:: L:: M:: N
1:STOCK CONTROL SHEET SOFT DRINKS
2:_____
3:
4:
5:
6:PLU ITEM  R.P.   C.P.    C/F       1       2       3       PLU  Book Actual Over/ Value Va
7:                       Open Stock                          SALES Stock Stock Short losses St
8:                                                                                   @ R.P. @ C
9:
10: 9 Cola  .24    .18     492      144     120             740    16   14    -2    -.48   2
11: 10 Diet .24    .18     228       48      48             290    34   36     2     .48   6.
12: 11 Cherry .24  .18     120       24      36             178     2    0    -2    -.48
13: 12 8 up  .24   .18     168       24      24             189    27   27     0     .00   4.
14: 40 Shandy .24  .18     240        0      24             200    64   64     0     .00  11.
15: 41 Orange .24  .18     120       36       0             100    56   55    -1    -.24
16: 42 Lemon .23   .17     100        0       0              78    22   22     0     .00   3.
17: 70 Fizer .24   .18      72       48      48             140    28   28     0     .00   5
18: 71 Citrus .12  .07     120       60     120             280    20   19     0     .96   1
19: 76 Mixed .23   .19       0       24      24              20    28   28     0     .96   5.
20: 77 Tropica .24 .21      24       48      48             101    19   19     0     .00   3.
21:                      ------------------------------           ------------------------
22:                      1684      456     492       0      2316   316  312     5     .24   5
23:                      ------------------------------           ------------------------
24:
25:SALES ANALYSIS
26:_____
27:                     % Margin   Sales   Profit  % of Total % of Total
28:                                                    Sales    Profit
29:
30:    Cola               33%     177.60   59.20      34%       33%
31:    Diet               33%      69.60   23.20      13%       13%
32:    Cherry             33%      42.72   14.24       8%        8%
33:    8 up               33%      45.36   15.12       9%        8%
34:    Shandy             33%      48.00   16.00       9%        9%
35:    Orange             33%      24.00    8.00       5%        4%
36:    Lemon              35%      17.94    6.33       3%        3%
37:    Fizer              33%      33.60   11.20       6%        6%
38:    Citrus             71%      33.60   24.00       6%       13%
39:    Mixed              21%       4.60     .97       1%        1%
40:    Tropical           14%      24.24    3.46       5%        2%
41:                              -------------------------------------
42:                              521.26   181.72     100%      100%
43:
44:          Overall profit margin:        35%
45:
46:
47:
48:
49:
50:
51:
52:
53:
54:
55:
56:
57:
58:
59:
60:
```

```
 : A::  B :: C::   D    ::    E    ::    F    ::    G    ::    H    ::    I    :
1:STOCK CONTROL SHEET SOFT DRINKS
2:_____
3:
4:
5:
6:PLU ITEM   R.P.   C.P.        C/F           1         2 3                 PLU
7:                         Open Stock                                     SALES
8:
9:
10: 9  Cola   .24 .18    492          144          120                    740
11: 10 Diet   .24 .18    228          48           48                     290
12: 11 Cherry .24 .18    120          24           36                     178
13: 12 8 up   .24 .18    168          24           24                     189
14: 40 Shandy .24 .18    240          0            24                     200
15: 41 Orange .24 .18    120          36           0                      100
16: 42 Lemon  .23 .17    100          0            0                      78
17: 70 Fizer  .24 .18    72           48           48                     140
18: 71 Citrus .12 .07    120          60           120                    280
19: 76 Mixed  .23 .19    0            24           24                     20
20: 77 Tropica .24 .21   24           48           48                     101
21:                   --------------------------------------------------------
22:                   SUM(E10:E20)  SUM(F10:F20)  SUM(G10:G20)  SUM(H10:H20)  SUM(I10:I20)
23:                   --------------------------------------------------------
24:
25:SALES ANALYSIS
26:_____
27:                     % Margin        Sales      Profit    % of Total   % of Total
28:                                                              Sales       Profit
29:
30:  Cola       (C10-D10)/D10   I10*C10   E30*F30   F30/F42   G30/G42
31:  Diet       (C11-D11)/D11   I11*C11   E31*F31   F31/F42   G31/G42
32:  Cherry     (C12-D12)/D12   I12*C12   E32*F32   F32/F42   G32/G42
33:  8 up       (C13-D13)/D13   I13*C13   E33*F33   F33/F42   G33/G42
34:  Shandy     (C14-D14)/D14   I14*C14   E34*F34   F34/F42   G34/G42
35:  Orange     (C15-D15)/D15   I15*C15   E35*F35   F35/F42   G35/G42
36:  Lemon      (C16-D16)/D16   I16*C16   E36*F36   F36/F42   G36/G42
37:  Fizer      (C17-D17)/D17   I17*C17   E37*F37   F37/F42   G37/G42
38:  Citrus     (C18-D18)/D18   I18*C18   E38*F38   F38/F42   G38/G42
39:  Mixed      (C19-D19)/D19   I19*C19   E39*F39   F39/F42   G39/G42
40:  Tropical   (C20-D20)/D20   I20*C20   E40*F40   F40/F42   G40/G42
41:                   --------------------------------------------------------
42:                           SUM(F30:F40)  SUM(G30:G40)  SUM(H30:H40)  SUM(I30:I40)
43:
44:           Overall profit margin:      G42/F42
```

```
      :    J    ::    K    ::    L    ::    M    ::    N    :
 1:
 2:
 3:
 4:
 5:
 6:          Book       Actual        Over/        Value        Value
 7:          Stock       Stock        Short        losses       Stock
 8:                                                @ R.P.        @ C.P.
 9:
 0: (SUM(E10:H10))-I10  14            K10-J10      C10*L10      D10*K10
 1: (SUM(E11:H11))-I11  36            K11-J11      C11*L11      D11*K11
 2: (SUM(E12:H12))-I12  0             K12-J12      C12*L12      D12*K12
 3: (SUM(E13:H13))-I13  27            K13-J13      C13*L13      D13*K13
 4: (SUM(E14:H14))-I14  64            K14-J14      C14*L14      D14*K14
 5: (SUM(E15:H15))-I15  55            K15-J15      C15*L15      D15*K15
 6: (SUM(E16:H16))-I16  22            K16-J16      C16*L16      D16*K16
 7: (SUM(E17:H17))-I17  28            K17-J17      C17*L17      D17*K17
 8: (SUM(E18:H18))-I18  19            K18-J18      C18*L18      D18*K18
 9: (SUM(E19:H19))-I19  28            K19-J19      C19*L19      D19*K19
 0: (SUM(E20:H20))-I20  19            K20-J20      C20*L20      D20*K20
 1: ----------------------------------------------------------------------
 2: SUM(J10:J20)    SUM(K10:K20)   SUM(L10:L20)  SUM(M10:M20)  SUM(N10:N20)
 3: ----------------------------------------------------------------------
 4:
 5:
 6:
 7:
 8:
 9:
 0:
 1:
 2:
 3:
 4:
 5:
 6:
 7:
 8:
 9:
 0:
 1:
 2:
 3:
 4:
```

Delivery analysis

```
 : A::  B  ::  C  ::  D  ::  E  ::  F  ::     G     ::    H    ::     I      ::   J    :
 :DATE: 15/10/1989    Order reference: 12
 ":
 »:Supplier:   Turner's Cash & Carry
 #:
 #:
 »:PLU ITEM      Retail Qty. per   Outer    VAT     Outers        Cost                 Retail      Margin
 ":            Price  outer    price    rate    Ordered       ex.vat               ex.VAT
 #:            inc.VAT         ex.VAT
 ":
 #: 1  Cola      .24    24     4.32    .15      5        E10*G10    (C10*D10*G10)*(1/(F10+1) (I10-H10)/I10
 .: 2  Diet      .23    24     3.84    .15      2        E11*G11    (C11*D11*G11)*(1/(F11+1) (I11-H11)/I11
 ": 3  Lemonade  .19    24     3.56    .15      1        E12*G12    (C12*D12*G12)*(1/(F12+1) (I12-H12)/I12
 #: 4  Fiz       .15    60     4.8     .15      3        E13*G13    (C13*D13*G13)*(1/(F13+1) (I13-H13)/I13
 #: 5  Citrus    .25    24     4.8     .15      5        E14*G14    (C14*D14*G14)*(1/(F14+1) (I14-H14)/I14
 5: 6  Tropical  .25    24     4.8     .15      3        E15*G15    (C15*D15*G15)*(1/(F15+1) (I15-H15)/I15
 ": 7  Orange    .22    24     3.36    .15      2        E16*G16    (C16*D16*G16)*(1/(F16+1) (I16-H16)/I16
 ": 8  Tangy     .18    24     3.36    .15      1        E17*G17    (C17*D17*G17)*(1/(F17+1) (I17-H17)/I17
 #:                                   =========================================================
 #:                           TOTALS   SUM(G10:G17)  SUM(H10:H17)  SUM(I10:I17)
 #:
 :
 #:
 #:                 Gross Profit on order:         I19-H19
 #:
 #:                 Percentage margin on order:    H23/I19
```

```
 : A::  B  ::  C  ::  D  ::  E  ::  F  ::     G     ::    H    ::     I      ::   J    :
 #:DATE: 15/10/1989    Order reference: 12
 ":
 #:Supplier:   Turner's Cash & Carry
 #:
 #:
 #:PLU ITEM      Retail Qty. per   Outer    VAT     Outers        Cost                 Retail      Margin
 ":            Price  outer    price    rate    Ordered       ex.vat               ex.VAT
 #:            inc.VAT         ex.VAT
 #:
```
```
 #: 1  Cola      .24    24     4.32    15.0%      5        21.6             25.04      13.7%
 .: 2  Diet      .23    24     3.84    15.0%      2         7.68             9.60      20.0%
 2: 3  Lemonade  .19    24     3.56    15.0%      1         3.56             2.97      10.2%
 #: 4  Fiz       .15    60     4.80    15.0%      3        14.4             23.48      38.7%
 #: 5  Citrus    .25    24     4.80    15.0%      5        24               26.09      8.0%
 #: 6  Tropical  .25    24     4.80    15.0%      3        14.4             15.65      8.0%
 »: 7  Orange    .22    24     3.36    15.0%      2         6.72             9.18      26.8%
 ": 8  Tangy     .18    24     3.36    15.0%      1         3.36             3.76      10.6%
 #:                                   =========================================================
 #:                           TOTALS          22        95.72            116.77
 D:
 #:
 #:
 #:                 Gross Profit on order:         21.05
 #:
 #:                 Percentage margin on order:    18.0%
```

```
   : A ::    B    :: C :: E :: F :: G :: I :: J :: K :: M :: N :: O :: P :
 1:CASH BOOK
 2:ENTRY DETAILS          :BALANCES            :RECEIPTS              :PAYMENTS                    :
 3:               Reference:                   :Till    Credit        :                            :
 4:Date   Details  or Chq.no:Cash  Bank   Total :Sales   Sales  Other :Stock  O/heads Other  Total :
 5:------------------------:--------------------:----------------------:----------------------------:
 6:Balances from acc1 c/f:  : 80.00 50.00 130.00 :                      :                        .00 :
 7:1/10   From till         :110.45       110.45 :110.45                :                        .00 :
 8:1/10   From J Smith      :       40.00  40.00 :        40.00         :                        .00 :
 9:1/10   Cash to Bank      :( 90.00) 90.00   .00 :                     :                        .00 :
10:1/10   To Brands cash/c  :      ( 97.80)( 97.80):                    : 97.80                97.80 :
11:1/10   Rental payment    :( 60.00)     ( 60.00):                    :        60.00         60.00 :
12:1/10   Stationery        :(  5.46)     (  5.46):                    :         5.46          5.46 :
13:2/10   From till         :114.98       114.98 :114.98                :                        .00 :
14:3/10   Cash from bank    : 98.00 ( 98.00)  .00 :                     :                        .00 :
15:3/10   To Gazette (advert):     ( 80.34)( 80.34):                   :        80.34         80.34 :
16:4/10   Legal fees        :( 75.90)     ( 75.90):                    :        75.90         75.90 :
17:5/10   To Brands cash/c  :( 82.34)     ( 82.34):                    : 82.34                82.34 :
18:5/10   Capital (loan)    :      200.00 200.00 :                200.00:                        .00 :
19:6/10   Petrol            :      ( 10.00)( 10.00):                   :        10.00         10.00 :
20:6/10   Drawings for self :( 50.00)     ( 50.00):                    :              50.00   50.00 :
21:------------------------:--------------------:----------------------:----------------------------:
22:                         : 39.73 93.86 133.59 :225.43   40.00 200.00:180.14 231.70  50.00 461.84 :
23:------------------------------------------------------------------------------------------------
```

```
   : R  :
 1:
 2:
 3:
 4:
 5:
 6:
 7:
 8:
 9:
10:
11:
12:
13:
14:
15:
16:
17:
18:
19:
20:
21:
22:
23:
```

```
  :  A   ::  B  ::  C  ::  E  ::  F  ::  G  ::  I  ::  J  ::  K  :
1:CASH BOOK
2:
3:ENTRY DETAILS                :BALANCES              :RECEIPTS                      :
4:              Reference      :                      :Till    Credit                :
5:Date   Details or Chq.no. :Cash    Bank    Total   :Sales   Sales    Other        :
6:-----------------------------:----------------------:-----------------------------:
7:Balances from accl c/f:      :              E7+F7   :                              :
8:                             :              E8+F8   :                              :
9:                             :              E9+F9   :                              :
10:                            :              E10+F10 :                              :
11:                            :              E11+F11 :                              :
12:                            :              E12+F12 :                              :
13:                            :              E13+F13 :                              :
14:                            :              E14+F14 :                              :
15:                            :              E15+F15 :                              :
16:                            :              E16+F16 :                              :
17:                            :              E17+F17 :                              :
18:                            :              E18+F18 :                              :
19:                            :              E19+F19 :                              :
20:                            :              E20+F20 :                              :
21:                            :              E21+F21 :                              :
22:-----------------------------:----------------------:-----------------------------:
23:             : SUM(E7:E21) SUM(F7:F21) SUM(G7:G21): SUM(I7:I21) SUM(J7:J21) SUM(K7:K21):
24:-------------------------------------------------------------------------------------

  :  M   ::  N   ::  0  ::  P  ::  R  :
1:
2:
3:PAYMENTS                       :
4:                               :
5:Stock   O/heads   Other   Total :
6:-------------------------------:
7:                        SUM(M7:07):
8:                        SUM(M8:08):
9:                        SUM(M9:09):
10:                       SUM(M10:01):
11:                       SUM(M11:01):
12:                       SUM(M12:01):
13:                       SUM(M13:01):
14:                       SUM(M14:01):
15:                       SUM(M15:01):
16:                       SUM(M16:01):
17:                       SUM(M17:01):
18:                       SUM(M18:01):
19:                       SUM(M19:01):
20:                       SUM(M20:02):
21:                       SUM(M21:02):
22:-------------------------------:
23: SUM(M7:M21) SUM(N7:N21) SUM(07:021) SUM(P7:P21):
24:-------------------------------
```

Appendix 7

Sources of further information and advice

The Small Firms Service

The Small Firms Service is operated by the Department of Trade and Industry. The service offers information and counselling to owners and managers of small businesses in dealing with their plans and problems. It is also an advisory service for those thinking of starting their own business. The service operates through a nationwide network of Small Firms Centres – 13 Small Firms Centres and 100 area counselling offices.

The information provided is in booklet form, usually well-written and informative, ranging from advice on marketing, importing and exporting, to employing people. The service can also put you in touch quickly with the right people in local authorities, government departments, the professions, libraries, chambers of commerce or any other body that can help with your problem.

As well as answering enquiries over the telephone, the service can arrange a counselling session with a Small Firms Business Counsellor, an experienced businessman who may well have faced a similar problem(s) to the one you are presently facing. He will help by offering you advice and guidance, impartially and in strictest confidence.

The information service is free. For counselling, the first three sessions are free. A 'modest charge' is made for further sessions if you require them. To contact the Small Firms Service simply dial 100 for the operator and ask for Freefone Enterprise.

Local Enterprise Agencies

Local Enterprise Agencies have been formed in many locations throughout the UK – the likelihood is that one exists in your locality. They all have in common the aim of helping new and small businesses start and thrive in the local area.

These agencies, although small, usually with a full-time staff of only two or three, can draw on a wealth of experience in the local business community. They are usually sponsored by local companies, local government, chambers of commerce, banks and other concerns.

Local Enterprise Agencies can be a valuable help where guidance on problems relating to the local business environment is sought: for instance, help with obtaining premises, planning permission, and sources of finance.

Usually, the service provided by local Enterprise Agencies is free of charge.

Council for Small Industries in Rural Areas (CoSIRA)

This organization is government financed with the objective of revitalizing areas in England by helping small rural businesses to grow. If you are going to open up in a rural area, contact them and see what advice you can obtain. Their service includes advice on management, accountancy, budgeting/planning, and so on. CoSIRA also has a limited loan fund.

CoSIRA can be contacted at 141 Castle Street, Salisbury, Wiltshire SP1 3TP (0722-336255).

Co-operative Development Agency

The agency gives advice on how to set up a co-operative. There is a network of local agencies – check your telephone directory for the nearest to you, or contact them at Broadmead House, 21 Panton Street, London SW1Y 4DR (01-839-2988).

The clearing banks

Recent years have seen the major clearing banks more interested in the small business community. Most of the main clearing banks now produce free booklets. They are of mixed quality so shop around and see what is on offer. Such information is useful in giving indications of what a bank is looking for' in a business, and a person, when they are considering a loan application for a small business start up. Raising finance is fully discussed in Chapter 7.

Counselling sessions with your bank manager can be useful – but also expensive!

Accountants and solicitors

This book cannot substitute for seeking professional advice on some aspects of your business start up and operation. However, accountants and solicitors should be used only when necessary, simply because of the expense. Make sure you are using the right professional for the problem in hand.

Your local college

Many local colleges and adult education centres now operate short courses on how to start your own business. The courses are usually inexpensive and quite informative.

One of the main advantages of attending such a course is the opportunity to meet people with similar ambitions, giving you a chance to share and learn from other people's experiences.

Glossary of retail and general business terminology

Asset: Anything owned by the business (see Chapter 6).

Balance sheet: This is a summary of what the business owns (the value of its assets) and what it owes (i.e., how it is presently financing its assets). The two lists must balance, for what it has must have been 'paid for'!

Bar code: Bar codes are now found on nearly all prepacked merchandise. The code consists of a series of bars which can be read by a scanner. The code consists of 13 digits. One set of the digits are available to the retailer to identify the merchandise in a way that is unique to his/her shop (i.e., price, description, department, etc.). Selling merchandise using bar code scanning enables the retailer to:

- gain detailed sales information
- increase the speed at which customers are served
- decrease the number of mistakes that are made at the till point
- effect price changes quickly and accurately.

Unfortunately the cost of such equipment is expensive – the cheapest effective system on the market at the time of writing was in excess of £2,500.

Similar benefits can be gained at a lower cost by using an electronic till with a PLU facility (see Chapters 12 and 13).

Break-even point: This is the sales level at which you will earn sufficient revenue to cover all costs (see Chapter 5).

Capital (see Chapter 6): Can have a number of meanings. Specifically:

- working capital (see later)
- share capital (amount put into the business by the shareholders)
- the value of fixed assets (see later).

Cash flow: The pattern of cash coming into and going out of the business over a period of time. Note a surplus or deficit of cash in a business does not necessarily mean that it is making a profit or a loss. All businesses should attempt to forecast their cash flow (see Chapter 6).

Catchment area: A term borrowed from geography, used to describe the principal area from which a particular shop or shopping centre draws the majority of its customers. (See Chapter 4.)

Closing stock: The value of stock remaining at the end of a trading period (see Chapters 9 & 12).

Cost: This can have many meanings, however, in accounting terms an item of expenditure does not become a cost until it has been used up in the course of trading. For example, the cost of stock sold is a cost but the expenditure on stock held in storage or on the fixtures is not a cost but an asset (i.e., something owned by the business). (See Chapter 5.)

Creditor: Somebody you owe money to.

Current assets: Anything owned by the business with the intention of turning into cash in the near future (certainly within one year). Includes, cash, stock, prepaid bills and debtors to the business (see Chapters 6 & 12).

Current liability: Total of short term debt (e.g., overdrafts, issued but unpaid invoices) owed to creditors by the business.

Debtor: Somebody who owes money to you.

Demand lines: Items of merchandise that are bought frequently and are usually the prime reason for the customer's shopping trip.

Depreciation: The cost of a fixed asset spread out over its working life (see Appendix 5 on methods of depreciation).

Drawings: The amount(s) you as the owner withdraw from the business. A common misconception is that you will be taxed on your drawings – this is not the case. Taxation in the case of a sole trader is based on net profits earned. Net profit is not affected by drawings.

Equity: The value of the owner(s)' stake in the business.

EPOS: Electronic Point of Sale – see 'Bar Codes' & 'PLU' (see Chapters 12 & 13).

Fixed asset: Something which the business intends to possess for a long time (i.e., longer than one year), typically, premises, fixtures and fittings.

Fixed costs: Those costs that do not significantly change with fluctuations in sales (see Chapter 5).

Good will: An intangible asset (that is one that cannot be directly measured) – a value given to a trading name or the customer loyalty a shop has built up. It is only shown on the balance sheet on purchase of the business and is then written off as a cost (see Chapter 9).

Gross profit: This is the difference between the cost and retail price of an item – or similarly between the sales for a period and the cost of stock in generating those sales.

Gross profit margin: The gross profit expressed as a percentage of the retail price or sales (i.e., gross profit/price or sales × 100). Specific types of retail businesses tend to operate on roughly similar profit margins (see Chapters 1 and 5). Do confuse gross profit margins with gross profit mark ups (see later).

Impulse lines: Items of merchandise that are purchased on impulse – as an afterthought. Careful attention to the positioning of merchandise can increase the sales of impulse lines (see Chapter 8).

Lead time: The time period between placing and receiving an order.

Marketing mix: A combination of various policies (pricing, location, promotional activities, service provisions and levels) aimed at improving sales.

Margin: See gross profit margin

Mark up: Not to be confused with margin. The mark up gives the **gross profit** as a percentage of the cost price (i.e. gross profit/cost price × 100). It is therefore possible to have mark ups of one thousand percent and more but a margin cannot be greater than 99.9% (see Chapter 5).

Net assets employed: This is the total value of all assets employed in the business less short term liabilities. That is the total value of assets financed by long term loans and capital introduced by the owner(s) (see Chapters 5, 9 & 12).

Net profit: The amount left, at the end of a trading period, after all fixed costs (overheads) have been paid for out of gross profit. This figure is not the same as the cash balance at the end of the trading period.

Open to buy: A method for calculation of a merchandise buying budget which can be adjusted to take into account present stocks and desired stock holding (see Chapter 13).

Opening stock: The value of stock at the beginning of a trading period (see Chapters 9 & 12).

Price sensitivity or elasticity: A measure of how sensitive sales levels are to price changes.

PLU ('Price Look Up'): A facility found on electronic tills to allow the price, department (and some times the description) of item to be recorded against a 'stock number' (PLU number). The facility allows the sales of PLU items to be individually recorded.

Profit and loss account: A statement (account) of sales and the costs involved in attaining those sales for a given period of time. After all costs have been deducted from the revenue earned from sales the account will either show a net profit or net loss (see Chapters 5, 9 and 12).

Rate of stock turn (RST): The number of times the average stock holding is sold (turned over) in a given trading period. The RST is usually given as an annual figure. When using RST figures always check on what basis they have been calculated (see Chapters 1, 5, 9 & 12).

Shrinkage: Loss of merchandise through theft, clerical errors, damage, etc.

Retail or business environment: The factors which directly or indirectly influence the business – ranging from local competition to national economic trends (see Chapter 2).

Retail mix: Same as the marketing mix (see Chapter 2, especially references to 'Unique Selling Proposition').

Target market: A group of customers, which can be described in some meaningful way, that represent a profitable group which the business seeks to reach and sell to.

Trading policy: The image and reputation that the shop seeks to build and project to its customers, based on its unique selling proposition (see Chapters 2 and 8).

Variable cost: Those costs that vary significantly with variations in sales – typically the cost of stock (see Chapter 5).

Voluntary group or chain: Where a group of retailers align themselves with a particular wholesaler (e.g. Spar) – the retailers will usually take on the name of the wholesaler but continue to trade on a mainly independent basis (see Chapter 1).

Working capital: In general terms it is that amount of money that flows from cash into stock and back into cash again via sales. In accounting terms the total amount of working capital tied up in the business is calculated by subtracting current liabilities from current assets (see Chapters 6 & 12).

Index